£3

UK AIRPORTS
AND AIRFIELDS
A SPOTTER'S GUIDE

UK AIRPORTS AND AIRFIELDS
A SPOTTER'S GUIDE

TIM LAMING

Airlife
England

First published in the UK in 2000
by Airlife Publishing Ltd

Second impression 2001

**British Library Cataloguing-in-Publication
Data**
A catalogue record for this book
is available from the British Library

ISBN 1 85310 978 9

Typeset by Phoenix Typesetting,
Ilkley, West Yorkshire

Printed in England by
St Edmundsbury Press Ltd, Bury St Edmunds,
Suffolk.

Airlife Publishing Ltd
101 Longden Road, Shrewsbury,
SY3 9EB England.
E-mail: airlife@airlifebooks.com
Website: www.airlifebooks.com

Contents

Introduction

Key

☺☺☺

The star rating gives an indication of the interest and activity to be found at the airfield in question. Maximum ten stars.

✿

Viewing locations are shown on the airfield charts.

Elevation – height above sea-level.

Tel – main switchboard number.

Runways –

TODA	take-off distance available
LDA	landing distance available

Radio –

Approach	–	used to control aircraft approaching or departing.
Radar	–	for control of aircraft in the airfield vicinity.
Tower	–	for control of aircraft flying the airfield circuit or on the ground

Compiling a directory of British airfields is something of a subjective exercise. Although in principle it may seem an easy task, it is sometimes difficult to decide precisely which airfields are worth mentioning and which are not. For example, a busy military aerodrome might not be of much interest to a collector of Cessna serials, whereas the local private landing strip would probably bore a typical fast jet enthusiast. Likewise, airfields which are virtually disused may be of little interest to most, but to those who have fond memories of plane spotting or even flying at long-abandoned bases, even the rarest of airborne visitors would make the site worthy of inclusion.

Consequently, I've endeavoured to take a fairly broad view of what is likely to be of general interest to most aviation enthusiasts, and in doing so, this book presents a detailed listing of the most active airfields in the UK, combined with excellent diagrams provided courtesy of the Royal Air Force to whom I am most grateful for their seemingly endless co-operation. A second section lists even more airfields which are not quite so busy, but still well worth including in this 'rough guide' to active sites. Space prevents me from listing absolutely every potentially interesting site, so a number of helicopter landing grounds, virtually disused airfields and other places have not been included, but I hope that this book will give the reader a comprehensive guide as to what can be seen, and where. If any seemingly obvious places have still been omitted I can only apologise!

Of course, it is also important to establish the purpose of this book, and in general terms I have assumed that the typical reader will be an aircraft spotter and/or photographer, who wants to know where the best places are to see military and/or civil aircraft. Consequently, each entry gives the precise grid co-ordinates for the airfield and also a broader location indication. The main telephone number is provided too, in case any specific enquiries need to be addressed to the base concerned (I would suggest that any callers ask to speak to the Community Relations Officer or Press Officer), and basic details of the runway lengths, radio frequencies and 'spotting' information are included. I have also included a (purely subjective) 'star rating' for each site, which gives a fair indication of whether the airfield is a 'must-see' (with ten stars) or simply worth checking-out if you happen to be passing (one star). Where appropriate, some recommended vantage points for spotting and/or photography are also marked on the airfield maps although in many instances viewing locations are many and varied.

However, it's worth remembering that the status of many airfields can change quite quickly, and places which are busy can suddenly become very quiet. For example, RAF Fairford is virtually abandoned for most of the year, but you might be surprised to find the airfield occupied by B-52 bombers on exercise, if not over-flowing with aircraft during the annual Air Tattoo week. Likewise, places such as St Mawgan are often inactive but regular exercises will see the base bursting with action, albeit for just a few days. My advice is to read enthusiast magazines and newsletters, or use the internet to find out what's happening on a week-by-week basis.

Another important consideration when observing aircraft is one of safety and security. The Cold War has certainly ended and you would be very unlucky to find yourself confronted with security-conscious policemen at the perimeter of most military bases these days. Most establishments now take a fairly relaxed view of public

spectators, and providing that spotters keep to public roads and paths, there should be little problem. However, some bases are still rather more sensitive than others, and Army establishments are good examples, where any close scrutiny and/or photography is not recommended. Research establishments are also sometimes sensitive but the most important consideration is to use some sound judgment. Keep to well-worn paths and stick with other spotters if possible. Don't be tempted to trespass on any land be it military or civil as the results can be serious and expensive. And don't assume that civil facilities will be any more forgiving of intruders than military ones – they won't be! It's also important to consider some basic safety points, such as keeping clear of runway approaches – you might be happy to risk getting your head knocked off by a passing undercarriage unit but you're certain to upset the local police, who simply won't allow such obvious acts of stupidity. Parking your car across a crash gate isn't a good idea either, and leaving a car on any unauthorised land or stretch of road is to be discouraged. At the very least you could well be ticketed.

But enough of the pitfalls. Plane spotting is a relatively safe pastime, at least in the UK, and it can be a rewarding one too, if you manage to be in the right place at the right time. Patience is certainly required, but a great deal of success in terms of spotting or photography can be attributed to careful planning. Some careful scrutiny of publications, newsletters, computer web sites or a chat with fellow enthusiasts will often provide the best advice as to where to be and when. Hopefully this book will help to steer a few people in the right direction!

Tim Laming

UK AIRFIELDS

Aberdeen (Dyce)

☺☺☺☺

Operator: Civilian
Location: N57 12.25 W002 12.2 (NW of Aberdeen on A96)
Elevation: 215ft
Tel: 01224 723714/722331
Hours:
(winter)   0630–2150 Mon–Sat,
           0650–2150 Sun
(summer)   0530–2050 Mon–Sat,
           0550–2050 Sun

Runways:
16/34 (158T slope 0.22% up) 6,000ft
Runway 16 TODA 6,660ft, LDA 6,000ft
Runway 34 TODA 6,693ft, LDA 6,000ft

Radio:
Approach – 120.4 353.55
Radar – 120.4 353.55
Tower – 118.1

Notes:
A busy regional airport with particular emphasis on helicopter operations, the nearby Scottish oil fields have made Aberdeen the busiest heliport in Europe. Associated business and scheduled services also contribute to a lively movements schedule, while a flying school is also located on the airfield. Having first opened in 1934, many wartime buildings remain, evoking memories of coastal patrols and convoy escorts. Military activities continued into the late 1950s. Viewing of present-day operations is easily achieved thanks to the network of surrounding access roads and car parks, which enable observation of all parts of the airfield to be obtained. The modern pyramidal control tower building reflects the equally modern terminal facilities which are also now available, and which include shopping and catering outlets.

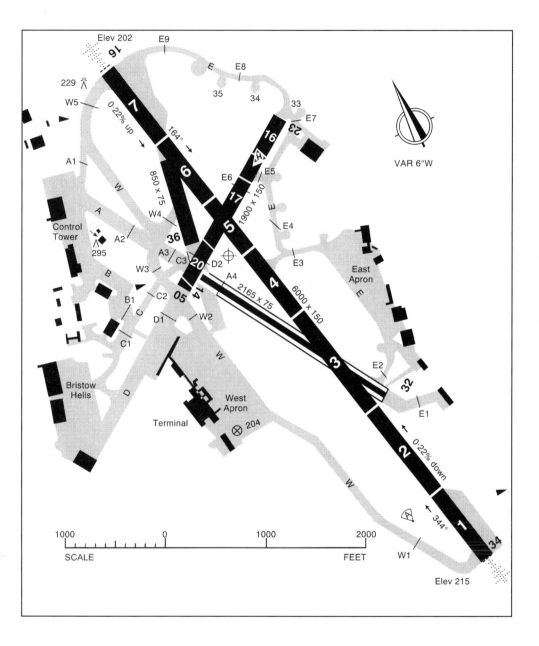

Alderney
☺☺

Operator: Civilian
Location: N49 42.37 W002 12.88 (1nm SW of St Anne's)
Elevation: 291ft
Tel: 01481 822851
Hours:

(winter)	0740–1830 Mon–Sat, 0855–1830 Sun
(summer)	0640–1730 Mon–Thu, 0640–1830 Fri–Sun

Runways:
08/26 (079T slope 0.14% up) 2,887ft
Runway 08 TODA/LDA 2,887ft
Runway 26 TODA 3,350ft, LDA 2,887ft

Radio:
Approach – 128.65
Tower – 125.35

Notes:
The oldest and smallest of the Channel Island airfields, Alderney is a relatively quiet airfield hosting services provided by Aurigny, with a small fleet of Trislanders. Small private aircraft also operate from the airfield and viewing access to most areas is straightforward. Private flying is actively encouraged and there is even a small duty-free shop on the site. Occasional fly-in events are also held here during summer months when more than a hundred aircraft gather on the airfield, literally filling the field to capacity.

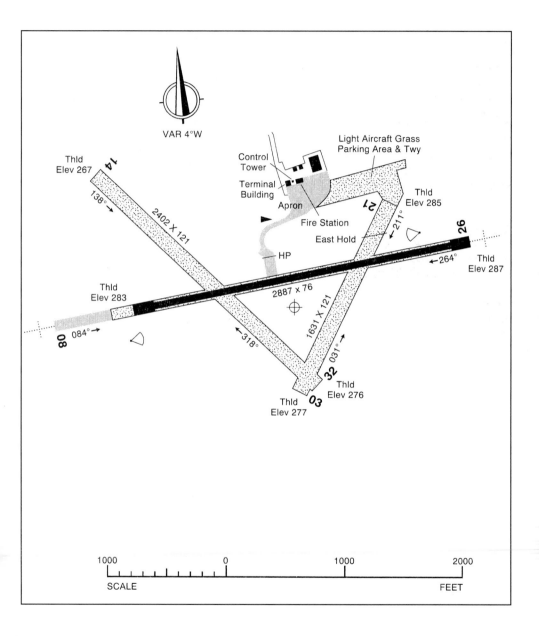

VAR 4°W

Thld
Elev 267

14

138°

2402 X 121

Control
Tower

Terminal
Building

Apron

Fire Station

HP

Light Aircraft Grass
Parking Area & Twy

21

211°

East Hold

Thld
Elev 285

26

264°

Thld
Elev 287

Thld
Elev 283

2887 x 76

1631 X 121

031°

08

084°→

318°

32

Thld
Elev 276

03

Thld
Elev 277

SCALE

1000   0   1000   2000

FEET

Barkston Heath

☺☺☺

Operator: Royal Air Force
Location: N52 57.74 W000 33.70 (4nm NE of Grantham)
Elevation: 367ft
Tel: 01400 261201
Hours: 0730–1730 Mon–Fri

Runways:

06/24 (057.42T slope 0.72% down) 6,007ft
Runway 06 TODA 6,056ft, LDA 5,502ft (first 500ft sterile)
Runway 24 TODA 6,030ft, LDA 6,001ft
11/29 (282.5T slope 0.762% down) 4,206ft
Runway 11 TODA 4,232ft, LDA 4,199ft
Runway 29 TODA 4,206ft, LDA 3,691ft (first 515ft sterile)

Radio:

Approach – 340.475
Director – 261.05
Departures – 291.7
Talkdown – 360.72
Tower – 342.075 120.425
Ground – 340.525

Notes:
Home to the distinctive yellow-painted Slingsby Fireflies of the Joint Elementary Flying Training School (JEFTS), Barkston Heath is also a Relief Landing Ground for nearby RAF Cranwell, and provides facilities for regular practice approaches when Cranwell's circuit is over-crowded. Famous as a major participant in D-Day operations (when the airfield's runways and dispersals were literally jammed with Dakotas and other transports), Barkston Heath opened in 1941 and was for many years the home to the USAAF's 61st Troop Carrier Group. Post-war, the station was also a Bloodhound SAM site, and although many traces of wartime connections are still visible, few signs of the once-prominent missile battery remain. Good views of the airfield can be obtained from surrounding roads, including excellent close-up access to runway 24's approach path. The JEFTS aircraft are normally hangared when inactive, but aircraft scheduled to fly are parked on the adjacent ramp, next to the eastern perimeter track (beside the B6403).

BARKSTON HEATH, illustrating the considerable size of the airfield, much of which is now unused.

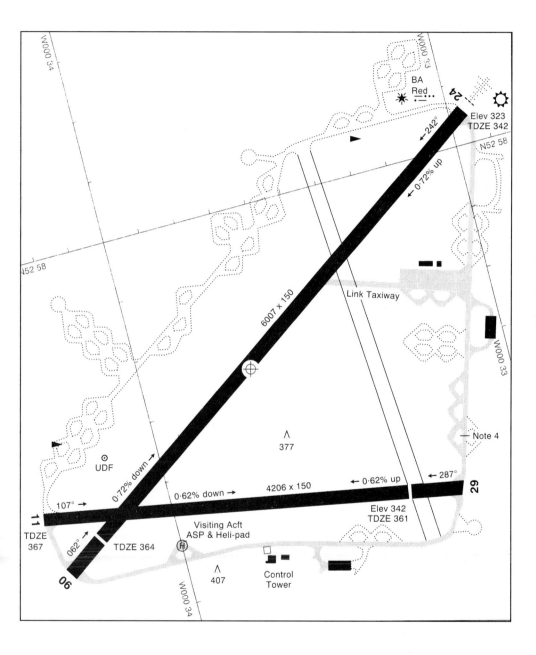

Belfast (Aldergrove)
☺☺☺

Operator: Civilian & Royal Air Force
Location: N54 39.45 W006 12.93 (10nm NW of Belfast off the M1 on the A57)
Elevation: 267ft
Tel: 028 9442 2888
Hours:
24hrs, RAF 0500–2100 Mon–Fri, 0700–1500 Sat–Sun

Runways:
07/25 (065T slope 0.67% up) 9,111ft
Runway 07 TODA 10,007ft, LDA 9,111ft
Runway 25 TODA 10,423ft, LDA 9,111ft
17/35 (342T) 6,401ft
Runway 17 TODA 6,201ft, LDA 5,899ft
Runway 35 TODA 6,926ft, LDA 5,899ft

Radio:
Approach – 120.9 310.0
Radar – 120.9 310.0
Tower – 118.3 310.0
Ground – 121.75
Operations – 241.825

Notes:
Opened in 1918 as a manufacturing site for Harland & Wolf (to build bombers for Handley Page), Aldergrove was a very active wartime RAF airfield. Since the early 1960s, however, the airfield has been developed into a major airport with more than 2.5 million passengers passing through the facility every year. In addition to charter and freight operations, regular (and international) scheduled services are provided by airlines such as Aer Lingus. The Royal Air Force maintains a presence at the airfield, and many RAF and Nato communications and transport aircraft visit the base. Most activities are in support of Army operations, and helicopter movements are common, with No. 230 Squadron (flying Pumas) and No. 72 Squadron (with Wessex and Pumas) being based here. In view of the sensitive nature of Army operations in Northern Ireland, photography and/or viewing of areas other than those connected with the civil terminal is not recommended.

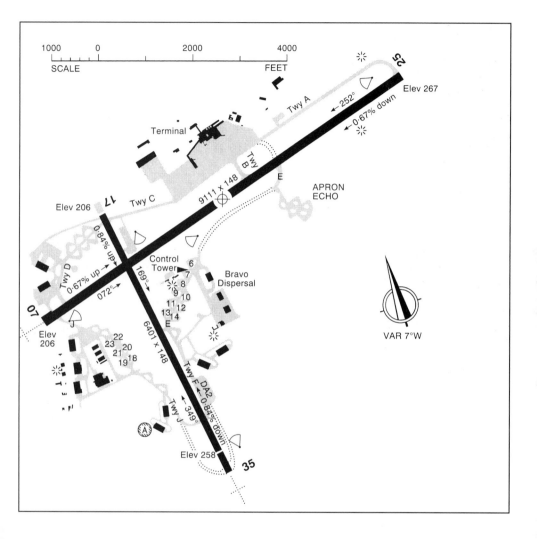

Belfast (City)
☺☺

Operator: Civilian
Location: N54 37.08 W005 52.35 (1nm from Belfast)
Elevation: 15ft
Tel: 028 9045 7745
Hours:
0630–2130 Sun–Fri, 0630–2115 Sat

Runways:
04/22 (035T) 6,001ft
Runway 04 TODA 6,657ft, LDA 5,699ft
Runway 22 TODA 6,260ft, LDA 5,797ft

Radio:
Approach – 130.85
Radar – 134.8 130.85
Tower – 130.75

Notes:
Although regarded as one of the relatively new 'City' airports, the airfield dates back to the 1930s. It was the manufacturing site for countless sea-planes (including the famous Sunderland) during World War Two, as Short Brothers had established their facility on this site. The company remains at the airfield to the present day, and in addition to Short 330 and 360 commuter aircraft, the agile Anglo-Brazilian Tucano can often be seen making test flights. Records show that other famous aircraft such as the Stirling, Skyvan, Sperrin and the mighty Belfast transport were also built here and flown from the site. Commercial operations began in 1983 and numerous regional airline services currently use the site, flying to airports across the United Kingdom. A small military presence is visible in the shape of two Vigilant gliders belonging to No. 664 Volunteer Gliding School, RAF. Observations of airfield operations are possible from adjacent roads.

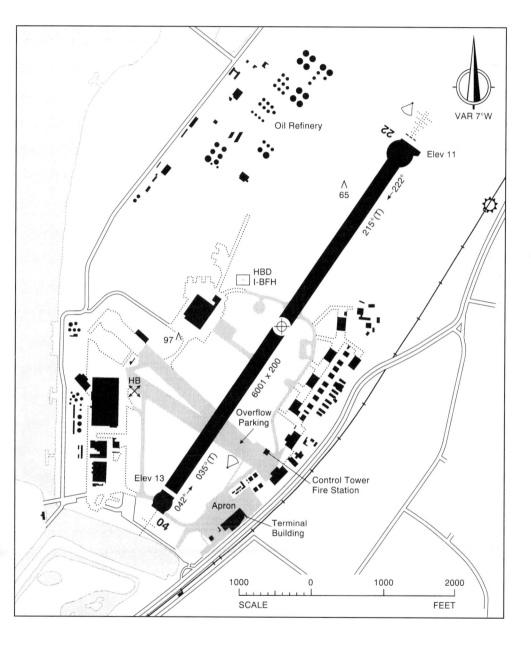

Oil Refinery

VAR 7°W

22

Elev 11

∧
65

215°(T)

←222°

HBD
I-BFH

97 ∧

6001 × 200

HB

Overflow
Parking

035°(T)

042°→

Elev 13

Control Tower
Fire Station

04

Apron

Terminal
Building

1000		0	1000	2000
SCALE				FEET

Benbecula

☺

Operator: Civilian
Location: N57 28.65 W007 21.98 (off
B892 at Balivanich)
Elevation: 19ft
Tel: 01870 602051
Hours:
(winter) 1000–1555 Mon–Fri,
1130–1300 Sat
(summer) 0900–1455 Mon–Fri,
0930–1100 Sat

Runways:
06/24 (055T slope 0.02% down) 5,528ft
Runway 06 TODA 6,014ft, LDA 5,028ft
Runway 24 TODA 5,528ft, LDA 5,036ft
18/36 4,002ft, TODA/LDA 4,002ft

Radio:
Approach/Tower – 119.2
Information – 119.2

Notes:
Initially developed as a Royal Air Force station, RAF Benbecula opened in 1942 and was associated chiefly with World War Two anti-submarine operations. In 1946 the airfield was transferred to civilian operations and BEA commenced flights to and from the site. Loganair then took over operations and the airline continues to operate today under the guise of British Airways Express. Military operations are still associated with the airfield thanks to the adjacent danger area which is used primarily for SAM test launches (most notably Rapiers). Not surprisingly, viewing the daily activities at the open and windswept airfield is easy, although photography of military operations isn't encouraged and aircraft movements are fairly minimal.

BENBECULA from the air, the small airport apron visible in the far distance.

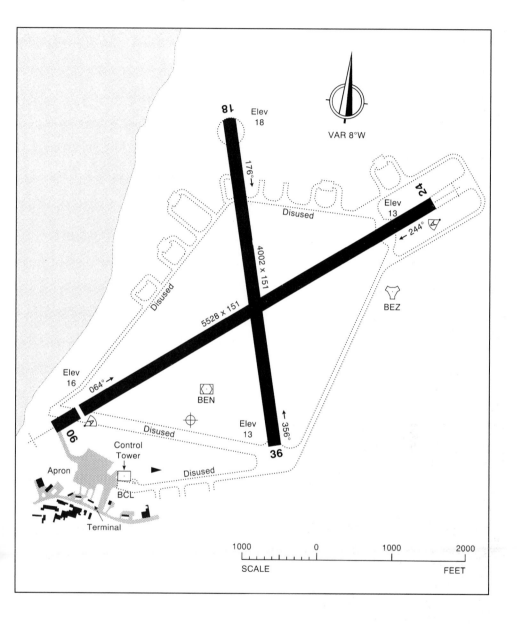

Benson
☺☺☺

Operator: Royal Air Force
Location: N51 36.98 W001 05.75 (2nm NE of Wallingford)
Elevation: 203ft
Tel: 01491 837766
Hours:
0800–1730 Mon–Fri

Runways:
01/19 (007.83T slope 0.42% up) 5,981ft
Runway 01 TODA 6,309ft, LDA 5,981ft
Runway 19 TODA 5,981ft, LDA 5,981ft

Radio:
Radar – 257.1 134.3
Approach – 268.825 127.15 362.3 122.1
Director – 315.75 127.15 344.0 122.1
Talkdown – 259.87 241.625 127.15 123.3
Tower – 279.35 130.25
Ground – 340.325

Notes:
Once the home to World-War-Two-vintage Fairey Battles, Benson was better known for its association with photographic reconnaissance Spitfires which were later joined by specially equipped Mosquitoes. In post-war years RAF Benson later became a major transport base, and the home to a large fleet of Argosy aircraft. The Queen's Flight was also based here for many years with Andovers, Wessex and BAe 146s. More recently, however, RAF Benson has become associated with helicopter activities, and after a brief period of operations with the Wessex, Benson is now a Puma base, and the home to No. 33 Squadron. Additionally, the University of London Air Squadron, the Oxford University Air Squadron and No. 6 Air Experience Flight are also based at Benson, operating a fleet of Bulldogs which are frequently active, especially at weekends. Benson will soon be the Royal Air Force's first Merlin HC3 base when the new helicopter enters RAF service. Viewing helicopter operations from adjacent roads (particularly the A423) is possible if not a little unpredictable; the runway thresholds are easily visible, but helicopter approaches are naturally rather flexible. However, RAF and other Nato transport and communications aircraft do visit the airfield occasionally.

BENSON is the home of the Royal Air Force's Puma fleet, and the first Merlin helicopters for the RAF will eventually enter service here.

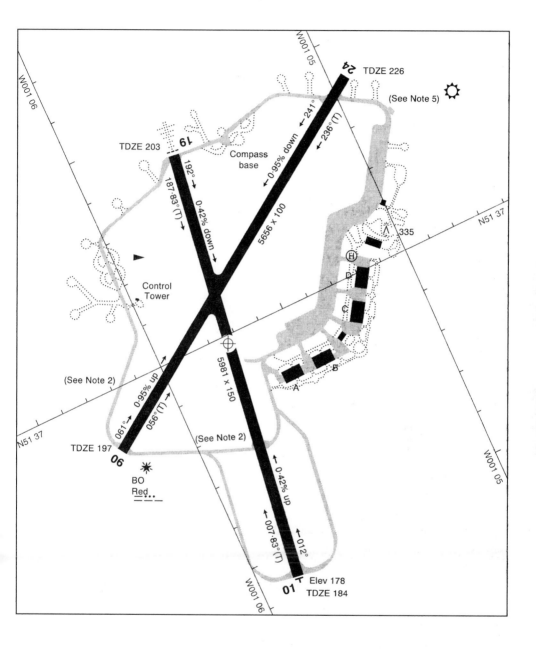

Biggin Hill
☺☺☺☺☺
Operator: Civilian
Location: N51 19.85 E000 01.95 (2nm SE of Bromley on A233)
Elevation: 600ft
Tel: 01959 571111
Hours:
0730–2100 Mon–Fri, 0900–2000 Sat–Sun

Runways:
03/21 (025T slope 0.96% down) 5,932ft
Runway 03 TODA 7,133ft, LDA 5,112ft
Runway 21 TODA 5,912ft, LDA 5,505ft
11/29 (104T) 2,677ft

Radio:
Approach – 129.4
Tower – 134.8
Departure – 121.875

BIGGIN HILL, illustrating a TTTE Tornado during an airshow visit from Cottesmore.

Notes:
One of the most famous and historic airfields in Britain, Biggin Hill is of course famous for its role in the Battle of Britain, and numerous reminders of the airfield's wartime connections remain, the station remaining essentially un-changed since World War Two. After a post-war period of Hunter operations, Biggin Hill was for many years a non-flying station where would-be RAF pilots were weeded-out prior to being selected for training, or rejected. Sadly, the RAF station is now abandoned and slowly deteriorating (with the exception of a small museum), but the airfield is very active as one of the busiest general aviation sites in the country, with a huge variety of based and visiting aircraft ranging from Cessnas to much larger Gulfstreams and even the odd former military jet. A small number of

preserved 'warbirds' have been based here too, but most have now been relocated to other airfields where surrounding airspace is less congested. Biggin Hill is also famous for its annual air display and for the infamous 'dip' beyond the threshold of Runway 03, which encouraged many display pilots to disappear below the horizon, until safety rules (and a fatal accident) forbade this speciality act. With a busy road crossing the runway threshold, observation of flying activities is certainly no problem.

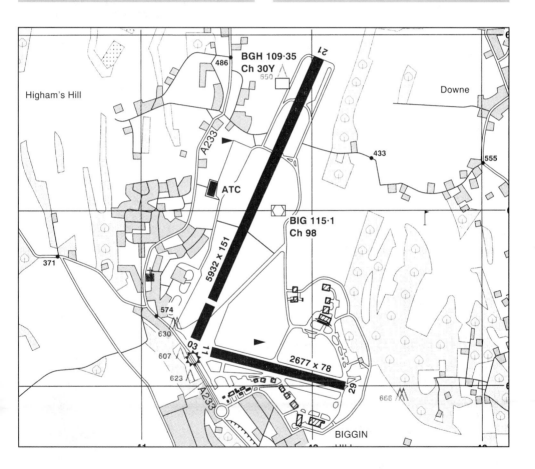

Birmingham

☺☺☺☺☺

Operator: Civilian
Location: N52 27.23 W001 44.88 (5nm S of Birmingham on the A45)
Elevation: 325ft
Tel: 0121 767 5511
Hours:
24hr

Runways:
15/33 (146T slope 0.25% up) 8,546ft
Runway 15 TODA 8,776ft, LDA 7,477ft
Runway 33 TODA 9,022ft, LDA 7,559ft
06/24 (237T) 4,314ft
Runway 06 TODA 4,541ft, LDA 3,363ft
Runway 24 TODA 4,734ft, LDA 3,898ft

Radio:
Approach – 118.05
Radar – 118.05 131.325
Tower – 118.3
Ground – 121.8
Information – 126.275

Notes:
Opened in 1939, Birmingham (Elmdon) Airport was associated with the test flying of newly built Stirlings and Lancasters during World War Two (constructed by the nearby Austin car factory), together with Tiger Moth training operations. Civilian flying began in 1946 and the site is now a major international airport serving over a hundred destinations. In addition to the numerous scheduled services, Birmingham provides facilities for general aviation flying, much of which takes place on the shorter Runway 06/24. Accessible by car, rail and bus, the airport boasts dedicated public viewing and shop facilities. A new terminal complex has been constructed from where aircraft movements can be observed, and plans to close the secondary runway have been shelved, largely as a result of protests from general aviation flyers who frequently use it. Movements are fairly frequent, and comprise mostly aircraft in the medium-capacity category (Boeing 737, A320, etc.).

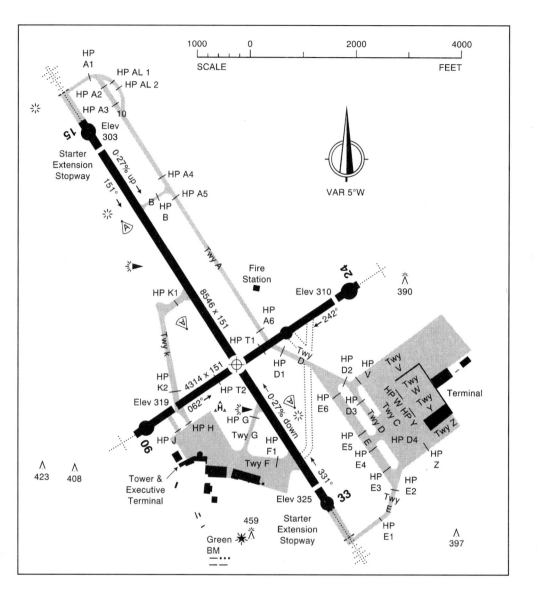

Blackbushe
☺☺☺

Operator: Civilian
Location: N51 19.43 W000 50.85 (8nm S of Reading on A30)
Elevation: 329ft
Tel: 01252 873338
Hours:
(winter) 0800–1700
(summer) 0700–1700

Runways:
08/26 (072T slope 0) 4,436ft
Runway 08 TODA 4,058ft, LDA 3,615ft
Runway 26 TODA 4,058ft, LDA 3,494ft

Radio:
Information – 122.33
Radar – 122.3

Notes:
A significant World War Two airfield, Blackbushe was transferred to civilian operation in 1947 and quickly became a popular destination along with Northolt, thanks to its proximity to London. The airfield regularly hosted visiting military aircraft, particularly during the SBAC Farnborough Show period, when Blackbushe often provided a base for aircraft associated with the event. More recently the late Doug Arnold housed his collection of preserved 'warbirds' here, and the airfield is currently the home to a thriving general aviation community. Aircraft other than typical general aviation types are now only rarely seen at Blackbushe. Access to the airfield and viewing of activities is relatively easy, and the clubhouse and café are normally open to visitors.

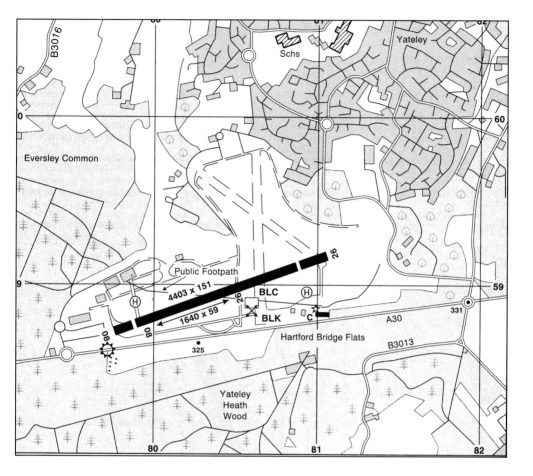

Blackpool (Squire's Gate)

☺☺☺

Operator: Civilian
Location: N53 46.29 W003 01.71 (2nm S of Blackpool off A584)
Elevation: 34ft
Tel: 01253 343434
Hours:
0700–2100

Runways:
10/28 (095T slope 0.07% down) 6,132ft
Runway 10 TODA 7,119ft, LDA 6,132ft
Runway 28 TODA 6,988ft, LDA 6,132ft
13/31 (307T slope 0) 3,524ft
Runway 13 TODA 3,937ft, LDA 3,031ft
Runway 31 TODA 3,934ft, LDA 3,524ft
07/25 (248T slope 0) 2,854ft
Runway 07 TODA 2,559ft, LDA 2,526ft
Runway 25 TODA 3,517ft, LDA 2,460ft

Radio:
Approach – 119.95 135.95
Tower – 118.4
Radar – 135.95
Information – 121.75

Notes:
An historic aviation site, the first aircraft landed on the site (which was then a racecourse) in 1909, although the airfield officially opened in 1919. A wartime manufacturer site, post-war aircraft were also completed at Squire's Gate, and military aircraft still occasionally visit the airfield, particularly during occasional air display weekends. The small passenger terminal was redeveloped in 1995 and the current facility handles a small but steady series of movements ranging from light aircraft to a handful of larger airliners. The general aircraft community thrives at Blackpool with four flying clubs on site. Indeed, the only part of Blackpool Airport which doesn't appear to be thriving is the Vulcan bomber situated near the airport entrance, which has sadly been allowed to seriously deteriorate since it flew in around fifteen years ago. Observation of aircraft from adjacent roads is possible, although movements (other than general aviation types) are fairly minimal.

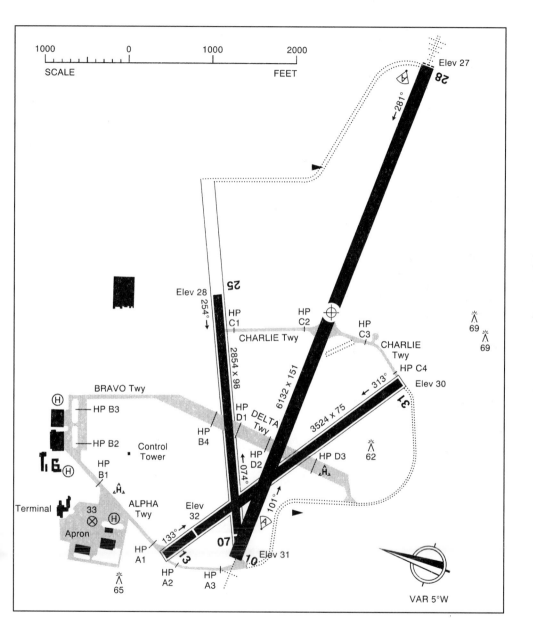

SCALE

FEET

1000   0   1000   2000

Elev 27

28

281°

Elev 28

25

254°

2854 x 98

HP C1

HP C2

CHARLIE Twy

HP C3

CHARLIE Twy

HP C4

69

69

Elev 30

313°

31

6132 x 151

3524 x 75

BRAVO Twy

HP B3

HP B2

Control Tower

HP B4

HP D1

DELTA Twy

HP D2

074°

HP D3

62

Terminal

HP B1

ALPHA Twy

Elev 32

33

Apron

07

133°

HP A1

13

Elev 31

10

101°

65

HP A2

HP A3

VAR 5°W

Boscombe Down

☺☺☺☺☺☺☺☺

Operator: Ministry of Defence
(Procurement Executive)
Location: N51 09.13 W001 44.84 (7nm
NE of Salisbury)
Elevation: 407ft
Tel: 01980 665431
Hours:
0830–1700 Mon–Thu, 0830–1600 Fri

Runways:
05/23 (050.13T slope 0.20% down)
10,538ft
Runway 05 TODA 10,538ft, LDA 10,528ft
Runway 23 TODA 10,594ft, LDA 10,202ft
17/35 (166.55T slope 0.39% down)
6,918ft
Runway 17 TODA 6,353ft, LDA 6,278ft
Runway 35 TODA 6,773ft, LDA 6,278ft

Radio:
Departures – 359.775 276.85 130.0
Director – 291.65 130.0
Talkdown – 336.15 130.0
Tower – 386.7 130.75
Ground – 299.4 130.75

Notes:
Undoubtedly a fascinating airfield, Boscombe Down is at the very centre of the Ministry of Defence's aviation research efforts, and all new aircraft and associated weapon development (other than that performed by manufacturers) is based here, with the Defence Evaluation and Research Agency. Additionally, the world-famous Empire Test Pilots School (ETPS) is also located at Boscombe Down, and their mixed fleet of aircraft (including the Jaguar, Hawk, Hunter and BAC1-11) can be seen operating at the airfield on most days. The Royal Air Force's Strike/ Attack Operational Evaluation Unit operates a fleet of Harriers, Jaguars and

BOSCOMBE DOWN is one of the UK's most fascinating airfields, where most of the MoD's test flying is based. The ETPS fleet is also based here.

Tornadoes, and the Southampton University Air Squadron/No. 2 Air Experience Flight operates Bulldogs. Test flying is by its very nature somewhat unpredictable, and so viewing of these activities can be difficult, but occasionally very rewarding. Good views of the airfield can be obtained close to the threshold of Runways 17 and 23, but despite the fact that aircraft enthusiasts regularly photograph aircraft from this location, signposts would suggest that picture-taking is still officially (and not surprisingly) discouraged. The cluster of aircraft shelters (built to house F-111s deployed from the USA) are now only rarely used to accommodate based aircraft. A small number of visiting types can also be seen occasionally.

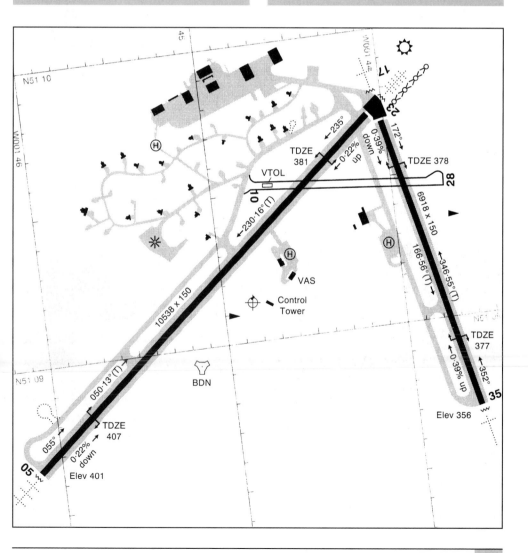

Bournemouth (Hurn)
☺☺☺☺

Operator: Civilian
Location: N50 46.80 W001 50.55 (3nm N of Bournemouth)
Elevation: 36ft
Tel: 01202 364152
Hours:
0630–2130

Runways:
08/26 (075T slope 0.10% down) 7,451ft
Runway 08 TODA 8,451ft, LDA 6,030ft
Runway 26 TODA 6,844ft, LDA 6,463ft
17/35 (345T slope 0) 4,843ft
Runway 17 TODA 4,866ft, LDA 4,446ft
Runway 35 TODA 4,810ft, LDA 4,446ft

Radio:
Approach – 119.625
Radar – 119.625 118.65
Tower – 125.6
Ground – 121.7
Information – 121.95

Notes:
Another historic World War Two airfield, Hurn was the base for bomber types and a variety of aircraft connected with the D–Day landings. Post-war, the airfield was a base for Vickers/British Aircraft Corporation, but more recently the site has become a fully fledged airport with a number of scheduled flights and a growing number of cargo movements. General aviation, air taxis and flying schools are also based here, together with FR Aviation, whose fleet of Falcon 20s is used in support of military exercises across the UK. Military aircraft are occasionally seen at Hurn, thanks to the various overhaul and repair companies based on the airfield. Access to the

BOURNEMOUTH is home to a variety of warbirds, and the Royal Jordanian Historic Flight (illustrated) was formed here, one Hunter from the Flight still remaining at Hurn.

airfield is easy, although the many companies and facilities are scattered across the relatively large airfield. Divided into three areas, the main terminal is signposted from the A31 and A338, while to the north-east, a further cluster of flying schools and air taxis share space with FR Aviation. To the north-west, the third area is less active, with a growing industrial estate and some aviation companies. Also based here is Jet Heritage, with its collection of preserved airworthy jets, including Hunters and a Meteor. Observation of movements is certainly possible but somewhat unpredictable, thanks to the spread of facilities over a very large area.

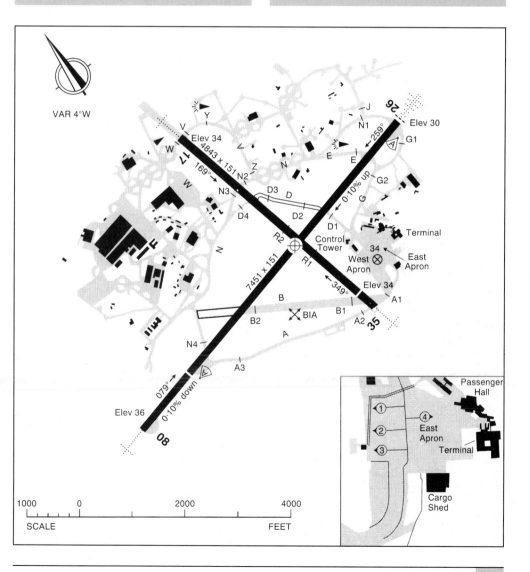

Bristol (Lulsgate)
☺☺☺☺

Operator: Civilian
Location: N51 22.96 W002 43.15 (6nm S of Bristol on A38)
Elevation: 622ft
Tel: 01275 474444
Hours:
24hrs

Runways:
09/27 (086T slope 0.15% down) 6,598ft
Runway 09 TODA 6,683ft, LDA 6,358ft
Runway 27 TODA 9,895ft, LDA 6,155ft

Radio:
Approach – 128.55
Radar – 124.35
Tower – 133.85

Notes:
A World-War-Two-vintage training airfield, this site was developed into an airport during the 1950s, the main runway having been extended twice for commercial use. Scheduled and charter flights share the airfield with general aviation, and a modern terminal has been constructed adjacent to the A38 from where movements can be observed. Military visitors are very rare, and largely confined to approaches and overshoots. Viewing the airport's operations was easily achieved thanks to a public enclosure, but this has recently been removed due to development of the site. Until it is reinstated, the best observations can be achieved from surrounding roads, although activity other than general aviation is fairly low.

BRISTOL airport caters for a variety of domestic scheduled services and occasional charter flights.

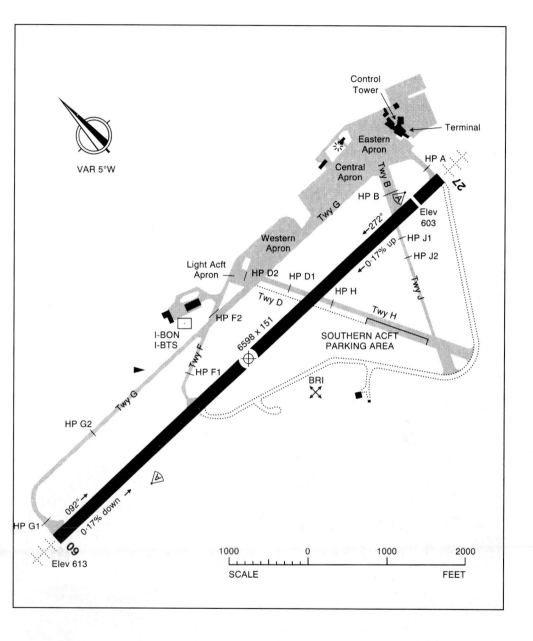

VAR 5°W

Control
Tower

Terminal

Eastern
Apron

HP A

27

Twy B

Central
Apron

HP B

←272°

Elev
603

Western
Apron

0·17% up

HP J1

HP J2

Twy G

Light Acft
Apron

HP D2

HP D1

HP H

Twy J

Twy D

Twy H

HP F2

6598 × 151

SOUTHERN ACFT
PARKING AREA

I-BON
I-BTS

Twy F

HP F1

BRI

Twy G

HP G2

092°→

0·17% down →

HP G1

09

Elev 613

1000		0		1000		2000

SCALE

FEET

Brize Norton

☺☺☺☺☺☺☺

Operator: Royal Air Force
Location: N51 45.00 W001 35.02 (1nm SE of Carterton)
Elevation: 288ft
Tel: 01993 842551
Hours:
24hrs

Radio:
Radar – 134.3 257.1
Zone – 119.0
Director – 124.275 356.875 344.0
Talkdown – 123.725 338.65 385.4
Tower – 126.5 396.7 257.8
Ground – 121.725 370.3

Notes:
The Royal Air Force's largest operational airfield, Brize Norton opened in 1937 and has always been associated with transport aircraft. The huge 10,000ft runway once enabled regular Strategic Air Command detachments to be made at Brize, which included types such as the B-47 and B-52 as well as the awesome B-58 Hustler. The station is currently home to the RAF's strategic transport fleet and its tactical/strategic refuelling tanker squadrons. VC10s make up the bulk of movements at Brize (Nos. 10 and 101 Squadrons) while 216 Squadron TriStars (the largest aircraft ever to operate in RAF service) are also frequently seen arriving or departing. Brize is also the home of No.1 Parachute Training School and the famous Falcons parachute team, although parachute drops are not made over the airfield. Visiting Nato transport aircraft are common, other military types less so, although RAF fast jets do perform practice approaches, en route to low-level corridors to the west of the airfield. Excellent views of operations can be made from the road crossing the approach to Runway 26, and with a

BRIZE NORTON, the huge VC10/TriStar servicing hangar is clearly visible.

large fleet of very active transports and tankers, aircraft movements are fairly continuous. Views of the Runway 08 threshold are not particularly reward-ing, thanks to its distance from the road network. Once the home of the mighty

Belfast freighter, Brize will soon be the new home for the RAF's fleet of leased C17 Globemaster transports, and new tanker and strategic tanker types will eventually replace the VC10 fleet at the base.

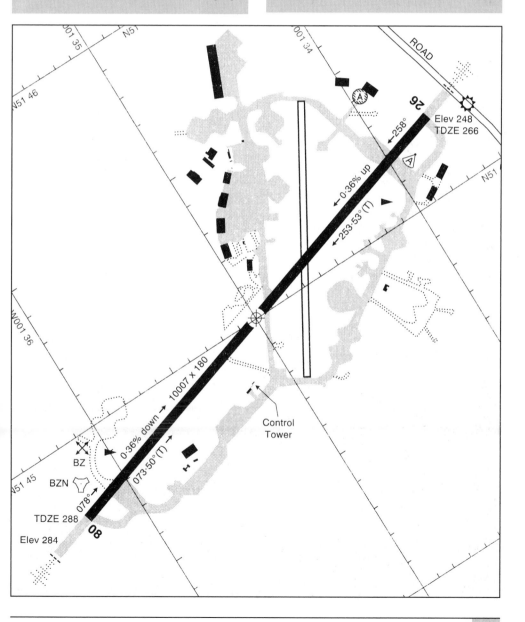

EGSC

Cambridge (Teversham)

☺☺☺☺

Operator: Civilian
Location: N52 12.30 E000 10.50 (1nm E of Cambridge on A1303)
Elevation: 50ft
Tel: 01223 293737/373213
Hours:
0900-1800

Runways:
05/23 (051T slope 0.15% up) 6,447ft
Runway 05 TODA 6,404ft, LDA 5,472ft
Runway 23 TODA 6,624ft, LDA 5,735ft

Radio:
Approach – 123.6
Radar – 130.75 372.425
Tower – 122.2 372.425

CAMBRIDGE, showing part of the Marshall commercial vehicle and aviation engineering site.

Notes:
Associated closely with Marshall Aerospace (the airfield owner and operator), Teversham provides a base for Marshall's heavy engineering facilities, which attract a variety of types, most notably TriStars and C-130 Hercules transports. A wide range of military aircraft visit the Marshall facility and RAF aircraft are regularly seen at Cambridge, especially Hercules aircraft from RAF Lyneham. Business and general aviation types also visit Teversham, and the Bulldogs of the Cambridge University Air Squadron/No. 5 Air Experience Flight are also frequently active, especially at weekends. Suckling Airways Dornier 228s fly a restricted scheduled service from the airfield and a few charter flights also use Teversham, especially during summer

months. Consequently, the airfield is fairly active with both military and civil types. Unfortunately, viewing the aircraft and associated movements isn't easy, as the sensitive nature of military contract work has encouraged Marshall to keep most areas of the airfield inaccessible. However, watching arrivals and departures from the adjacent public roads is possible.

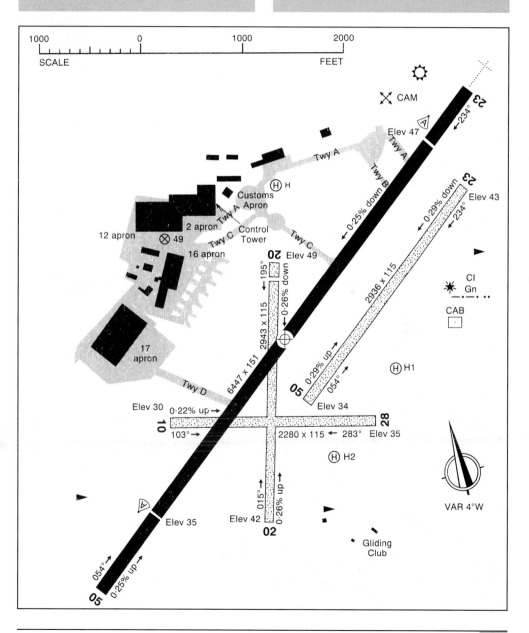

Cardiff (Rhoose)
☺☺☺☺

Operator: Civilian
Location: N51 23.80 W003 20.60 (6nm SW of Cardiff off A4226)
Elevation: 220ft
Tel: 01446 712562
Hours:
24hrs

Runways:
12/30 (117T slope 0.07% up) 7,723ft
Runway 12 TODA 8,045ft, LDA 7,001ft
Runway 30 TODA 8,215ft, LDA 7,221ft

Radio:
Approach – 125.85 277.225
Radar – 125.85 124.100 277.225
Tower – 125.0
Information – 119.475

CARDIFF is home to a major British Airways maintenance site, in addition to being an active regional airport.

Notes:
A fairly small regional airport, Cardiff boasts approximately one million passengers per year, together with roughly a dozen regular scheduled services. Charter flights are fairly common during summer months, but otherwise aircraft activity is fairly low, apart from steady general aviation traffic. The airfield was once home to a fascinating collection of preserved aircraft, but rather tragically, most of the collection was deliberately destroyed some years ago and now the airfield is dominated by a huge maintenance hangar built by British Airways to house Boeing 747s. Military visitors are rare, although RAF types do perform overshoots en route to nearby low-level routes. Observation of the airfield can be achieved in comfort from the terminal's café, while a public viewing area is also available, situated on the southern side of the airfield, within the general aviation area.

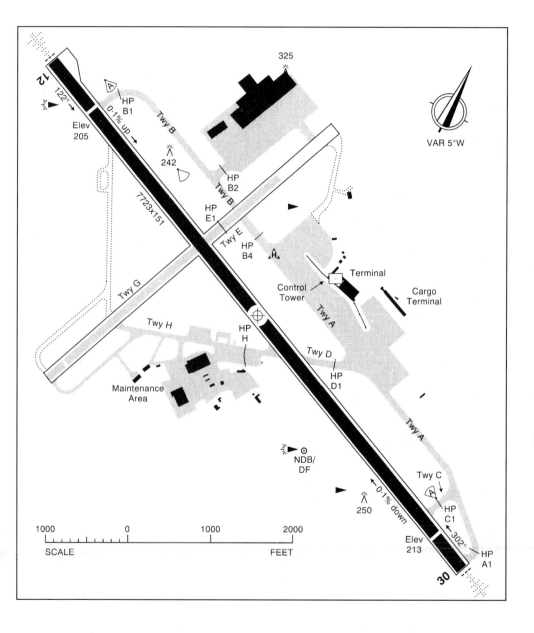

VAR 5°W

12

122°

Elev
205

0.1% up

HP
B1

Twy B

242

HP
B2

Twy B

7723x151

HP
E1

Twy E

HP
B4

325

Twy G

Terminal

Control
Tower

Cargo
Terminal

Twy A

Twy H

HP
H

Twy D

HP
D1

Maintenance
Area

Twy A

NDB/
DF

0.1% down

250

Twy C

A

HP
C1

302°

Elev
213

HP
A1

30

SCALE   FEET

1000   0   1000   2000

Carlisle
☺☺☺
Operator: Civilian
Location: N54 56.25 W002 48.55 (3nm E of Carlisle off A689)
Elevation: 190ft
Tel: 01228 573641
Hours:
0830–1900 Mon–Fri, 0900–1700 Sat–Sun

Runways:
07/25 (060T slope 0.70% up) 6,027ft
Runway 07 TODA 5,380ft, LDA 4,334ft
Runway 25 TODA 5,984ft, LDA 4,820ft
01/19 (002T) 4,226ft
Runway 01 TODA 4,127ft, LDA 3,343ft
Runway 19 TODA 4,226ft, LDA 3,310ft

Radio:
Approach – 123.6
Tower – 123.6
Radar – 123.6

Notes:
A former Royal Air Force airfield (Crosby-on-Eden), Carlisle is a fairly quiet airfield devoted to general aviation activity. Scheduled services have yet to be established (although various attempts have been made without success), but the airfield is maintained in good condition. Military aircraft are few, although some transport and communications aircraft do use the airfield, usually in connection with the nearby weapons range at Spadeadam. With three flying schools based at the airfield, light aircraft activity is common and viewing activity is actively encouraged, with a small terminal facility from where good views of the airfield can be obtained. Also on the airfield is a small collection of preserved aircraft, which include a Lightning and a Vulcan, the latter aircraft flying into Carlisle after retirement from RAF service. A third (disused) runway is regularly used to store commercial vehicles.

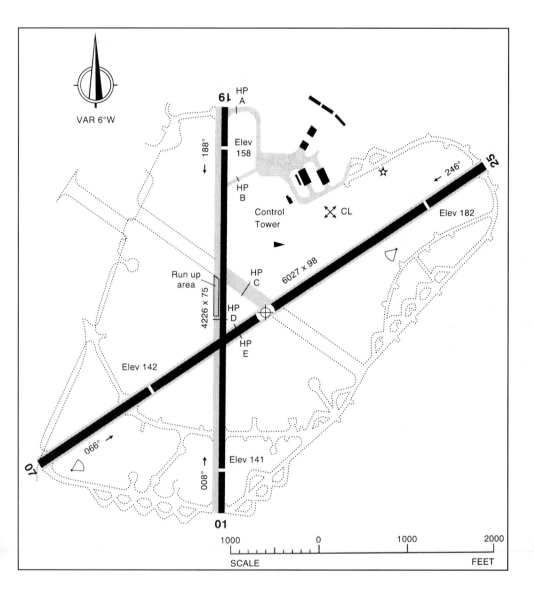

Chivenor
☺☺

Operator: Royal Marines
Location: N51 05.23 W004 09.02 (2nm
W of Barnstaple off A361)
Elevation: 50ft
Tel: 01271 813662
Hours:
24hrs

Runways:
10/28 (6,012ft)
16/34 (4,434ft)

Radio:
Radio – 252.8   130.2

---

*CHIVENOR no longer houses Hawk trainers,
but a military presence remains, thanks to the
Royal Marines. Whether the airfield returns to
a more active flying status remains to be
seen.*

Notes:
Once a very active RAF base, Chivenor is
now virtually inactive, since the withdrawal of the last RAF unit (No. 7 Flying
Training School with a fleet of Hawks) in
1994. Now a Royal Marines Base, helicopter activity is confined to Lynx,
Gazelle and Sea Kings, together with
operations associated with the remaining RAF unit, No. 22 Squadron's 'A'
Flight, with Sea King Search and Rescue
helicopters. Fixed-wing activity is all but
gone, apart from very occasional visiting
aircraft and the Vigilant gliders
belonging to No. 642 Volunteer Gliding
School. A former Coastal Command
base, little remains of Chivenor's World
War Two history, and the base is more
often remembered for its 24-year
association with the Hunters of No. 229
Operational Conversion Unit, and the
fondly remembered annual air days

which usually included mass launches of the based Hunters. Observation of the airfield is possible although there is obviously little to see by way of activity, despite the fact that the airfield is maintained in good condition. Observation of No. 22 Squadron's Sea Kings can be made via the disused railway line track which skirts the northern boundary of the airfield. The airfield has been activated for Harrier exercise deployments and may well be used again in the future. It is also possible that Chivenor may resume fixed-wing operations again at some stage, at it has done in the past.

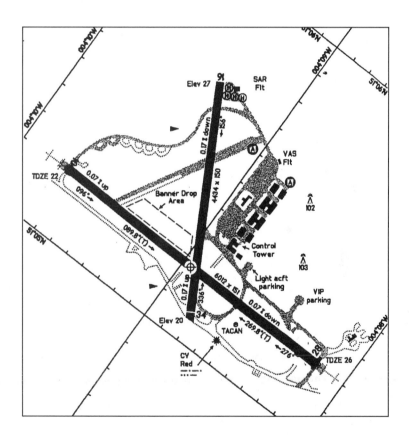

Church Fenton

☺☺☺☺

Operator: Royal Air Force
Location: N53 50.06 W001 11.73 (12nm E of Leeds off the B1223)
Elevation: 29ft
Tel: 01347 848261
Hours:
0800–1715 Mon–Thu, 0800–1700 Fri, 0830–1700 Sat–Sun

Runways:
06/24 (054.68T) 5,773ft
Runway 06 TODA 5,768ft, LDA 5,615ft
Runway 24 TODA 5,773ft, LDA 5,615ft
16/34 (155.67T) 5,466ft
Runway 16 TODA 5,597ft, LDA 5,466ft
Runway 34 TODA 5,581ft, LDA 4,811ft

Radio:
Approach – 254.525 362.3 126.5
Director – 375.325 344.0
Talkdown – 386.725 385.4 123.3
Tower – 262.7 257.8 122.1
Ground – 340.2 122.1

Notes:
A famous World-War-Two-era RAF station, Church Fenton was opened as a Fighter Command airfield, and a variety of RAF fighter types were stationed here at various times, including relatively unusual types such as the Hornet. From the 1960s onwards the station was transferred to training operations, and the base began a long association with the Jet Provost which continued until 1989 when Tucanos arrived. The resident unit (No. 7 Flying Training School) then disbanded and the Tucanos transferred to nearby Linton-on-Ouse. However, Church Fenton has remained active as a Relief Landing Ground for Linton-on-Ouse and the once-resident Tucanos are still regularly seen in Church Fenton's circuit. The Yorkshire Universities Air Squadron/No. 9 Air Experience Flight operates Bulldogs from one of the station's rather unusual (shortened) hangars, and other RAF types occasionally perform overshoots. In all other respects the base is fairly inactive, and visitors are very rare. The once-annual air display has now gone, and it remains to be seen if this popular event is reinstated at some stage. Viewing operations is easy, and a public viewing area is located on the B1222 road, close to the threshold of Runway 06. Good observations of the secondary runway can also be made from the roadside.

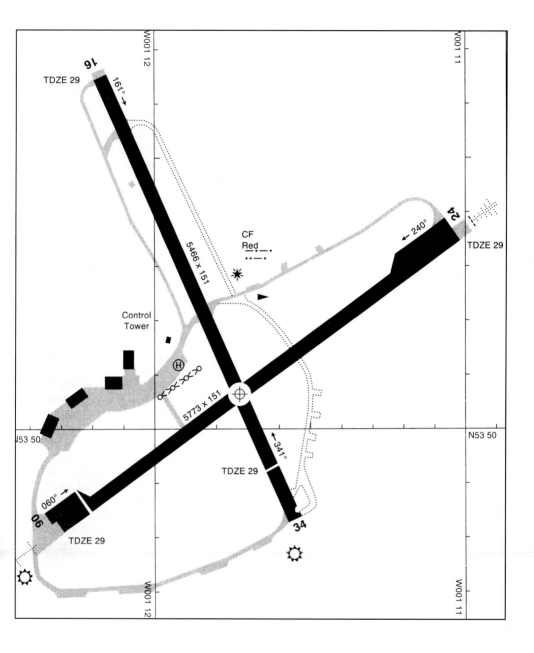

Colerne
☺

Operator: Royal Air Force
Location: N51 26.45 W002 16.80 (2nm NE of Bath)
Elevation: 593ft
Tel: 01225 743249
Hours:
Variable

Runways:
07/25 (065.21T slope 0.01% down) 4,084ft
Runway 07 TODA 5,875ft, LDA 4,658ft
Runway 25 TODA 5,449ft, LDA 4,402ft
01/19 (005.25T slope 0.001% down) 2,969ft
Runway 01 TODA 3,989ft, LDA 2,933ft
Runway 19 TODA 3,684ft, LDA 3,684ft

Radio:
Approach – 277.275 362.3 122.1
Tower – 258.975 122.1
Ground – 360.75

COLERNE is one of a number of fairly inactive airfields from where the RAF operates powered and non-powered gliders for Air Cadet flying experience.

Notes:
RAF Colerne was initially constructed as a Maintenance Unit airfield, although the station became a Fighter Command base in 1941 until the end of World War Two. After a period of Brigand and Meteor operations, Colerne became a major Hastings base, and more recently had a brief association with Hercules operations. The base was largely vacated by the RAF in 1978, after which the Army became the major occupant. However, the Bulldogs of the Bristol University Air Squadron/No. 3 Air Experience Flight remain at the airfield and provide the bulk of the station's flying activities, although Army helicopters are also regularly seen. Visitors are rare and the base is now largely inactive. Good views of the airfield can be obtained from adjacent roads, particularly Fosse Way, which crosses the threshold of Runway 07. The once-sizeable collection of preserved aircraft stored at the base has now been dispersed to other sites, such as Cosford.

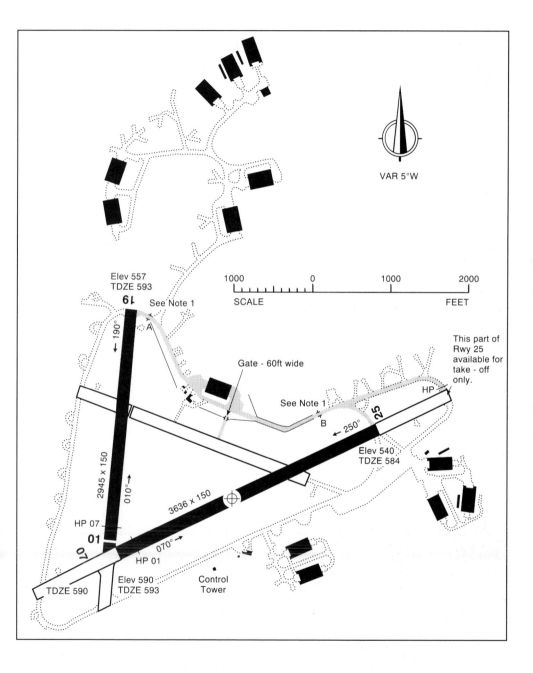

Elev 557
TDZE 593

6Ɫ

See Note 1

190°

A

Gate - 60ft wide

See Note 1

B

250°

25

This part of
Rwy 25
available for
take - off
only.

HP

1000   0   1000   2000

SCALE   FEET

VAR 5°W

Elev 540
TDZE 584

2945 x 150

010°

3636 x 150

070°

HP 07

01

07

HP 01

TDZE 590

Elev 590
TDZE 593

Control
Tower

Coltishall

☺☺☺☺☺☺☺☺

Operator: Royal Air Force
Location: N52 45.30 E001 21.44 (6nm N of Norwich on the B1150)
Elevation: 66ft
Tel: 01603 737361
Hours:
0830–1730 Mon–Thu, 0830–1700 Fri

Runways:
04/22 (035.80T slope 0.16% up) 7,500ft
Runway 04 TODA 7,500ft, LDA 7,500ft
Runway 22 TODA 7,620ft, LDA 7,500ft

Radio:
Approach – 315.325 342.25 122.1
Director – 342.25 125.9 123.3
Talkdown – 275.975 254.25 123.3
Tower – 339.95 122.1 142.29
Ground – 387.775
Operations – 364.8

COLTISHALL remains active as the RAF's Jaguar base, the home of Nos. 6, 41 and 54 Squadrons, together with the Jaguar OCU.

Notes:
A famous Battle of Britain airfield opened in 1940, Coltishall was the home to a variety of famous World-War-Two-era types such as the Walrus and Beaufighter, as well as the Spitfire and, most notably, the Hurricane. Post-war, the station hosted Mosquitoes, Vampires, Venoms, Meteors and Javelins before becoming the Royal Air Force's first Lightning base in 1960. After a long period of association with Lightning operations, the station transferred to strike/attack and recon-naissance operations, becoming a Jaguar base in 1974. Currently, Coltishall is the home of Nos. 6, 54 and 41 Squadrons, the RAF's three remaining operational Jaguar units, joined by No.16 (R) Squadron (the Jaguar Operational Conversion Unit) in 1999 following its transfer from Lossiemouth. A very active RAF base, Coltishall's Jaguars are normally visible on the station's ramp, as (unlike other Strike Command bases) the base does

not have a Hardened Aircraft Shelter complex. Excellent views of aircraft movements can be obtained from adjacent roads, and a small access road leads to an outstanding vantage point next to the threshold of Runway 22. Visiting RAF types are also regularly seen, and many Nato types can be observed during exercise periods, making Coltishall a particularly popular airfield for observation and photography.

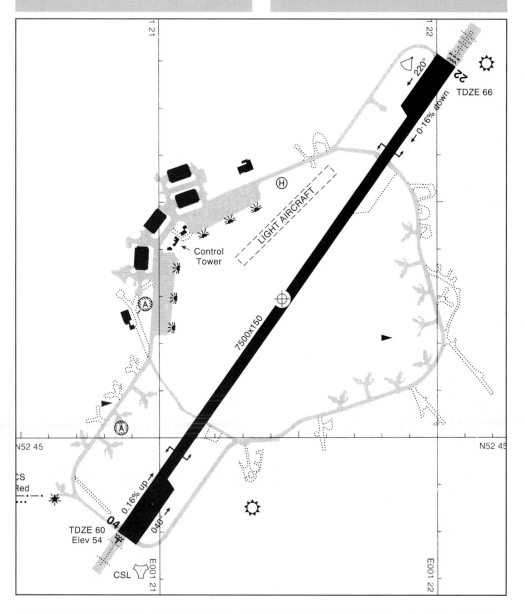

Coningsby

☺☺☺☺☺☺☺☺☺

Operator: Royal Air Force
Location: N53 05.58 W000 09.96 (1nm
SE of Tattershall off A153)
Elevation: 25ft
Tel: 01526 342581
Hours:
0800–1700 Mon–Fri

Runways:
08/26 (071.91T slope 0.06% up) 9,000ft
Runway 08 TODA 9,672ft, LDA 9,000ft
Runway 26 TODA 9,157ft, LDA 9,000ft

Radio:
Approach – 312.225 362.3 344.625
120.8 122.1
Director – 262.95 344.0
Talkdown – 300.925 337.975 123.3
Tower – 275.875 119.975 120.8 122.1
Ground – 358.55 122.1

---

*CONINGSBY is an excellent site for
over-the-fence aircraft photography, as
illustrated by this photograph of a visiting
Tornado F3 from Leeming.*

Notes:
Having opened in 1940 as a bomber
base, Coningsby operated Hampdens,
Manchesters and Lancasters during the
war, with Mosquitoes, Lincolns and
B-29 Washingtons during the early
post-war years. After a period of
Canberra operations the base was
developed into a V-bomber station prior
to the arrival of Vulcans. The base was
then closed to prepare for the arrival of
the TSR2, but following the cancellation
of that project, Coningsby received
Phantoms in 1966 which remained at
the base until Tornado F2s and F3s took
over during the late 1980s. Coningsby
currently provides a home to Nos. 5
and 56(R) Squadrons with Tornado F3s,
the Air Warfare Centre's Tornado
F3 unit, and of course the Battle of
Britain Memorial Flight (BBMF) with
Spitfires, Hurricanes, Lancasters,
Dakotas and Chipmunks. Excellent
views of the airfield can be obtained

from minor roads which cross the approaches to both ends of the runway, and the base regularly receives a variety of Nato and RAF visitors, especially during exercises. The Battle of Britain Flight is also active during most summer weekends, and public tours of the BBMF facility are usually available.

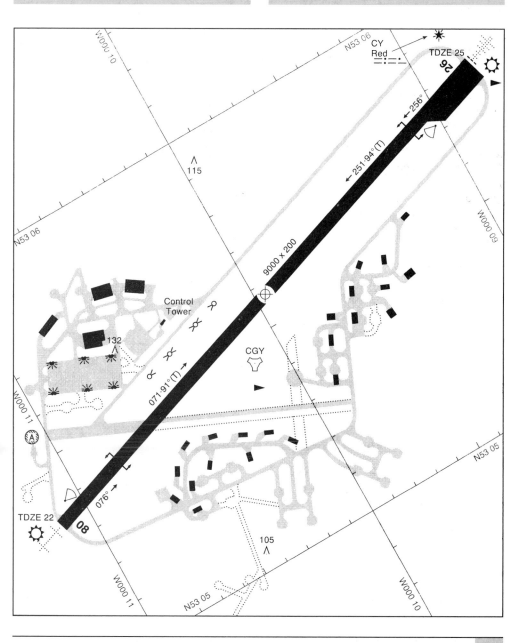

Cosford

☺☺☺☺☺☺☺

Operator: Royal Air Force
Location: N52 38.40 W002 18.33 (5nm E of Telford off A464)
Elevation: 271ft
Tel: 01902 372393
Hours:
As required

Runways:
06/24 (057T slope 0.37% up) 3,770ft
Runway 06 TODA 3,770ft, LDA 3,695ft
Runway 24 TODA 3,770ft, LDA 3,671ft

Radio:
Approach – 276.125 118.925
Tower – 357.125 118.925
Ground – 121.95

Notes:
Although rather quiet in terms of aircraft movements, Cosford's adjacent Aerospace Museum makes a visit well worth while. The only resident flying units are the Birmingham University Air Squadron/No. 8 Air Experience Flight with Bulldogs, and No. 633 Volunteer Gliding School with Vigilants. Visitors are rare, although aircraft are occasionally delivered by air to the resident technical school or to the Aerospace Museum, and the majority of aircraft on the base were originally flown in. Other aircraft movements are confined to Jet Provosts and Harrier GR3s belonging to the ground training school, and these can often be seen on the flight line, or taxiing around the perimeter tracks. Excellent views of the airfield and activity can be obtained from the Museum access road.

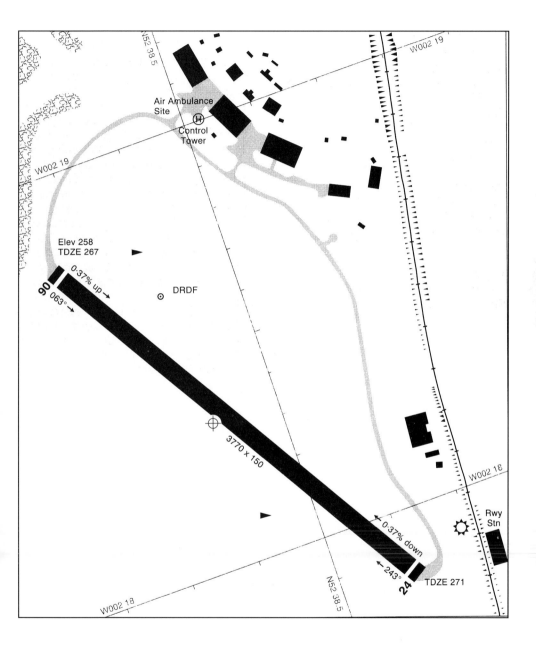

Air Ambulance Site

Control Tower

Elev 258
TDZE 267

0.37% up →

90

063° →

DRDF

3770 x 150

90

0.37% down

243°

24

TDZE 271

Rwy Stn

W002 19

N52 38 5

W002 19

W002 18

W002 18

N52 38 5

Cottesmore

☺☺☺☺☺☺☺☺

Operator: Royal Air Force
Location: N52 44.14 W000 38.93 (12nm SE of Melton Mowbray off A1)
Elevation: 461ft
Tel: 01572 812241
Hours:
0800–1700 Mon–Fri

Runways:
05/23 (041.32T slope 0.75% down) 9,004ft
Runway 05 TODA 9,070ft, LDA 9,004ft
Runway 23 TODA 9,103ft, LDA 9,004ft

Radio:
Approach – 312.075 340.575 130.2
Director – 312.075 358.725 123.3
Talkdown – 262.9 337.875 123.3
Tower – 370.05 122.1 257.8 130.2
Ground – 336.375 122.1

COTTESMORE was the home of the TTTE until 1999, when the Tornadoes were dispersed to their respective national owners, leaving the base to prepare for Harrier operations.

Notes:
A large bomber airfield opened during the Royal Air Force's expansion in World War Two, Cottesmore was further expanded in the 1950s to accommodate Vulcan and Victor V-bombers. The station also enjoyed a long association with the Canberra, No. 231 Operational Conversion Unit being based at Cottesmore for many years, along with ECM Canberra units. In 1980 the airfield received the Royal Air Force's first operational Tornado aircraft, and the Tri-national Tornado Training Establishment (TTTE) was subsequently opened, operating a large fleet of British, Italian and German Tornadoes. Following the disbandment of the TTTE in 1999, Cottesmore became a Harrier base, with Nos. 3 and 4 Squadrons relocating from Laarbruch, together with No. 1 Squadron from nearby Wittering, the two airfields effectively becoming one large 'twin base' for Harrier operations. Viewing aircraft movements is possible at Cottesmore, the best vantage point being from a small road which leads to a position close to the eastern edge of the flight line. Although photography

of the flight line is difficult from this point, aircraft do operate on the adjacent taxiway which is easily observed. The approach to Runway 05 is virtually inaccessible, but a fairly close look at the Runway 23 approach is possible, although the airfield is obscured from view at this point. Aircraft activity is likely to be fairly high when the Harrier units have settled into their new environment, especially during exercise periods.

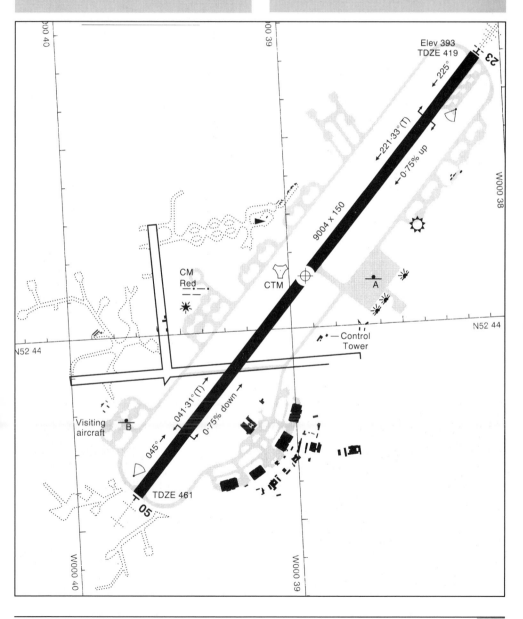

Coventry (Baginton)

☺☺☺☺☺☺

Operator: Civilian
Location: N52 22.18 W001 28.78 (SE of central Coventry off A45)
Elevation: 281ft
Tel: 024 7630 1717
Hours:
0730–2359 Mon, 24hrs Tue–Fri,
0001–2000 Sat, 0830–2100 Sun

Runways:
05/23 (047T slope 0.02% down) 5,299ft
Runway 05 TODA 6,119ft, LDA 5,299ft
Runway 23 TODA 6,690ft, LDA 5,299ft

Radio:
Approach – 119.25
Radar – 122.0
Tower – 119.25 124.8
Ground – 121.7

COVENTRY is Air Atlantique's home base. A sizable fleet of Dakotas remains active at the airfield.

Notes:
Coventry was for many years associated with the aircraft manufacturer Armstrong Whitworth, and countless bombers (including Whitleys and Lancasters) were completed and first flown from the airfield during World War Two. Post-war, aircraft production included Sea Hawks, Meteors (especially night-fighter versions), Hunters and Argosy transports. The site of the Armstrong Whitworth factory is now devoted to car production, but the airfield is still very active as both a general aviation site and a popular cargo base. The main resident is Air Atlantique with a fleet of Dakotas, DC-6s and a growing number of 'warbirds' ranging from a Devon and Twin Pioneer to a pair of Shackletons. Cargo flights are sporadic but can include exotic types such as the Boeing 707. The small terminal handles a few services, but the most regular activity is

provided by flying clubs. The adjacent Midlands Air Museum houses a fascinating collection of aircraft such as a Vulcan, Argosy, Lightning, Voodoo, Phantom and Starfighter, and aircraft

movements can also be observed from this area, although a more convenient viewing area is available at the airport site. Access to good views of the runway approaches is also possible.

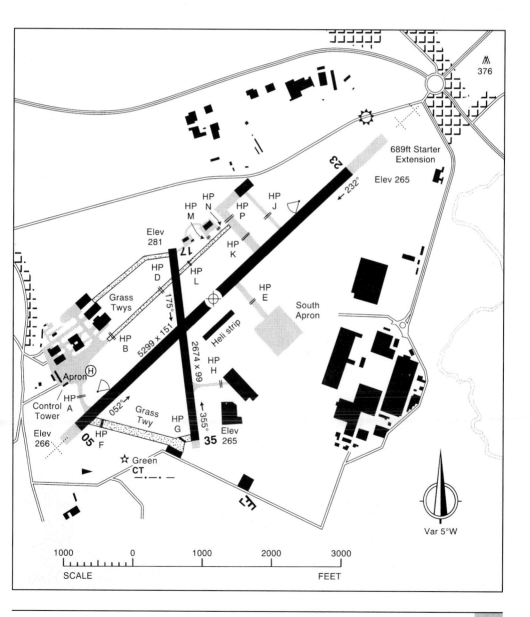

Cranfield

☺☺☺☺☺☺

Operator: Civilian
Location: N52 04.33 W000 37.00 (5nm SW of Bedford off A509)
Elevation: 364ft
Tel: 01234 754761
Hours:
0830–1900 Mon–Fri, 0900–1800 Sat–Sun

Runways:
04/22 (032T slope 0.03% down) 5,928ft
Runway 04 TODA 6,335ft, LDA 5,256ft
Runway 22 TODA 6,004ft, LDA 5,512ft

Radio:
Approach – 122.85
Tower – 134.925 122.85

Notes:
Cranfield has for many years been associated with the Institute of Technology, and this organisation still dominates the site, although a growing number of smaller companies have seen Cranfield continue to grow as a general aviation base. Both flying clubs and air taxi operators are located here, together with maintenance companies and a variety of civilian 'warbird' (particularly jet) operators. Indeed, Cranfield is probably the only place where Cessnas can be seen sharing a taxiway with a Lightning! The annual Popular Flying Association attracts hundreds of light aircraft, and other air shows are regularly staged at Cranfield, again with an emphasis on jet operations, and the RAF gave its last Vulcan display over the airfield. The Empire Test Pilots School was also based here prior to moving to Farnborough, although Cranfield's military connections have all but gone now. Vantage points are plenty, including a café which overlooks the airfield.

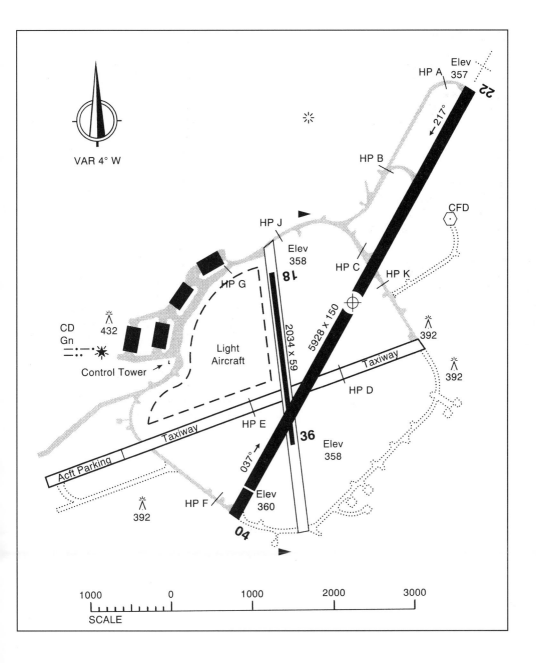

Cranwell

☺☺☺☺☺☺☺

Operator: Royal Air Force
Location: N53 01.82 W000 28.99 (5nm NW of Sleaford off A17)
Elevation: 218ft
Tel: 01400 261201
Hours:
As required

Runways:
09/27 (082.7T slope 0.65% down) 6,831ft
Runway 09 TODA 6,909ft, LDA 6,293ft
Runway 27 TODA 6,909ft, LDA 6,526ft
01/19 (008.2T slope 0.13% up) 4,803ft
Runway 01 TODA 4,803ft, LDA 4,803ft
Runway 19 TODA 4,803ft, LDA 4,803ft

Radio:
Approach – 340.475 362.3 119.375
Departures – 250.05
Director – 282.0 123.3 344.0
Talkdown – 356.925 122.1 257.8
Tower – 379.525 122.1 257.8
Ground – 297.9

CRANWELL as viewed from the south, with the smaller grass field (Cranwell North) discernible beyond the domestic site.

Notes:
Originally opened in 1916 as a Royal Naval Air Station, Cranwell was transferred to the RAF in 1918, the famous RAF College opening here in 1934. Traditionally associated with training operations, most RAF trainer types have been based here at some stage, ranging from the Harvard and Vampire to the Varsity, with the Jet Provost being the longest-serving resident aircraft type. Following the withdrawal of the Royal Air Force's Jet Provosts, Cranwell became a Tucano base. More recently the latter type has moved to Linton-on-Ouse, making way for the Dominies of No. 55(R) Squadron, the Jetstreams of No. 45(R) Squadron and the Bulldogs of the Central Flying School. The world-famous Red Arrows are also based at Cranwell, although formation flying training is conducted some miles away overhead their former base at Scampton. Good views of the very busy airfield circuit can be obtained, particularly on the approach to all four runway thresholds. Further light aircraft activity (including gliders) takes place at

Cranwell North airfield (a grass strip) situated to the north of the B1429. Visitors are few, other than occasional overshoots performed by RAF types, most notably the JEFTS Fireflies from nearby Barkston Heath. Jaguars belonging to a resident ground school can also sometimes be seen on the airfield.

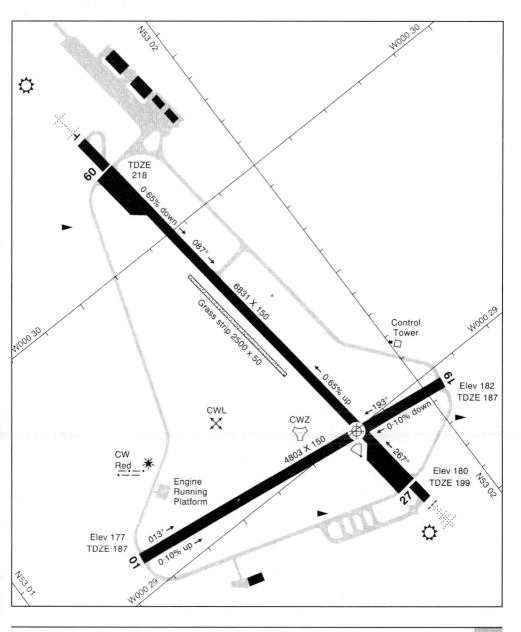

Culdrose

☺☺☺☺☺☺☺☺

Operator: Royal Navy
Location: N50 05.17 W005 15.34 (1nm SE of Helston)
Elevation: 267ft
Tel: 01326 574121
Hours:
0830–1700 Mon–Thu, 0830–1400 Fri

Runways:
12/30 (112.82T slope 0.16% up) 6,006ft
Runway 12 TODA 6,097ft, LDA 6,006ft
Runway 30 TODA 6,102ft, LDA 6,006ft
07/25 (243T slope 0.36% up) 3,420ft
Runway 07 TODA 3,370ft, LDA 3,370ft
Runway 25 TODA 3,370ft, LDA 3,370ft
18/36 (178.46T slope 0.23% down) 3,455ft
Runway 18 TODA 3,455ft, LDA 3,455ft
Runway 36 TODA 3,455ft, LDA 3,455ft

Radio:
Approach – 241.95 134.05
Radar – 241.95 134.05 339.95 122.1
Talkdown – 388.0 123.3 259.75 122.1
Tower – 386.525 122.1 123.3
Ground – 299.4

Notes:
Despite boasting no fewer than three active runways, Royal Naval Air Station Culdrose is most closely associated with helicopter flying, and the base is currently one of the world's busiest helicopter sites. Home to the Fleet Air Arm's Sea King ASW and AEW squadrons, all of these assets are based here when they are not embarked upon ships. Additionally, a SAR Sea King unit provides cover for the Cornwall area. Fixed-wing flying includes the Jetstreams of 750 Naval Air Squadron and the all-black Hawks belonging to the Fleet Requirements And Direction Unit (FRADU), together with some weekend glider flying. Visiting aircraft are fairly common, and various RAF types perform practice approaches from time to time. An excellent public viewing

CULDROSE is a busy naval helicopter base, with a public viewing enclosure designed to enable easy observation of the base's activities.

area (including a shop and café) is provided, from where activities can be observed, with the approach to the main runway just a short walk from this location. However, despite the station's reputation as a busy helicopter base, operations can be sporadic, ending early on Fridays, and ceasing completely during the annual summer leave period.

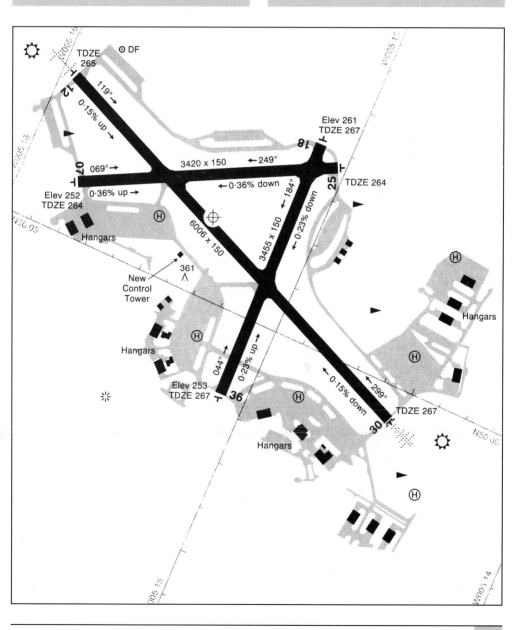

Dishforth
☺

Operator: Royal Air Force
Location: N54 08.23 W001 25.22 (8nm
NE of York off A1)
Elevation: 117ft
Tel: 01748 832521
Hours:
0730–1610 Mon–Thu, 0730–1600 Fri

Runways:

16/34 (150.79T) 6,096ft
Runway 16 TODA 6,588ft, LDA 5,630ft
Runway 34 TODA 6,588ft, LDA 5,846ft
10/28 (092.4T) 4,469ft
Runway 10 TODA 5,026ft, LDA 3,071ft
Runway 28 TODA 4,793ft, LDA 4,469ft

Radio:

Approach – 357.375 125.0 362.3 122.1
Tower – 259.825 122.1
Ground – 379.675 122.1
Operations – 252.9

Notes:
Once a busy Royal Air Force bomber station, later transferred to transport operations, Dishforth is now a joint RAF/Army station, largely devoted to Army helicopter (Lynx and Gazelle) flying. However, the circuit is regularly occupied by Tucanos from nearby Linton-on-Ouse, as Dishforth is used as a Relief Landing Ground (RLG). Glider flying takes place at weekends and some evenings, but visitors are rare. Excellent views of operations can be obtained from the road adjacent to the A1, which runs parallel with the main runway.

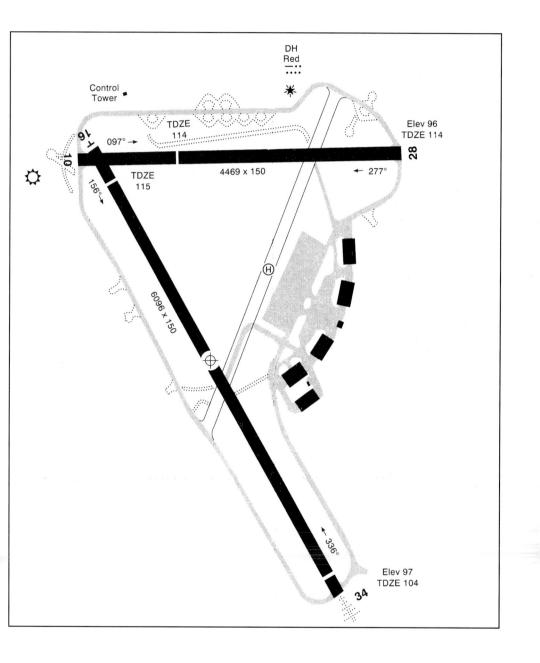

Dundee
☺

Operator: Civilian
Location: N56 27.15 W003 01.55 (1nm S of Dundee on A85)
Elevation: 13ft
Tel: 01382 669414
Hours:
0645–2030 Mon–Fri, 0930–1600 Sat–Sun

Runways:
10/28 (090T) 4,593ft
Runway 10 TODA 4,327ft, LDA 4,593ft
Runway 28 TODA 4,327ft, LDA 4,593ft

Radio:
Approach – 122.9
Tower – 122.9

Notes:
A small 'city airport', Dundee occupies a small strip of land alongside the River Tay. The emphasis is on business operations, with only a limited scheduled service. Private flying also takes place and a flying club is based at the airfield. Observing the activity is possible from the A85, and medium-level overflights from Tornado F3s approaching RAF Leuchars are quite common.

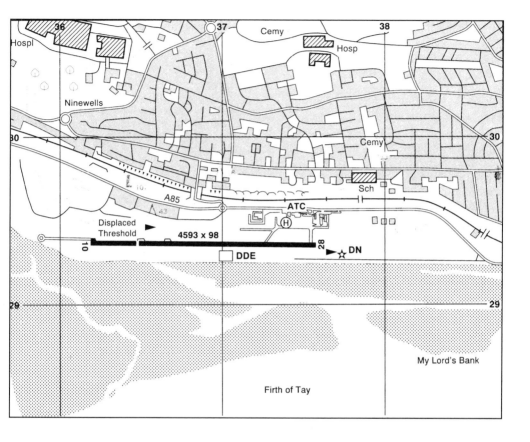

Dunkeswell
☺☺

Operator: Civilian
Location: N50 51.60 W003 14.08 (10nm E of Exeter off the A373)
Elevation: 850ft
Tel: 01404 891643
Hours:
(winter) 0900–1800 Mon–Sun
(summer) 0800–1800 Mon–Sun

Runways:
05/23 (041T) 4,268ft
Runway 05 TODA 3,159ft, LDA 3,159ft
Runway 23 TODA 3,159ft, LDA 3,159ft
18/36 (170T) 4,350ft
Runway 18 TODA 2,103ft, LDA 2,103ft
Runway 36 TODA 2,103ft, LDA 2,103ft

Radio:
Station – 123.475

Notes:
A well-known World War Two USAAF base, Dunkeswell was the home to numerous Liberators, which were later replaced by similar aircraft operated by the United States Navy. After closing in 1948 the airfield reverted to use as a glider field, but a flying club was formed in 1967 and light aircraft activity has been present on the site ever since. Now the home of the Devon School of Flying, general aviation occupies the active portion of the larger (and mostly disused) wartime airfield site. Parachuting also takes place, as well as gliding, and access to most parts of the airfield is relatively easy. However, flying activity is fairly low.

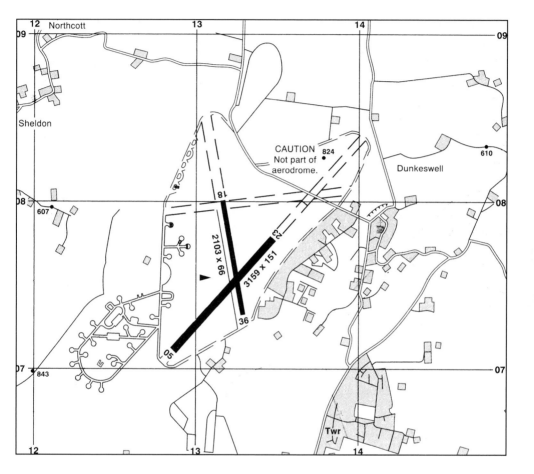

Dunsfold
☺

Operator: Civilian
Location: N51 07.03 W000 32.13 (2nm SW of Cranleigh off A281)
Elevation: 172ft
Tel: 01483 272121
Hours:
0800–1830 Mon–Fri

Runways:
07/26 (066.53T) 6,167ft
Runway 07 TODA 7,060ft, LDA 5,636ft
Runway 25 TODA 6,184ft, LDA 5,692ft

Radio:
Approach – 367.375 312.625 135.175
Radar – 367.375 135.175 122.55
Tower – 375.4 124.325

Notes:
Owned and operated by British Aerospace (BAe), relatively little activity takes place, with no resident aircraft and most movements confined to business aircraft. Hawk and Harrier test flying did take place at Dunsfold but many of these operations have now been transferred to Warton. Views of the airfield are possible, and the approach to Runway 25 can be seen from the A281 with a smaller road crossing the approach to Runway 07 at some distance. Not surprisingly, photography of the airfield facilities and/or aircraft is discouraged. The future of the airfield remains uncertain.

DUNSFOLD is a relatively inactive airfield, used sporadically for BAe test flying or communications movements. A few warbirds operate from the airfield, and this Sea Hawk was refurbished at Dunsfold on behalf of the FAA.

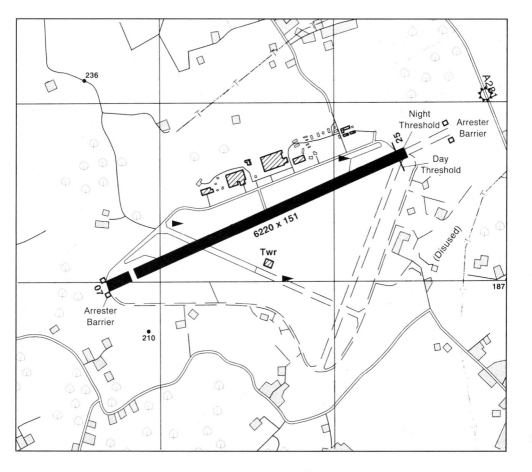

East Midlands (Castle Donington)

☺☺☺☺☺☺

Operator: Civilian
Location: N52 49.86 W001 19.60 (5nm SE of Derby off M1)
Elevation: 310ft
Tel: 01332 852852
Hours:
24hrs

Runways:
09/27 (088T slope 0.32% down) 7,480ft
Runway 09 TODA 8,497ft, LDA 7,480ft
Runway 27 TODA 8,241ft, LDA 7,480ft

Radio:
Approach – 119.65
Radar – 119.65 120.125 124.0
Tower – 124.0
Ground – 121.9

Notes:
Opened in 1942 as a Royal Air Force training and transport station, Castle Donington closed in 1946. It remained inactive until the early 1960s, when a local business consortium purchased the airfield and built an airport on the former RAF site. Although essentially a regional airport, East Midlands handles a variety of traffic, particularly cargo aircraft and parcel company movements. Scheduled services are also fairly frequent, and various aircraft are often seen visiting maintenance facilities at the airport. Military traffic is relatively rare, although some Royal Air Force aircraft are overhauled at East Midlands. Otherwise, military connections are few now that the Andover calibration aircraft operated on behalf of the RAF (and based at East Midlands) have been withdrawn. Light aircraft are not very common, although flying clubs are based at the airport. A small collection of preserved aircraft is situated next to the airport and should be available for viewing once a new location has been developed (the original site making way for a new cargo apron). Viewing movements is fairly easy, the best vantage point being the approach to Runway 27 which crosses over the M1.

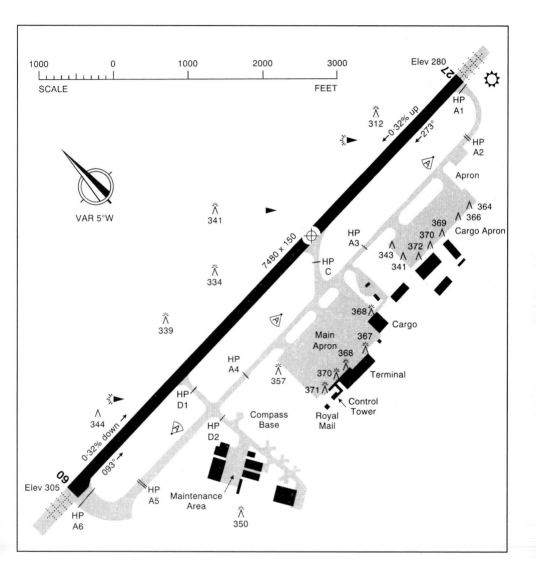

SCALE — 1000 0 1000 2000 3000 FEET

VAR 5°W

Elev 280

27

HP A1

HP A2

Apron

312
0·32% up
273°

341

364
366
369
370
372
343
341

7480 x 150

HP A3

HP C

334

339

368
Cargo

Main Apron
367
368
370
371

HP A4
357

HP D1

Compass Base

Control Tower

Royal Mail

Terminal

344
0·32% down
093°

HP D2

HP A5

09
Elev 305

HP A6

Maintenance Area

350

Edinburgh (Turnhouse)

☺ ☺ ☺ ☺ ☺ ☺

Operator: Civilian
Location: N55 57.15 W003 21.77 (3nm W of Edinburgh off the A8)
Elevation: 135ft
Tel: 0131 399 1888
Hours:
24hrs

Runways:

07/25 (059T slope 0.12% down) 8,400ft
Runway 07 TODA 8,599ft, LDA 7,700ft
Runway 25 TODA 9,865ft, LDA 7,700ft
13/31 (119T slope 0.6% up) 5,892ft
Runway 13 TODA 6,492ft, LDA 5,688ft
Runway 31 TODA 6,499ft, LDA 5,688ft
08/26 (070T slope 0.38% up) 2,621ft
Runway 08 TODA 2,621ft, LDA 2,621ft
Runway 26 TODA 2,621ft, LDA 2,621ft

Radio:

Approach – 121.2
Radar – 121.2 128.975
Tower – 118.7
Ground – 121.75

Notes:
Effectively two airfields joined together, the original Turnhouse site was opened as a Royal Air Force station prior to World War Two, acting as a base for both Spitfires and Hurricanes, and a staging post for numerous USAAF bombers during the war. More recently the remaining RAF enclave (which included a University Air Squadron) departed, and military activity is now confined to fewer visiting types. The main airport site was developed to the west of Turnhouse, with a new passenger terminal off the A8 and a new 8,000-foot runway which attracts a number of scheduled flights, charters and a variety of business aircraft, together with some helicopter traffic. Flying clubs are also present and light aircraft activity is fairly common, creating a somewhat varied aircraft movements schedule. Viewing opportunities are plenty in view of the sprawling nature of the airfield.

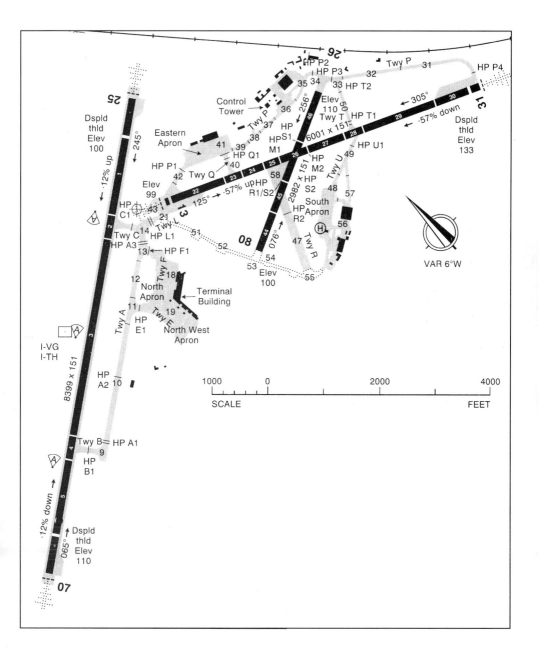

Exeter
☺ ☺ ☺ ☺ ☺

Operator: Civilian
Location: N50 44.07 W003 24.83 (3nm NE of Exeter off A30)
Elevation: 102ft
Tel: 01392 367433
Hours:
0600–2359 Mon, 0001–0100, 0600–2359 Tue–Fri, 0001–0100, 0530–2000 Sat, 0700–2359 Sun

Runways:
08/26 (076T slope 0.05% up) 6,834ft
Runway 08 TODA 8,704ft, LDA 6,683ft
Runway 26 TODA 8,704ft, LDA 6,683ft
13/31 (121T slope 0.05% up) 4,393ft
Runway 13 TODA 4,462ft, LDA 3,924ft
Runway 31 TODA 4,396ft, LDA 3,970ft

Radio:
Approach – 128.15
Radar – 128.15 119.05
Tower – 119.8

Notes:
First opened as a municipal airport in 1937, the airfield was developed into a Royal Air Force station during World War Two and the RAF maintained a presence at the airport throughout the 1960s with target-towing Meteors remaining on the airfield into the 1970s. Scheduled and charter flights have gradually increased since the 1950s and the airport currently caters for both types of aircraft, together with some business traffic, light aircraft (flying clubs being based on the airfield) and even jet warbirds, largely in the shape of Hunters (the collection of Lightnings went to South Africa, thanks to the CAA's refusal to permit their operation in the UK). Military movements are rare, but the varied traffic provides plenty to see, and observation is possible from various vantage points around the airfield, where many World War Two remains can still be seen.

EXETER is a well-established regional airport. A number of warbirds have been relocated to the airfield, these Hunters having been resident for some time.

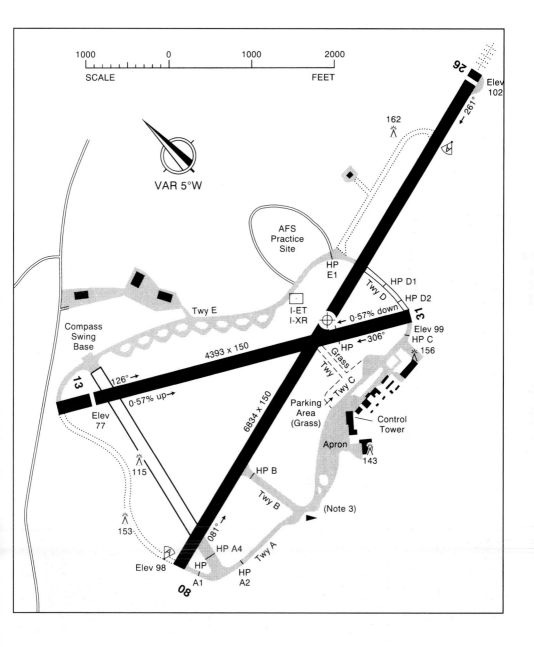

SCALE   FEET

1000   0   1000   2000

VAR 5°W

AFS Practice Site

HP E1

Twy D

HP D1

HP D2

Twy E

I-ET
I-XR

0·57% down

31

Elev 99
HP C

306°

156

Compass Swing Base

4393 x 150

Grass Twy

HP

13

126°

0·57% up

6834 x 150

Twy C

Parking Area (Grass)

Control Tower

Elev 77

Apron

143

115

HP B

Twy B

(Note 3)

153

081°

HP A4

Twy A

Elev 98

HP A1

HP A2

08

Elev 102

26

261°

162

Fairford
☺

Operator: United States Air Force
Location: N51 41.01 W001 47.41 (8nm N of Swindon)
Elevation: 268ft
Tel: 01285 714805
Hours:
As required

Runways:
09/27 (0.88.06T slope 0.37% down) 9,997ft
Runway 09 TODA 10,023ft, LDA 9,997ft
Runway 27 TODA 10,033ft, LDA 9,997ft

Radio:
Radar – 257.1 134.3
Director – 376.625 119.0
Tower – 337.575 119.15
Ground – 259.975
Operations – 379.475

FAIRFORD is deactivated for most of the year, with a brief spell of intense activity during the annual International Air Tattoo week. Occasional exercise deployments are made by B-52s and B-1Bs.

Notes:
Although Fairford is a long-established Royal Air Force base, it is perhaps best known for more modern activities, notably as the home of the Red Arrows, an operating base for Concorde development aircraft, and even more recently as the home of the world-famous International Air Tattoo. Despite the fact that Fairford is one of the busiest military airfields in the world for one weekend every year, the airfield is virtually inactive for the rest of the year, apart from very occasional visitors. Fairford is activated for brief periods once or twice a year, when USAF B-52 or B-1 bombers deploy to the base on exercise, from the continental USA. Fairford has also hosted B-52 deployments for long-range operational bombing missions over Iraq. Apart from activity connected with the International Air Tattoo (which can obviously be observed from inside the spectator positions on the show site), there is very

little to see unless an exercise is in progress. The best vantage point is on the road crossing the approach to Runway 27, although more distant views of the opposite end of the runway can also be obtained. On a day-to-day basis however, the airfield is almost always deactivated.

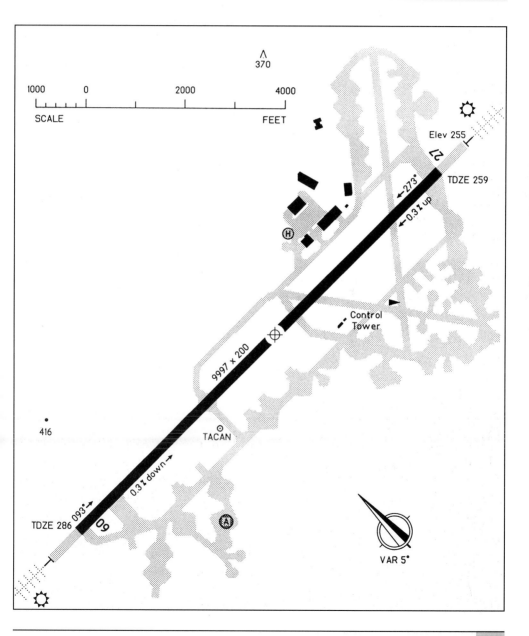

Farnborough

☺☺☺

Operator: Civilian
Location: N51 16.55 W000 46.56 (1nm N
of Aldershot off the A325)
Elevation: 237ft
Tel: 01252 392231
Hours:
0700–2200 Mon–Fri, 0800–2000 Sat–Sun

Runways:
07/25 (062.02T slope 0.17% down)
7,874ft
Runway 07 TODA 8,031ft, LDA 6,824ft
Runway 25 TODA 8,045ft, LDA 6,804ft
11/29 (107.53T slope 0.47% up) 4,494ft
Runway 11 TODA 4,494ft, LDA 4,494ft
Runway 29 TODA 4,494ft, LDA 3,641ft

Radio:
Approach – 376.9 134.35
Radar – 376.9 134.35 125.25 315.525
Talkdown – 259.0 130.05
Tower – 357.4 122.5
Operations – 130.375

*FARNBOROUGH is now a business aircraft
centre, although the airfield is still the home
of the world-famous SBAC show, held on
alternate years with the Paris Salon.*

Notes:
Possibly the most famous military airfield in Britain, Farnborough has always been linked with experimental flying, and known as the birthplace of British aviation. It is interesting to note that balloon and dirigibles were first flown here as long ago as 1915, only two years after the Wright brothers made their first flight in the USA. Home of the Royal Aircraft Establishment for a long time, a huge variety of British aircraft types have been operated from the base at various times. In 1947 the first SBAC show took place at Farnborough, and ever since then the airfield has been closely linked with what is now a biennial show, attracting a huge range of exotic aircraft types from all over the world. Indeed, there are very few aircraft types which have not visited Farnborough at some time. The Royal Aircraft Establishment no longer conducts test flying from Farnborough, even though a significant presence is still at the site (test flying is now conducted almost exclusively at Boscombe Down). The airfield is now in civilian hands, and most flying is connected with business

and general aviation. There are still occasional military visitors, however, connected with the Defence Research Agency (DRA), the Air Accident Investigation Branch (AAIB), or the RAF Institute of Aviation Medicine. Observing the movements is possible, but good vantage points are few. The best position is on the road crossing the approach to Runway 25, close to the north apron where visiting military aircraft will stop (most of the others, including DRA and AIB visitors, being parked on the south apron).

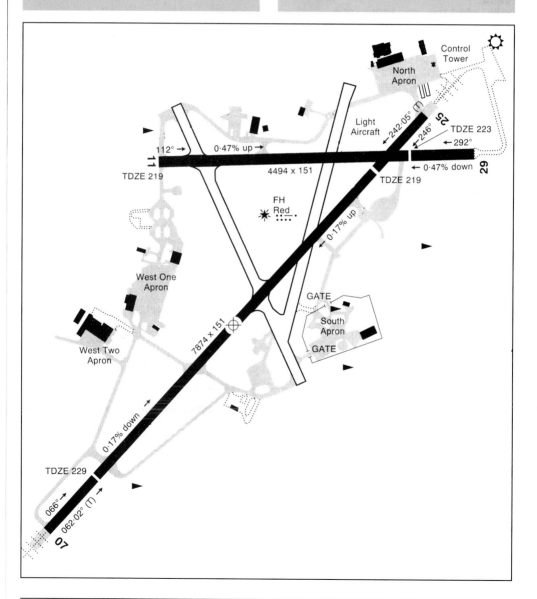

Glasgow (Abbotsinch)

☺☺☺☺☺

Operator: Civilian
Location: N55 52.32 W004 26.00
Elevation: 26ft
Tel: 0141 840 8029
Hours:
24 hrs

Runways:
05/23 (046T slope 0.09% down) 8,720ft
Runway 05 TODA 9,144ft, LDA 8,720ft
Runway 23 TODA 10,141ft, LDA 7,720ft
10/28 (271T) 3,622ft
Runway 10 TODA 3,819ft, LDA 3,419ft
Runway 28 TODA 3,819ft, LDA 3,622ft

Radio:
Approach – 119.1 362.3
Radar – 119.1 119.3 121.3 362.3
Tower – 118.8
Ground – 121.7

Notes:
Opened in 1932 as a municipal airport, Abbotsinch was later transferred to RAF and Royal Navy command, until the RAF left during World War Two, when operations continued under naval control, with a few flights made by Scottish Airways. Following the departure of the Fleet Air Arm in 1963, the airfield was gradually developed into a sizable airport, and Glasgow is now the busiest Scottish airport, with more than a dozen airlines operating from the base serving more than forty destinations, including the USA. Only one flying club remains at Glasgow (others having been encouraged to leave in anticipation of growing commercial traffic), but general aviation still forms a major part of the airport's daily movements schedule. Military visitors are rare. Observation of activity is best achieved from the A2 road, which passes close to the threshold of Runway 23 and Runway 28.

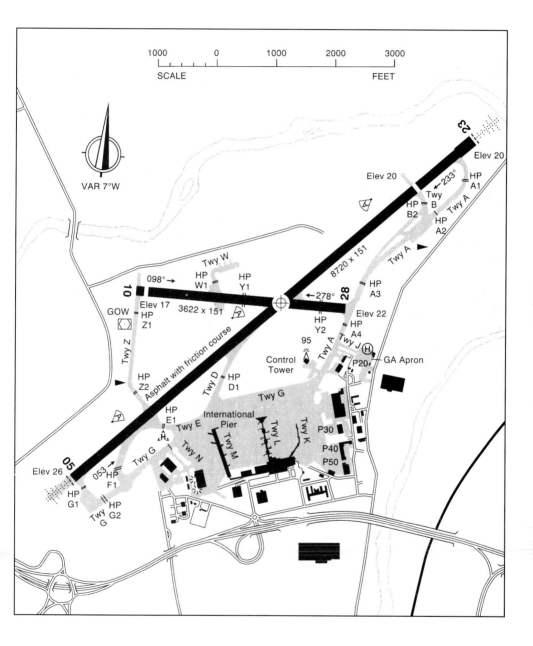

SCALE

FEET

VAR 7°W

23

Elev 20

Elev 20

HP A1

← 233°

Twy B

HP B2

Twy A

Twy A

HP A2

8720 x 151

Twy A

Twy W

098° →

HP W1

HP Y1

HP A3

10

Elev 17

3622 x 151

← 278°

28

Elev 22

GOW

HP Z1

HP Y2

HP A4

95

Twy J

Twy Z

Twy A

Control Tower

P20

GA Apron

Asphalt with friction course

HP Z2

Twy D

HP D1

Twy G

HP E1

International Pier

Twy L

Twy K

P30

05

Twy E

Twy M

P40

Elev 26

053 →

HP F1

Twy G

Twy N

P50

HP G1

HP G2

Twy G

Gloucestershire (Staverton)

☺☺☺

Operator: Civilian
Location: N51 53.65 W002 10.03 (3nm W of Cheltenham off the A40)
Elevation: 95ft
Tel: 01452 857700
Hours:

(winter)	0830–1930 Mon–Fri, 0900–1800 Sat–Sun
(summer)	0730–1830 Mon–Fri, 0800–1830 Sat–Sun

Runways:
09/27 (084T slope 0.37% up) 4,662ft
Runway 09 TODA 4,301ft, LDA 3,809ft
Runway 27 TODA 4,793ft, LDA 3,369ft
04/22 (214T) 3,190ft
Runway 04 TODA 3,547ft, LDA 3,190ft
Runway 22 TODA 3,655ft, LDA 2,936ft
18/36 2,297ft
Runway 18 TODA 2,625ft, LDA 2,625ft
Runway 36 TODA 2,625ft, LDA 2,625ft

Radio:
Approach – 125.65
Radar – 120.975
Tower – 122.9

Notes:
Often referred to as Staverton, this small airfield was opened in 1936 as a new site for the Cotswold Aero Club. The airfield was later developed by the Royal Air Force as a training base, and several well-known aviation companies operated from the airfield, including Rotol, Folland and Gloster. Reverting to civilian operations in 1950, the airfield has continued to thrive as a busy general and business aviation site with a variety of flying clubs, training companies and maintenance businesses. Military activity is rare, although the nearby RAF Training Command headquarters may see an increase in communications aircraft activity. Air shows no longer appear to be regular fixtures, despite the airfield having staged some very successful events, attracting aircraft up to the size of a Shackleton on one occasion. Observation of the daily movements is possible from many vantage points around the airfield perimeter.

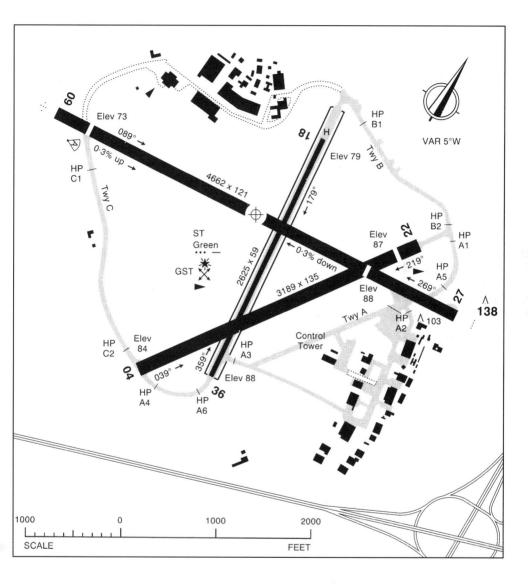

60

Elev 73

089°

0·3% up →

HP
C1

Twy C

HP
C2

Elev
84

04

039° →

HP
A4

2625 x 59

359°

18

H

Elev 79

179°

4662 x 121

⊕

0·3% down →

3189 x 135

ST
Green

GST

HP
A3

Elev 88

36

HP
A6

HP
B1

Twy B

VAR 5°W

HP
B2

HP
A1

Elev
87

22

219°

HP
A5

269°

27

∧
138

Elev
88

Twy A

HP
A2

∧ 103

Control
Tower

SCALE

1000   0   1000   2000

FEET

Guernsey

☺☺☺☺

Operator: Civilian
Location: N49 26.10 W002 36.12 (2nm W of St Peter Port)
Elevation: 336ft
Tel: 01481 37766
Hours:
0615–2100 Mon–Sun

Runways:
09/27 (088T slope 0.65% up) 4,800ft
Runway 09 TODA 5,341ft, LDA 4,800ft
Runway 27 TODA 5,699ft, LDA 4,800ft

Radio:
Approach – 128.65
Radar – 118.9 124.5
Tower – 119.95
Ground – 121.8

Notes:
Opening in 1939 with scheduled services to the UK mainland and other Channel Islands, this airfield enjoyed the dubious distinction of becoming a *Luftwaffe* base when the island was occupied in 1940. The *Luftwaffe* left (as one might expect) in 1945 and civilian operations quickly resumed. Today, more than twenty destinations are regularly served from Guernsey, and freight movements are also quite common. The general aviation community is also well catered for and a flying club is based at the airport. Observation of activity is possible from various points around the airport perimeter, although activity can be sporadic or fairly low at times.

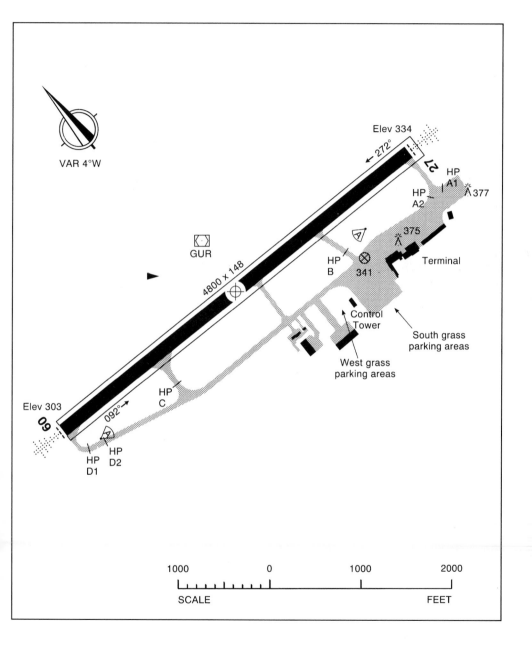

VAR 4°W

Elev 334

272°

27

HP
A1

HP
A2

377

GUR

4800 x 148

A

375

HP
B

341

Terminal

Control
Tower

South grass
parking areas

West grass
parking areas

Elev 303

092°

HP
C

09

HP
D1

HP
D2

1000	0	1000	2000

SCALE   FEET

Hawarden
☺

Operator: Civilian
Location: N53 10.68 W002 58.67 (2nm W of Chester off the A55)
Elevation: 35ft
Tel: 01244 522012
Hours:
0800–1900 Mon–Fri, 0930–1600 Sat–Sun

Runways:
05/23 (043T slope 0.30% down) 6,673ft
Runway 05 TODA 6,929ft, LDA 5,453ft
Runway 23 TODA 7,165ft, LDA 5,702ft
14/32 (312T) 3,295ft
Runway 14 TODA 4,245ft, LDA 3,295ft
Runway 23 TODA 4,170ft, LDA 3,295ft

Radio:
Approach – 123.35
Radar – 130.25
Tower – 124.95 336.325

Notes:
Initially built as a manufacturer's airfield (producing Wellington bombers), Royal Air Force Spitfire training was also conducted at this base during World War Two. In post-war years, aircraft production included Doves, Vampires and Mosquitoes, and a particularly famous example of the latter type was based here for many years (maintained by British Aerospace), making countless air show appearances until its tragic loss a few years ago. Hawarden is perhaps best known for the production of the HS125 business jet, better known as the Dominie in RAF service. More recently, however, Hawarden has become closely associated with Airbus production, and entire wing units are manufactured at the site before being moved (rather

HAWARDEN is a busy manufacturing site, although civilian flying at the airfield is slowly becoming more popular.

ironically) by road to Manchester Airport, for transportation by Beluga to Toulouse for final assembly. General aviation is now becoming more popular at the airfield, and a flying school is based on the site. Observation of the limited activity is possible from many vantage points, although the number of aircraft movements hardly reflect the size of the airfield.

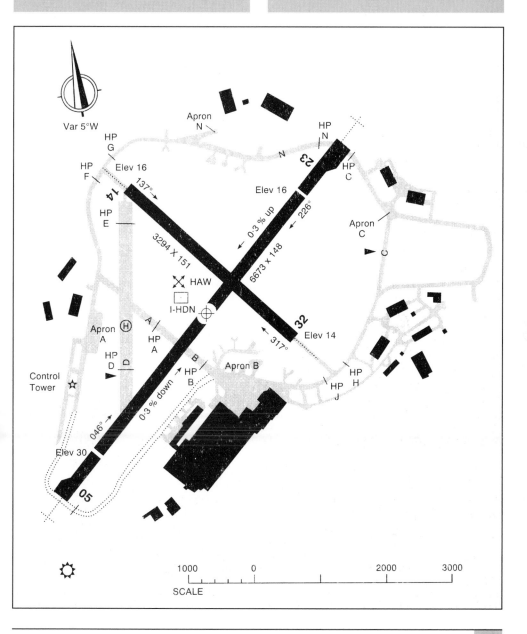

Honington
☺

Operator: Royal Air Force
Location: N52 20.56 E000 46.38 (6nm SE of Thetford)
Elevation: 174ft
Tel: 01359 269561
Hours:
As required

Runways:
09/27 (081.28T slope 0.07% down) 9,012ft
Runway 09 TODA 7,347ft, LDA 9,012ft
Runway 27 TODA 9,472ft, LDA 9,012ft

Radio:
Radar – 128.9 264.675
Approach – 254.875 309.95 257.8 123.3 315.575
Director – 309.95 358.75 385.4 344.0 123.3
Tower – 282.275 122.1
Ground – 241.975

HONINGTON was for many years a busy Tornado base (as illustrated), but the base is currently virtually inactive. However, Honington may well resume flying activities in the future.

Notes:
A long-established Royal Air Force base, Honington is currently deactivated, despite being a fully equipped bomber base, with a huge complex of aircraft shelters, a large parking apron, bomber-sized hangars and full supporting facilities. The RAF maintains the base although only non-flying activities are now based here. Famous as the home of the RAF's Buccaneer operations, Honington became a Tornado station following the gradual withdrawal of the former type (and relocation to Lossie-mouth). When the Cold War ended, the RAF's Tornado force was down-sized and Honington's units were dispersed to other stations, leaving the station bereft of flying units. The airfield has occasionally been reactivated for exercises, and as a 'bolt hole' for aircraft while other airfields have undergone runway resurfacing work. It is likely that Honington will remain available for such duties, but on a day-to-day basis the airfield remains closed at least for the forseeable future.

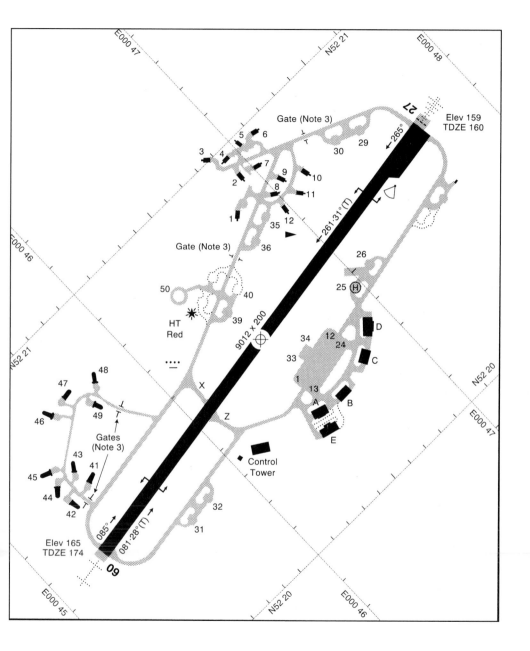

Humberside (Kirmington)

☺☺☺☺☺

Operator: Civilian
Location: N53 34.48 W000 21.05 (8nm W of Grimsby off the M180)
Elevation: 122ft
Tel: 01652 688456
Hours:
(winter)   0630–2145 Mon–Fri,
            0630–1830 Sat,
            0630–1945 Sun
(summer)   0530–2045 Sun–Fri,
            0530–1900 Sat

Runways:

03/21 (022T slope 0.66% down) 6,791ft
Runway 03 TODA 7,244ft, LDA 6,791ft
Runway 21 TODA 7,205ft, LDA 6,398ft
09/27 (081T) 3,458ft
Runway 09 TODA 3,458ft, LDA 3,261ft
Runway 27 TODA 3,963ft, LDA 3,018ft

Radio:

Approach – 124.675
Radar – 124.675 123.15
Tower – 118.55 124.675
Information – 124.125

Notes:
Formerly a World-War-Two-era Royal Air Force airfield operating Wellington bombers, Kirmington has gradually been developed into a large regional airport with a growing scheduled of airline and charter traffic of various capacities. The airport is certainly capable of handling most aircraft types, and Concordes have made occasional appearances at the facility, usually on charter flights. Helicopters supporting nearby offshore oil and gas rigs provide a significant number of aircraft movements, and general aviation also enjoys a fairly major presence. A handful of flying clubs are based at the airport and visitors are common, although military types much less so. However, occasional (and increasingly rare) air shows attract a wide range of interesting aircraft types. The terminal building is small but activities can be observed from the area, and good views of the runway approach can be made from the adjacent public road.

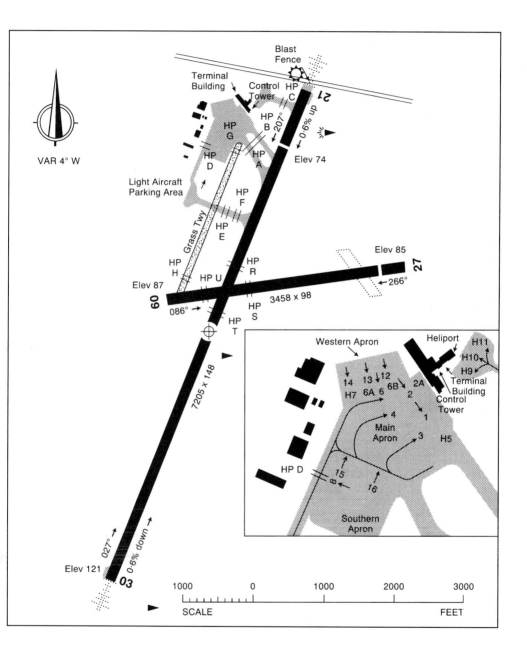

VAR 4° W

Blast
Fence

Terminal
Building

Control
Tower

HP
C

21

207°

0.6% up

Elev 74

HP
B

HP
G

HP
D

HP
A

Light Aircraft
Parking Area

HP
F

Grass Twy

HP
E

HP
H

HP
R

HP U

Elev 87

60

086°

3458 x 98

HP
S

Elev 85

27

266°

HP
T

7205 x 148

027°

0.6% down

Elev 121

03

Western Apron

Heliport

H11

H10

H9

Terminal
Building

Control
Tower

14 13 12

H7 6A 6 6B

2A

2

1

4

Main
Apron

3

H5

HP D

15

16

Southern
Apron

SCALE

1000   0   1000   2000   3000

FEET

Inverness

☺☺☺

Operator: Civilian
Location: N57 32.40 W004 03.00 (5nm NE of Inverness off the A96)
Elevation: 31ft
Tel: 01463 232471
Hours:
(winter)   0615–2200 Mon–Fri,
           0615–1915 Sat,
           0830–2200 Sun
(summer) 0530–2200 Mon–Sun

Runways:
06/24 (049T slope 0.09% down) 6,191ft
Runway 06 TODA 6,683ft, LDA 5,459ft
Runway 24 TODA 6,282ft, LDA 5,791ft

Radio:
Approach – 122.6
Tower – 122.6

Notes:
Opened as a Royal Air Force station in 1940, the airfield was subsequently developed into a regional airport. Following the completion of a major runway extension in 1974, the site is now the major airport for the Highlands region. With a number of scheduled services (mostly provided by British Airways) and some charter and business flights, Inverness is a fairly active airport despite its relatively small size. Flying training and air taxi operations are also present, as are Air Atlantique DC-3s, detached to the airport for pollution control duties, connected with the nearby oil and gas rigs. A small air strip (2,297ft x 59ft) is also incorporated into the former Runway 12/30, and is sometimes used for light aircraft traffic. Observation of aircraft movements is possible from various locations, including the terminal facility. Visitors are fairly few in numbers, and military types are rare.

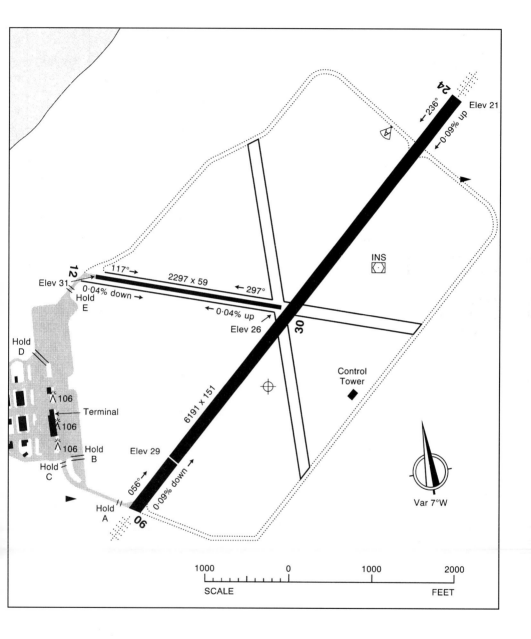

Jersey

☺ ☺ ☺ ☺ ☺

Operator: Civilian
Location: N49 12.48 W002 11.73 (3nm NW of St Helier)
Elevation: 277ft
Tel:　　01534 492000
Hours:
(winter)　　0700–2100 Mon–Sun
(summer)　　0600–2030 Mon–Sun

Runways:
09/27 (262.5T slope 0.13% down) 5,597ft
Runway 09 TODA 6,198ft, LDA 5,400ft
Runway 27 TODA 8,097ft, LDA 5,098ft

Radio:
Zone – 125.2 120.45
Radar – 118.55 120.3 120.45 125.2
Approach – 120.3
Tower – 119.45
Ground – 121.9

Notes:
The largest and most active of the Channel Islands airfields, Jersey caters for a variety of scheduled and charter flights, and is a particularly busy airport during the holiday season, attracting general aviation types from both the UK and French mainland. The small but modern terminal complex provides opportunities to view aircraft movements, although surrounding roads will also provide good vantage points. Annual fly-in events attract large numbers of light aircraft, and the airport's annual air show includes many well-known performers such as the Red Arrows. Normally, however, military visitors are quite rare.

JERSEY is a busy Channel Islands airport, with an annual air show which attracts a variety of interesting aircraft, often including warbirds such as Duxford's B-17.

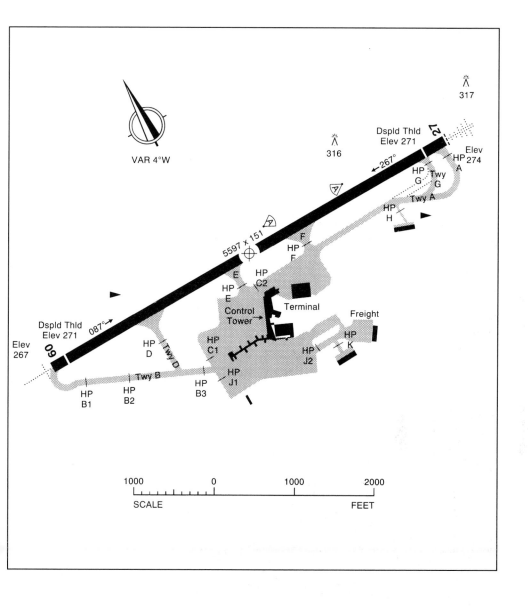

VAR 4°W

Dspld Thld
Elev 271

Elev
274

317

316

267°

HP
A

HP Twy
G G

Twy A

HP
H

5597 x 151

F

HP
F

E

HP
C2

HP
E

Control
Tower

Terminal

Freight

Dspld Thld
Elev 271

087°

HP
D

Twy D

HP
C1

HP
K

Elev
267

60

27

Twy B

HP
B3

HP
J1

HP
J2

HP
B1

HP
B2

| 1000 | 0 | 1000 | 2000 |

SCALE

FEET

Kinloss

☺☺☺☺☺☺☺

Operator: Royal Air Force
Location: N57 38.96 W003 33.64 (5nm NE of Forres on the B9089)
Elevation: 22ft
Tel: 01309 672161
Hours:
24 hrs

Runways:

08/26 (070.51T slope 0.13% up) 7,582ft
Runway 08 TODA 10,207ft, LDA 7,582ft
Runway 26 TODA 8,123ft, LDA 7,582ft

Radio:

Approach – 376.65 119.35 362.3
Director – 259.975 311.325 123.3
Talkdown – 370.05 123.3 376.525
Tower – 336.35 122.1 257.8
Ground – 296.725
Operations – 358.475

Notes:
Opened in 1939, Kinloss has always been associated with maritime operations, ever since the end of World War Two when the station was transferred from Bomber Command to Coastal Command (having previously been the home of No.19 OTU). Operating the Lancaster, Neptune and Shackleton, the station eventually received the Nimrod towards the end of the 1960s and has remained active as a Nimrod base ever since. No. 8 Squadron's Shackletons were based here briefly before moving to nearby Lossiemouth, and Kinloss is now the home of Nos. 120, 201 and 206 Squadrons, together with No. 22(R) Squadron, the Nimrod Operational Conversion Unit. No. 633 Volunteer

KINLOSS is the RAF's Nimrod base, and often handles foreign maritime aircraft during exercise periods.

Gliding School is also based here. Visiting maritime types are common, especially during exercises, and other RAF and Nato types regularly use the airfield facilities, although the bulk of the station's daily movements are naturally provided by the resident Nimrods. Observation of activity is best achieved from the B9011 road which crosses the approach to Runway 08.

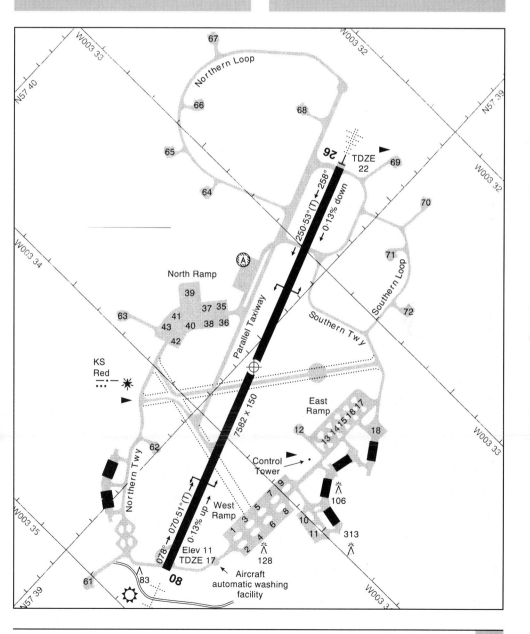

Lakenheath

☺☺☺☺☺☺☺☺☺

Operator: United States Air Force
Location: N52 24.56 E000 33.66 (8nm W of Thetford)
Elevation: 32ft
Tel: 01638 524186
Hours:
0600–2200 Mon–Thu, 0600–2000 Fri, 0800–2000 Sat–Sun

Runways:
06/24 (055.7T) 9,000ft
Runway 06 TODA 9,000ft, LDA 9,000ft
Runway 24 TODA 9,000ft, LDA 9,000ft

Radio:
Approach – 128.9
Departure – 123.3 137.2 242.075
Radar – 309.075 290.875 338.675
123.3 264.1 279.250
Tower – 358.675 122.1 257.8
Ground – 397.975
Operations – 300.825 269.075

Notes:
One of countless World-War-Two-era Royal Air Force stations transferred to USAAF (later USAF) control, Lakenheath is currently one of the biggest and most active United States Air Force airfields outside continental USA. A long-time home of the 48th Tactical Fighter Wing, the base enjoyed a long association with the F-100 Super Sabre, followed by the F-4C/D Phantom. More recently (through the 1980s) Lakenheath was the home to a huge fleet of F-111 bombers, many of which were deployed to the Middle East during operation Desert Storm. F-111s operated directly from and to Lakenheath when air strikes were launched against Libya. Lakenheath is now an F-15C/E Eagle

LAKENHEATH is one of the largest and most active USAF bases outside continental USA, and is currently home to F-15E and F-15C Eagles.

base, remaining active with a steady stream of visiting aircraft, particularly during exercises. Observation of Lakenheath's activities is possible, although all of the resident F-15s are housed in the base's complex of sixty aircraft shelters, scattered around the airfield. Visiting aircraft can sometimes be seen, but the sprawling nature of the base makes viewing rather difficult. The best observations are from the road crossing the approach to Runway 24, where good views of movements can be obtained.

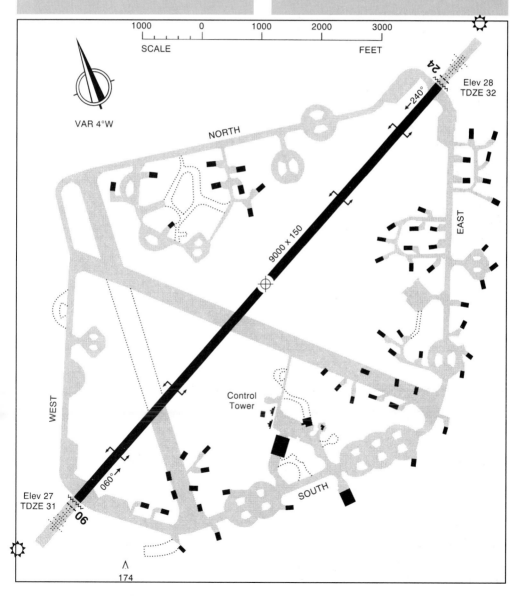

SCALE

FEET

1000   0   1000   2000   3000

VAR 4°W

NORTH

NORTH

EAST

WEST

SOUTH

9000 x 150

←240°

060°→

24

06

Elev 28
TDZE 32

Elev 27
TDZE 31

Control
Tower

Λ
174

Leeds/Bradford (Yeadon)

☺☺☺☺☺☺

Operator: Civilian
Location: N53 51.95 W001 39.63 (4nm NW of Leeds off the A658)
Elevation: 682ft
Tel: 0113 2509696
Hours:
(winter) 0700–2245 Mon–Fri,
          0700–1930 Sat–Sun
(summer) 0600–2200 Mon–Sun

Runways:

14/32 (138T slope 0.39% down) 7,382ft
Runway 14 TODA 10,397ft, LDA 5,912ft
Runway 32 TODA 7,477ft, LDA 6,286ft
10/28 (271T) 3,609ft
Runway 10 TODA 5,184ft, LDA 3,110ft
Runway 28 TODA 3,451ft, LDA 3,294ft

Radio:

Approach – 123.75
Radar – 121.05
Tower – 120.3
Information – 118.025

Notes:
Originally established as the home of the Yorkshire Aeroplane Club (which still resides at the airfield today), Yeadon is best known as a manufacturing base for Avro during World War Two, producing countless Ansons, Lancasters, Lincolns and Yorks. Post-war, the airfield was developed as a regional airport, and continual improvements have been made to the site (including a significant runway extension), enabling Leeds/Bradford to become a truly international airport, handling aircraft up to the size of Boeing 747s and Concordes (occasionally). General aviation is also a major part of the airport's modest number of daily movements, and a flying school is based on the airfield. Military visitors are rare. Viewing is possible from various sites, including the terminal area.

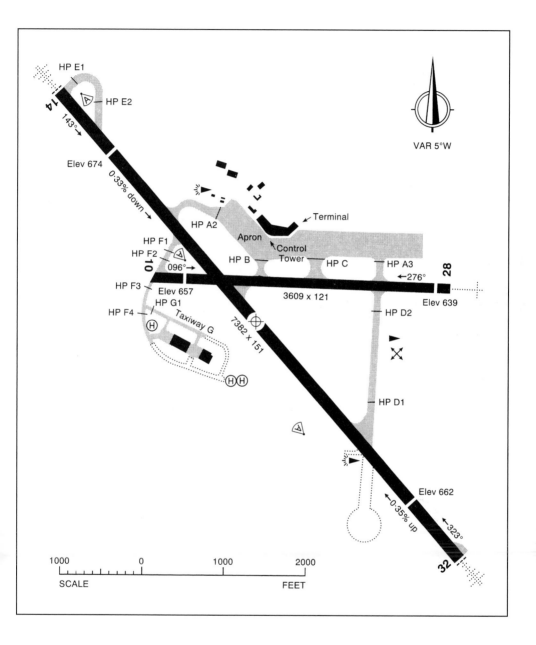

HP E1

HP E2

14

143°

Elev 674

0.33% down

HP A2

Terminal

HP F1

Apron

HP F2

Control
Tower

096°

HP B

HP C

HP A3

10

276°

28

HP F3

Elev 657

3609 x 121

Elev 639

HP G1

HP F4

Taxiway G

7382 x 151

HP D2

HP D1

VAR 5°W

Elev 662

0.35% up

323°

32

1000   0   1000   2000

SCALE   FEET

Leeming
☺☺☺☺☺☺

Operator: Royal Air Force
Location: N54 17.54 W001 32.11 (6nm SW of Northallerton off the A1)
Elevation: 132ft
Tel: 01677 423041
Hours:
0800–2359 Mon–Thu, 0800–1800 Fri, 0900–1715 Sat–Sun

Runways:
16/34 (155.77T slope 0.29% up) 7,520ft
Runway 16 TODA 8,412ft, LDA 7,520ft
Runway 34 TODA 7,986ft, LDA 7,520ft

Radio:
Approach – 337.825 127.75 362.3 123.3
Radar – 292.7 127.75
Director – 358.65 127.75 344.0 123.3
Talkdown – 336.35 309.875 385.4 123.3
Tower – 344.575 120.5 122.1 257.8
Ground – 386.725
Operations – 356.725

Notes:
A former Royal Air Force World War Two bomber base (operating Whitleys and Halifaxes), Leeming later became established as a fighter station with Javelins and Canberra trainers. The station then transferred to Training Command and became the home to numerous Jet Provosts. Following a major refurbishment, Leeming reopened as a fighter base, with the arrival of Tornado F3s in 1988, and the station is now the home to Nos. 11 and 25 Squadrons (23 Squadron having disbanded). No. 100 Squadron also relocated to the base from Finningley, operating a fleet of target facilities Hawks. The Bulldogs of the Northumbrian University Air Squadron/No. 11 Air Experience Flight are also resident at Leeming. Observation of activities at Leeming was once relatively easy, with an access road

LEEMING is one of the RAF's front-line fighter bases, and home to Nos. 11 and 25 Squadrons. The base's new control tower has been nicknamed (not surprisingly) the 'Happy Eater'.

literally crossing the main runway. Since reopening as a fighter base, access to the airfield has become much more difficult, and the only reasonable view is from the small road which runs parallel to the main runway. A viewing area is available close to the Willow Tree public house, but the runway is fairly distant from this position, and although some Tornado F3s and visiting aircraft can be seen on the main apron, most resident Tornado F3s are housed in the base's shelter complex. However, adequate views under the approach to Runway 34 are possible from the base access road.

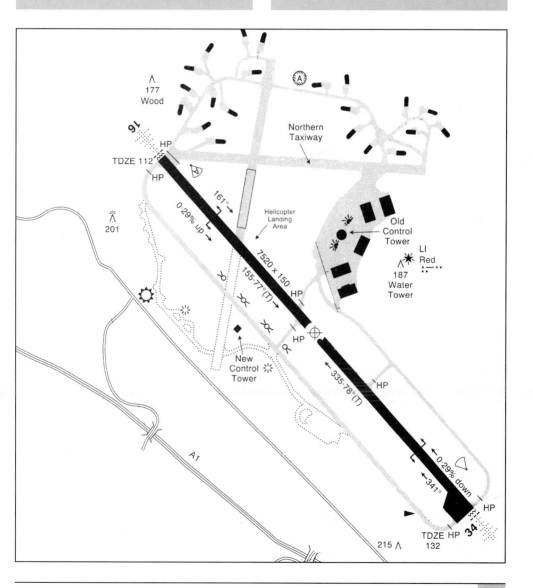

Leuchars

☺☺☺☺☺☺☺☺

Operator: Royal Air Force
Location: N56 22.37 W002 52.11 (3nm NW of St Andrews off the A919)
Elevation: 38ft
Tel: 01334 839471
Hours: 24hrs

Runways:
09/27 (081.73T slope 0.19% down) 8,491ft
Runway 09 TODA 8,642ft, LDA 7,605ft
Runway 27 TODA 8,645ft, LDA 8,491ft
04/22 (216.75T slope 0.17% up) 4,803ft
Runway 04 TODA 5,013ft, LDA 4,803ft
Runway 22 TODA 5,180ft, LDA 4,803ft

Radio:
Approach – 255.4 126.5 362.3
Director – 292.475 123.3
Talkdown – 370.075 123.3 259.925
Tower – 259.125 122.1
Ground – 297.9 122.1
Operations – 285.025

Notes:
A particularly historic site of military aviation, the site was first used for balloon flights as long ago as 1911, but Fleet Air Arm fighter operations began here in 1918. Coastal Command operations during World War Two used Beauforts and Beaufighters, as well as Hudsons and Mosquitoes. BOAC operated Mosquitoes from the airfield during the war. Post-war, the Royal Air Force operated Meteors, Vampires, Javelins, and Hunters from the airfield, which was followed by a long association with the Lightning, and an equally long period of Phantom operations. In 1989 the first Tornado F3s arrived, and Leuchars is currently the home to Nos. 43 and 111 Squadrons, both operating Tornado F3s. The East Lowlands University Air Squadron also maintains

LEUCHARS is a major RAF fighter base where a variety of visiting Nato aircraft types can often be seen on deployment or exercise.

a small fleet of Bulldogs at the base. Visiting aircraft from RAF and Nato units are fairly common, and the base regularly hosts exercises and squadron exchanges, deployments, etc. Observation of aircraft movements is fairly restricted thanks to the airfield's position close to the River Eden. The only reasonable viewpoint is from the road crossing the approach to Runway 09, from where the main apron is visible. The resident Tornado F3s are usually housed in the base's shelter complex.

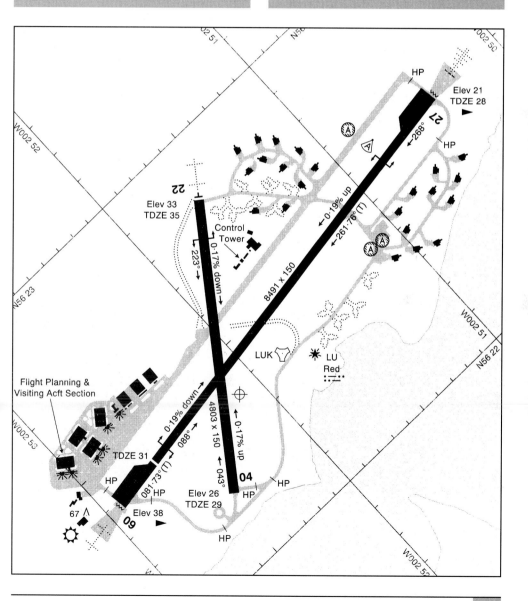

Linton-on-Ouse

☺☺☺☺☺☺☺

Operator: Royal Air Force
Location: N54 02.95 W001 15.17 (8nm NW of York off the A19)
Elevation: 53ft
Tel:　01347 848261
Hours:
0745–1715 Mon–Thu, 0745–1700 Fri

Runways:

04/22 (031.51T) 6,020ft
Runway 04 TODA 6,106ft, LDA 5,515ft
Runway 22 TODA 6,109ft, LDA 6,014ft
10/28 (096.11T) 4,394ft
Runway 10 TODA 4,394ft, LDA 4,394ft
Runway 28 TODA 4,394ft, LDA 4,394ft

Radio:

Approach – 362.675 362.3 129.15 292.8
Radar – 292.8 129.15 344.0 122.1
Director – 344.475 344.0 123.3 129.15
Departures – 277.625 292.8 129.15
Talkdown – 358.525 259.875 123.3
129.15
Tower – 300.425 257.8 122.1
Ground – 340.025 122.1

Notes:
A well-known World War Two Royal Air Force Bomber Command station, Linton operated substantial numbers of Whitleys, Lancasters and Halifaxes. Post-war, the airfield was transferred to Fighter Command, and various types were based here, including Vampires, Meteors and F-86 Sabres. In 1957 Linton transferred to Training Command and has remained active in this role ever since. After a very long association with the Jet Provost, the Tucano now equips the resident No. 1 Flying Training School (FTS), while No. 642 Volunteer Gliding School maintains a small number of Vigilants at the base. Aircraft movements are largely confined to the training activities conducted by No. 1 FTS, and some of the unit's flying training is exported to nearby Topcliffe

LINTON-ON-OUSE is a very active RAF training base, where numerous Tucanos are active on most weekdays.

and Dishforth, in order to ease congestion at Linton. Visitors are normally confined to occasional appearances by other RAF aircraft types, and Nato aircraft are fairly uncommon. Viewing Tucano operations at Linton can easily

be achieved thanks to a viewing area located close to the threshold of Runway 04, just off the minor road which crosses the runway approach at this point. The main apron/flight line can also be seen from this location.

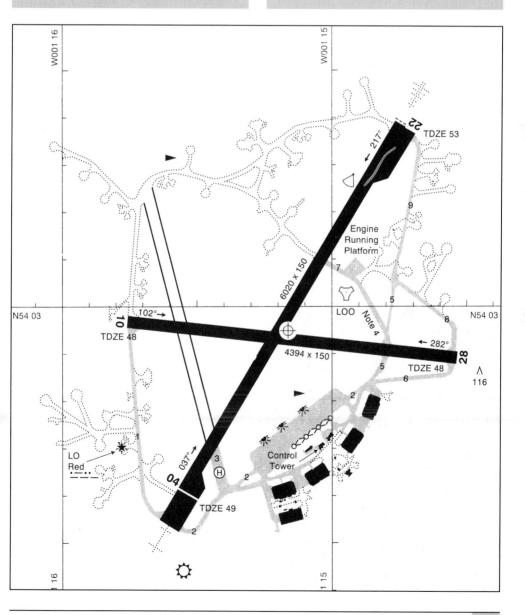

Liverpool (Speke)

☺☺☺☺☺☺☺

Operator: Civilian
Location: N53 20.02 W002 51.00 (5nm SE of Liverpool, off the A561)
Elevation: 81ft
Tel: 0151 486 8877
Hours:
24 hrs

Runways:
09/27 (086T slope 0.25% up) 7,500ft
Runway 09 TODA 7,769ft, LDA 7,300ft
Runway 27 TODA 8,100ft, LDA 7,500ft

Radio:
Approach – 119.85
Radar – 118.45 119.85
Tower – 118.1

Notes:
Dating back to 1928, Speke was originally developed as Liverpool Airport North, on a site south-west of the present airport complex. As part of the airport's expansion and development programme, a new (longer) runway was constructed adjacent to the River Mersey, together with a new terminal facility and apron. The former airport site was connected to the new runway by a long taxiway link, but flying from the original site ceased in the early 1980s. All flying is now conducted from the 'new' runway, while the original airport site is used as a base for flying clubs and maintenance facilities. Viewing is possible from the new terminal area, with the best views of flying being from the approach area near the threshold of Runway 27.

LIVERPOOL. The 'new' main runway is connected to the older airport site by a long taxiway link, visible in the foreground.

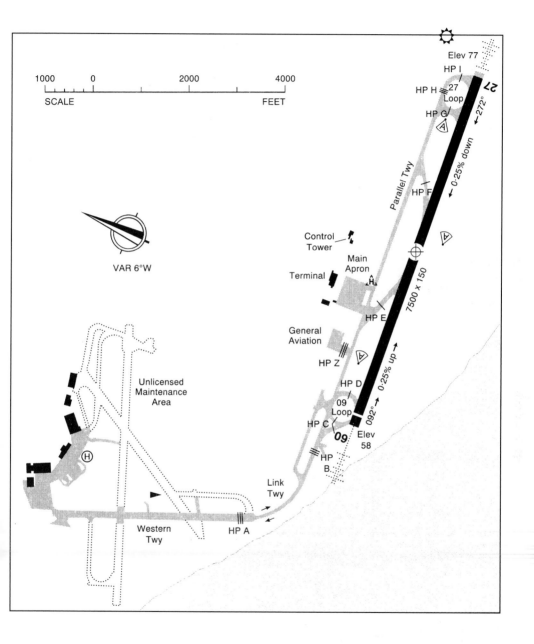

SCALE
1000 0 2000 4000
FEET

VAR 6°W

Elev 77
HP I
HP H — 27
Loop
HP G
272°
0·25% down
Parallel Twy
HP F
7500 x 150
Control
Tower
Main
Apron
Terminal
HP E
General
Aviation
HP Z
Unlicensed
Maintenance
Area
HP D
092°
0·25% up
09
Loop
HP C
09
Elev
58
HP
B
Link
Twy
Western
Twy
HP A

Llanbedr
☺

Operator: Ministry of Defence
Location: N52 48.70 W004 07.41 (8nm S of Porthmadog)
Elevation: 30ft
Tel: 01341 241321
Hours:
0900–1200 & 1300–1630 Mon–Thu,
0900–1200 & 1300–1500 Fri

Runways:
18/36 (349.8T slope 0.14% up) 7,500ft
Runway 18 TODA 7,996ft, LDA 7,195ft
Runway 36 TODA 7,687ft, LDA 7,305ft
05/23 (225.6T) 4,328ft
Runway 05 TODA 4,328ft, LDA 4,328ft
Runway 23 TODA 4,328ft, LDA 4,328ft
16/34 (328.9T) 4,207ft
Runway 16 TODA 4,207ft, LDA 4,207ft
Runway 34 TODA 4,207ft, LDA 4,207ft

Radio:
Approach – 386.675 122.5
Radar – 386.675 122.5
Talkdown – 370.3 122.5
Tower – 387.75 122.5

Notes:
Tucked away on the western coast of Wales, much of Llanbedr's history is obscured in relative secrecy. The airfield remains committed to the needs of the Defence Research Agency (DRA), although most of the aerial activity is normally provided in support of the Royal Air Force. Based aircraft are few, and although exotic types of unmanned 'drone' aircraft such as the Firefly, Meteor and Sea Vixen have been based here, the current residents are confined to a handful of aircraft such as a Hunter and Canberra target tug. Apart from the sporadic test flights conducted by the DRA, most activity concerns the launching and recovery of Jindivik unmanned target aircraft, which operate in the

LLANBEDR is a relatively quiet airfield, but home to a small and interesting variety of aircraft, including this Canberra B2(mod).

adjacent restricted airspace. They provide 'live' targets for RAF fighter pilots flying out of nearby RAF Valley (on detachment). The sensitive nature of some of Llanbedr's activities suggest that observing or photographing activities might not be encouraged. Aircraft movements are relatively few, with only occasional visiting types, and long periods of inactivity, combined with Jindivik operations which block the runway for considerable periods of time. However, the airfield can be easily observed from surrounding roads.

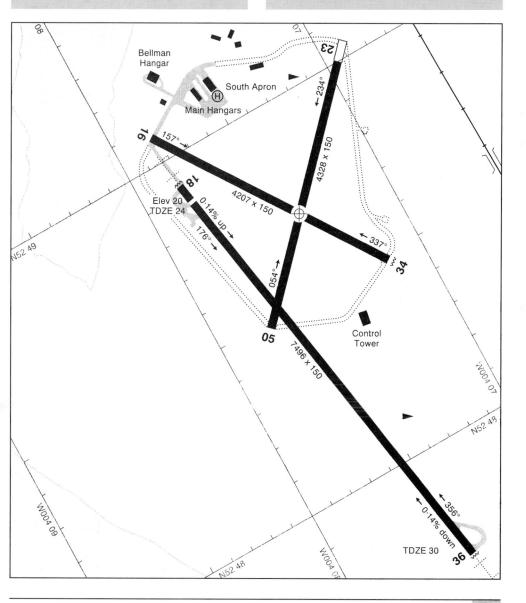

London City
☺☺☺☺☺☺☺

Operator: Civilian
Location: N51 30.32 E000 03.26 (4nm E of central London off the A1011)
Elevation: 17ft
Tel: 020 7474 5555
Hours:
0630–2230 Mon–Fri, 0630–1300 Sat, 1200–2230 Sun

Runways:
10/28 (093T slope 0.03% up) 3,934ft
Runway 10 TODA 4,091ft, LDA 3,934ft
Runway 28 TODA 4,544ft, LDA 3,934ft

Radio:
Approach – 132.7
Radar – 128.025
Tower – 127.95 118.075

Notes:
Perhaps the most famous example of the modern 'city airport', the site was first earmarked for aviation operations in the early 1980s, the first aircraft (a Dash 7) landing here on a trial flight in 1982. The airport opened in 1987, but the steep approach path and short runway placed severe restrictions on the aircraft types which could use the facility. However, the runway was extended in 1992, enabling types such as the BAe146 to safely operate from the airport. With new transport links to central London, the airport has gradually grown in popularity and currently caters for more than half a million passengers every year, accommodating a variety of aircraft types, chiefly the Dash7/8, Fokker 50 and RJ70 class of regional airliner. Business jets are also common visitors, but military visitors are very rare. Observation of movements is possible from the vicinity of the terminal, but the airport's position almost literally in the Thames makes wide access rather difficult.

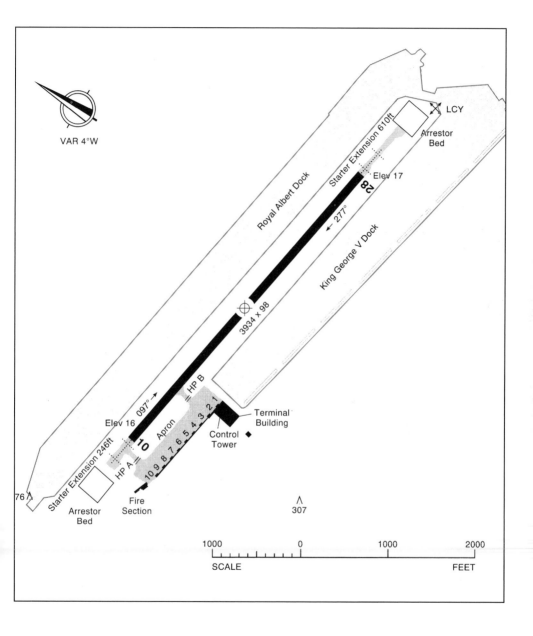

VAR 4°W

Royal Albert Dock

Starter Extension 610ft

LCY

Arrestor
Bed

Elev 17

28

← 277°

King George V Dock

3934 x 98

HP B

097° →

Elev 16

Apron

10 9 8 7 6 5 4 3 2 1

10

Terminal
Building

Control
Tower

HP A

Starter Extension 246ft

76

∧
307

Arrestor
Bed

Fire
Section

1000   0   1000   2000

SCALE   FEET

London Gatwick

☺☺☺☺☺☺☺☺☺☺

Operator: Civilian
Location: N51 08.88 W000 11.42 (2nm N of Crawley off the M23)
Elevation: 196ft
Tel: 01293 535353
Hours:
24 hrs

Runways:
08R/26L (078T) 10,879ft
Runway 08R TODA 10,863ft, LDA 9,075ft
Runway 26L TODA 11,178ft, LDA 9,288ft
08L/26R (078T) 8,415ft
Runway 08L TODA 9,770ft, LDA 7,359ft
Runway 26R TODA 8,868ft, LDA 7,047ft

Radio:
Approach – 126.825 118.95 135.575 129.025
Tower – 124.225 134.225
Ground – 121.8
Information – 136.525

GATWICK is second only to Heathrow in terms of aircraft movement numbers. Virgin is one of many airlines that operate from the airfield.

Notes:
Traditionally seen as Heathrow's 'over-spill', Gatwick has always been associated with charter flights, but in recent years the airport has gradually moved away from this image, and scheduled domestic and international flights now make up most of Gatwick's movements. Although airlines have traditionally aimed to operate from Heathrow, with Gatwick as a second choice, the situation is now changing. Gatwick has become a fully fledged second London airport, with two huge terminal areas, and two very long runways, combined with acres of parking space, maintenance facilities and excellent transport links. Not surprisingly, there are plenty of good vantage points from which to observe the busy schedule of arrivals and departures, not least a viewing area in the South Terminal. Apart from a wide range of Boeing and Airbus 'regulars', and just about every other imaginable airliner type, regional and business jets can also be seen, and quite a few military transports visit Gatwick.

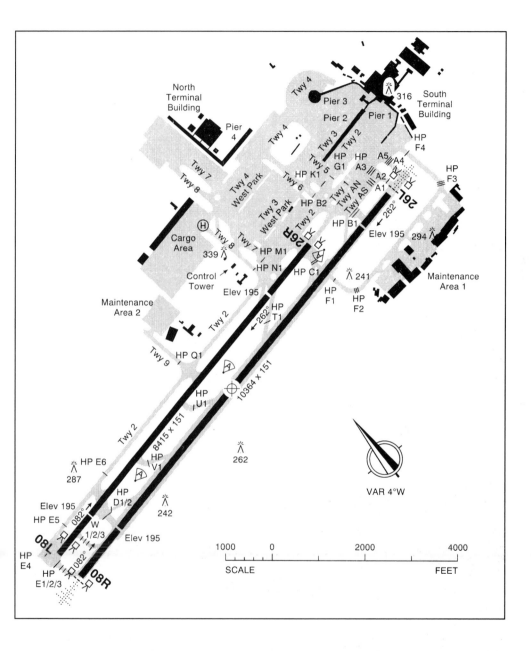

North Terminal Building

South Terminal Building

Pier 4

Pier 3
Pier 2
Pier 1

Twy 4

316

HP F4

Twy 4

Twy 3
Twy 2

HP
A5
A4

HP K1
G1
A3
A2

HP F3

Twy 5

Twy 1
A1

Twy 7

Twy 4
West Park

Twy 6

Twy AN

Twy 8

Twy 3
West Park

HP B2
Twy AS

Cargo Area

HP M1

HP B1

Elev 195
294

339

HP N1

HP C1

241

Maintenance Area 1

Control Tower
Elev 195

262
HP F1
HP F2

Maintenance Area 2

Twy 2

262
HP T1

Twy 9
HP Q1

HP U1

10364 × 151

8415 × 151

Twy 2

262

HP E6
287

HP V1

HP D1/2

Elev 195

HP E5

242

082°
W
1/2/3

Elev 195

08L

082°

HP E4

HP E1/2/3

08R

VAR 4°W

1000   0   2000   4000

SCALE   FEET

123

London Heathrow

☺☺☺☺☺☺☺☺☺☺

Operator: Civilian
Location: N51 28.65 W000 27.68 (10nm W of central London off the M25)
Elevation: 80ft
Tel: 020 8745 5566
Hours:
24hrs

Runways:

09R/09L (090T) 12,000ft
Runway 09R TODA 12,000ft, LDA 11,000ft
Runway 09L TODA 12,800ft, LDA 11,800ft
27R/27L (270T) 12,800ft
Runway 27R TODA 11,456ft, LDA 12,800ft
Runway 27L TODA 12,000ft, LDA 12,000ft

Radio:

Approach – 119.725 134.975 120.4
127.525
Radar – 119.9 125.625
Tower – 118.7 118.5 124.475
Ground – 121.9

HEATHROW, undoubtedly the busiest location for aircraft movements, and the only UK airfield where Concorde operations take place on a daily basis.

Notes:
The world's busiest international airport, Heathrow handles more than 380,000 flights every year, boasts the longest runways in Britain, and almost every imaginable commercial aircraft type passes through the airport at some time or other. It is of course the main base for British Airways Concorde operations, and a major hub for European, domestic and USA flights. Business aircraft also visit Heathrow, together with a fair number of cargo types. Although some evidence of the original hexagonal runway layout is still visible, Heathrow is now built around two main parallel runways, with a central 'core' of terminals, and the more recently constructed terminal positioned on the airfield perimeter. Activity is almost continuous, and on a clear day it's possible to observe perhaps half a dozen aircraft on approach to the same runway. Viewing facilities are confined to a rather grubby enclosure on top of the Queen's building which affords an adequate view of just part of the huge airport. Unfortunately, most other areas

are virtually impossible to see unless approached on foot, and it is a great shame that such a famous airport doesn't offer better facilities to aircraft enthusiasts. However, good views of the runway approaches are possible.

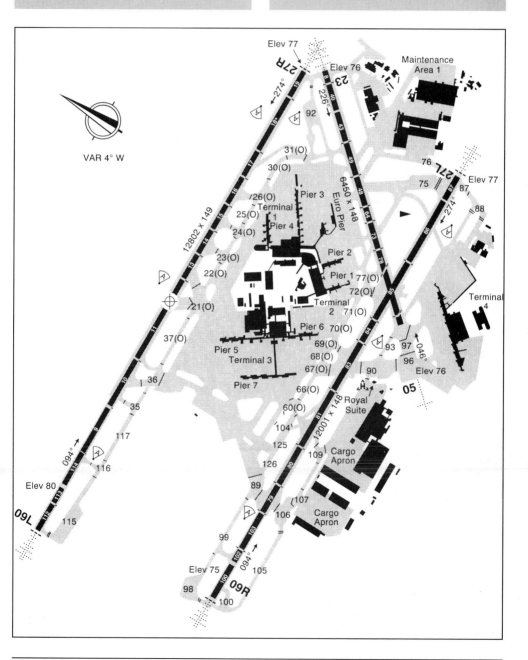

London Luton

☺☺☺☺☺☺☺

Operator: Civilian
Location: N51 52.47 W000 22.12 (1nm E of Luton off the A505)
Elevation: 526ft
Tel: 01582 395395
Hours:
24hrs

Runways:
08/26 (074T slope 0.13% down) 7,087ft
Runway 08 TODA 10,630ft, LDA 7,087ft
Runway 26 TODA 10.630ft, LDA 6,808ft

Radio:
Approach – 129.55 128.75 126.725
Radar – 128.75 126.725
Tower – 132.55
Ground – 121.75
Information – 120.575

Notes:
Although a significantly smaller airport than either Gatwick or Heathrow, Luton is becoming an increasingly popular choice as London's third airport. Once a popular site for general aviation, few light aircraft now use the airfield (landing and handling fees have been increased dramatically, presumably in order to discourage potential users). Medium-sized airliners and business jets are most common, together with a variety of cargo aircraft. Charter flights are Luton's most common use, and both Britannia and Monarch Airways are based here. Aircraft movements are frequent but by no means in the same league as the larger London airports. Spectators are catered for with a good viewing area, and the airport activities can be observed easily from a number of locations.

LUTON. This photograph illustrates the main aprons and the sizable runway.

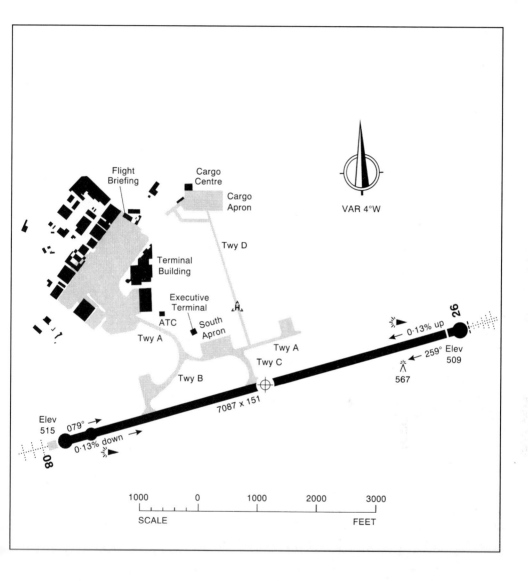

London Stansted

☺☺☺☺☺☺

Operator: Civilian
Location: N51 5.10 E000 14.10 (2nm E of Bishop's Stortford off the M11)
Elevation: 348ft
Tel: 01279 680500
Hours:
24hrs

Runways:
05/23 (223T slope 0.24% down) 10,000ft
Runway 05 TODA 10,951ft, LDA 10,000ft
Runway 23 TODA 10,879ft, LDA 10,000ft

Radio:
Approach – 120.625
Radar – 120.625 126.95
Tower – 123.8 125.55
Ground – 121.725
Information – 114.55

STANSTED is a fairly quiet airport despite being classed as one of the 'London group'. Unusual visitors have included this Nasa 747, complete with a space shuttle orbiter mounted on the fuselage.

Notes:
Originally opened as a USAAF bomber base in 1943, little remains of Stansted's wartime heritage apart from some hard standings, particularly in the business aircraft park. Although the airfield began civilian operations shortly after World War Two, the USAF returned in the 1950s and constructed a long runway before abandoning the airfield again, thankfully leaving behind a huge runway which provided the basis for a new airport. However, despite the considerable size of the airfield, facilities remained poor and business continued to be slow. Things are slowly changing, however, because as the other London airports continue to grow, greater interest is being shown in Stansted, and the emphasis is slowly shifting away from its long-standing association with freight operations. Aircraft movements are relatively few but the airfield can be observed from a variety of locations. Stansted does occasionally host some interesting visitors, the Space Shuttle Enterprise being the most famous so far, but military activity is very rare.

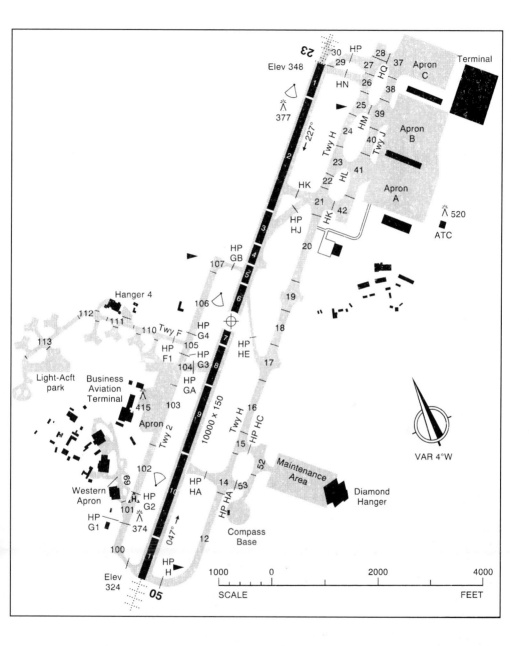

Elev 348
377
227°
Twy H
HN
HK
HP
HJ
HP
GB
107
106
Hanger 4
112
111
110 Twy F
113
HP
G4
105
HP
F1
HP
G3
104
HP
HE
Light-Acft park
Business Aviation Terminal
415
103
Apron 2
Twy 2
102
99
Western Apron
HP
G2
101
374
HP
G1
100
Elev 324
05
047°

30 HP 28
29 27 37 Apron C
26 38
25 39
24 HM Twy J 40
23 HL 41
22 42 Apron A
21
20
19
18
17
HK
HP HC
16
Twy H
15
52
14 53
HP HA
HP HA
13
12
Compass Base
HP H

Terminal
520
ATC
Maintenance Area
Diamond Hanger
VAR 4°W

10000 x 150

1000   0   2000   4000
SCALE   FEET

Lossiemouth

☺☺☺☺☺☺☺☺☺

Operator: Royal Air Force
Location: N57 42.31 W003 20.35 (4nm N of Elgin off the B9135)
Elevation: 42ft
Tel: 0134 3812121
Hours:
0800–1800 Mon–Thu, 0800–1700 Fri

Runways:
05/23 (043.69T slope 0.04% up) 9,091ft
Runway 05 TODA 9,242ft, LDA 9,091ft
Runway 23 TODA 9,170ft, LDA 8,786ft
10/28 (096.44T slope 0.06% down) 6,176ft
Runway 10 TODA 6,488ft, LDA 6,102ft
Runway 28 TODA 6,616ft, LDA 6,176ft

Radio:
Approach – 376.65 362.3
Director – 259.975 311.325 123.3
Departures – 258.85 119.35
Talkdown – 250.05 312.4 123.3
Tower – 337.75 118.9 122.1
Ground – 299.4

Notes:
Although Lossiemouth was opened in 1942 as a Royal Air Force bomber station (No. 20 OTU was based here) the station became more closely associated with the Fleet Air Arm, after being transferred to Navy control after the war. Types such as the Sea Hawk, Hunter and Buccaneer were common sights during the 1960s, and the station returned to the RAF in 1972, becoming the home to No. 8 Squadron's Shackletons, No. 226 OCU's Jaguars, and the Buccaneers of Nos. 12 and 208 Squadrons, and No. 237 OCU. Following the demise of both the Shackleton and Buccaneer, and the departure of the remaining Jaguars to Coltishall in 1999, Lossiemouth has become an all-Tornado base,

with Nos. 12 and 617 Squadrons and No.15(R) Squadron all based at the station. Two Sea Kings from No. 202 Squadron are also based here to provide SAR cover for the region, and a wide variety of RAF and Nato types visit the station on deployment, or during exercises. Observation of aircraft movements is possible from various sites, the best being the approach to Runway 23, which is crossed by the B9040. Although seeing Buccaneers streak over the road at bush-top height is no longer a possibility, the number of based aircraft and variety of visitors makes Lossiemouth one of Britain's best 'spotting' locations.

LOSSIEMOUTH, showing part of the base's extensive hardened aircraft shelter complex.

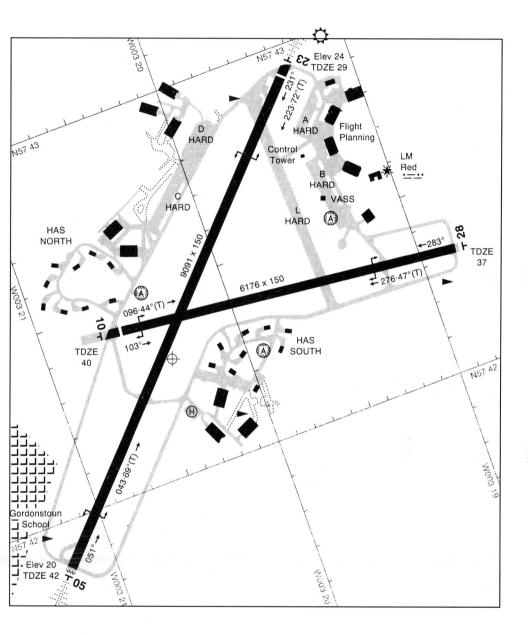

Lyneham
☺☺☺☺☺☺☺☺

Operator: Royal Air Force
Location: N51 30.31 W001 59.60 (6nm
NE of Chippenham off the A3102)
Elevation: 513ft
Tel:　　　01249 890381
Hours:
24hrs

Runways:
07/25 (060.21T slope 0.82% down)
7,830ft
Runway 07 TODA 7,853ft, LDA 7,830ft
Runway 25 TODA 11,744ft, LDA 7,233ft
18/36 (174.94T slope 0.18% down)
5,991ft
Runway 18 TODA 6,319ft, LDA 5,991ft
Runway 36 TODA 6,089ft, LDA 5,991ft

Radio:
Radar – 257.1 134.3
Approach – 359.5 118.425 362.3 123.4
Zone – 345.025 123.4
Director – 300.475 344.0 118.425
Talkdown – 375.2 123.3 385.4
Tower – 386.825 119.225 122.1
Ground – 340.175 129.475 122.1
Operations – 254.65

Notes:
Traditionally connected with transport operations, Lyneham opened in 1940, and after a period of flying training operations the station quickly began transport flights, first with Liberators, followed by Dakotas and Yorks. The first jet transports arrived here after World War Two in the shape of Comet C2s, and these were later joined by a fleet of Britannias. The Hercules first arrived at Lyneham in 1967, and the type has remained here ever since. Lyneham is now the home of the entire RAF Hercules fleet, the Lyneham Transport Wing (LTW) divided into Nos. 24, 30, 47, 57(R) and 70 Squadrons. The new Hercules C4/C5 is due to gradually replace the existing fleet of C1/C3 aircraft. As might be expected, Lyneham is a busy station supporting the RAF's world-wide Hercules operations, and a variety of visiting transport types can be seen here. Observation is possible from

LYNEHAM is the home to the RAF's Hercules fleet, and C-130 operations take place around the clock on a daily basis.

sites around the airfield perimeter, the best location being the approach to Runway 36, although this runway is only occasionally used. The main runway is easily observed near the

Runway 07 threshold (best approached on foot), and good landing views can be obtained at the Runway 25 end, although the airfield is obscured by a hill at this location.

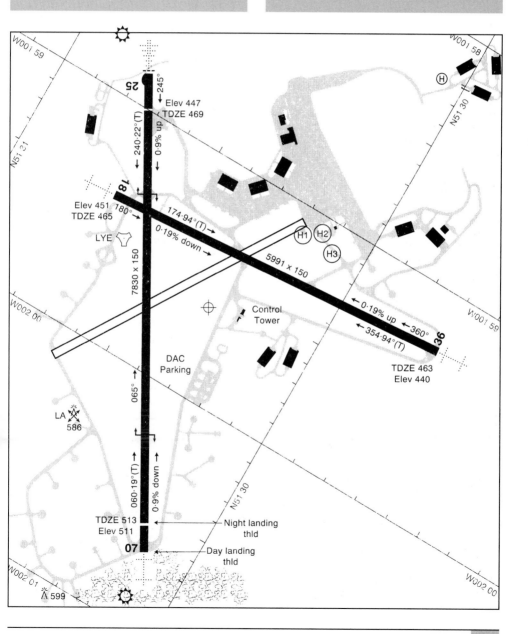

Manchester (Ringway)

☺☺☺☺☺☺☺☺☺

Operator: Civilian
Location: N53 21.22 W002 16.50 (6nm SW of Manchester off the M56)
Elevation: 256ft
Tel: 0161 489 3331
Hours:
24hrs

Runways:
06L/24R (051T slope 0.49% up) 10,000ft
Runway 06L TODA 10,600ft, LDA 8,602ft
Runway 24R TODA 10,499ft, LDA 9,400ft

Radio:
Approach – 119.4 118.575
Director – 121.35
Tower – 118.625
Ground – 121.7
Information – 128.175

Notes:
Another former Royal Air Force station, Ringway assumed the role of Manchester's airport in 1938, taking over from the smaller field at Barton, some miles away. The site emerged during World War Two (when aircraft production was the main activity) as a small airport, but development began in 1962 with a new terminal and a runway extension. Following more recent modifications, Manchester became a truly international airport, with a growing number of scheduled services, together with charter flights, freight operations, business aircraft and private flying. Activity is fairly high, with movements taking place throughout the day, although most are domestic flights, with only an occasional international aircraft. Military aircraft are rare but can sometimes be seen. Viewing facilities are available at the airport, but the terminal pier roof areas have long since been closed for security reasons (although it's difficult to establish exactly what security risk the pier roof presents). Perhaps the best views are from the approach to Runway 24R, particularly from the garden of the adjacent pub, where departures and arrivals can be observed in ideal conditions! Construction of a new parallel runway will enable a new viewing park to be opened soon.

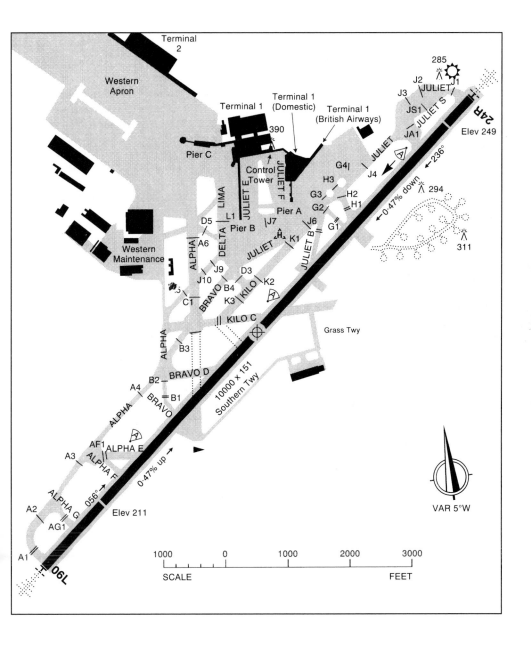

Terminal 2

Western Apron

Terminal 1
Terminal 1 (Domestic)
Terminal 1 (British Airways)

Pier C

390

Control Tower

285
JULIET
J2
J1
J3
JS1
JULIET S
JA1
24R
Elev 249

JULIET
236°

G4
H3
J4
0.47% down
294

Pier A
G3
H2
G2
H1

LIMA
DELTA
JULIET E
JULIET F

D5
L1
Pier B
J7
J6
G1
311

Western Maintenance

ALPHA
A6
J9
D3
JULIET
A
K1
JULIET B

J10
B4
KILO
K2

C1
K3
KILO
BRAVO

KILO C
Grass Twy

ALPHA
B3

BRAVO D
B2
A4
BRAVO
B1
10000 x 151
Southern Twy

ALPHA

AF1
ALPHA E
A3
ALPHA F
0.47% up
A2
ALPHA G
056°
Elev 211
AG1

A1
06L

VAR 5°W

| 1000 | 0 | 1000 | 2000 | 3000 |

SCALE   FEET

Manston
☺☺
Operator: Royal Air Force
Location: N51 20.52 E001 20.77 (2nm W of Ramsgate off the A253)
Elevation: 178ft
Tel: 01843 823351
Hours:
0800–1800 Mon–Fri, 0900–1700 Sat–Sun

Runways:
10/28 (101.24T slope 0.01% down)
9,029ft
Runway 10 TODA 9,232ft, LDA 9,029ft
Runway 28 TODA 9,213ft, LDA 9,029ft

Radio:
Approach – 321.6 126.35 362.3 122.1 129.45
Director – 338.625 126.35 344.0 123.3
Talkdown – 312.325 123.3 385.4 119.925
Tower – 344.35 119.275 257.8 122.1

Notes:
A famous wartime Royal Air Force base, Manston has faded into relative obscurity in post-war years, although the station is still very much in business. Unfortunately, flying activity is now very rare, the only permanent military aircraft presence being provided by Vikings of No. 617 Volunteer Gliding School. Most of the aircraft movements are now provided by freight operators who are also based on the airfield, the resident civil flying clubs and occasional general aviation visitors. Military aircraft are normally only seen during occasional exercises or deployments, and one-off deliveries to the fire school. Observation of most of the airfield is easy, but aircraft are very few and far between, despite the sprawling nature of the airfield, and the huge runway.

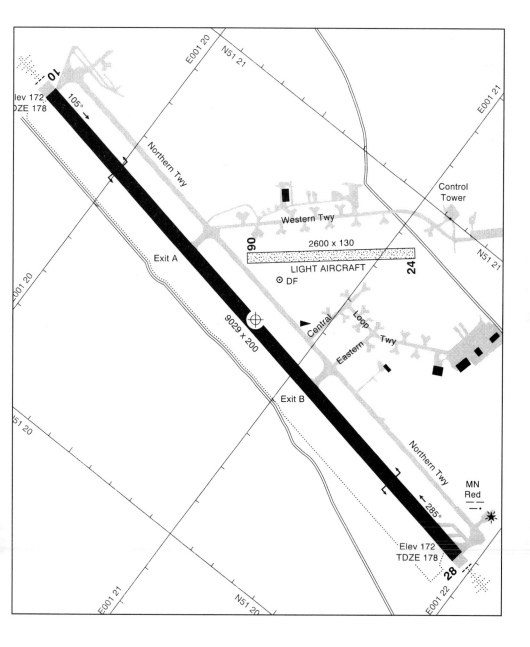

Elev 172
TDZE 178
10
105°
Northern Twy
Western Twy
Control Tower
N51 21
E001 20
N51 21
E001 21
E001 21
90
2600 x 130
24
LIGHT AIRCRAFT
⊙ DF
Exit A
E001 20
9029 x 200
Central
Loop
Twy
Eastern
Exit B
N51 20
Northern Twy
MN
Red
285°
Elev 172
TDZE 178
28
N51 20
E001 21
N51 20
E001 22

Marham

☺☺☺☺☺☺☺

Operator: Royal Air Force
Location: N52 38.90 E000 33.03 (5nm SW of King's Lynn off the A1122)
Elevation: 75ft
Tel: 01760 337261
Hours:
0800–2359 Mon–Thu, 0800–1800 Fri

Runways:
06/24 (055.42T slope 0.03% up) 9,141ft
Runway 06 TODA 9,790ft, LDA 9,141ft
Runway 24 TODA 9,879ft, LDA 9,141ft
01/19 (188.57T) 5,905ft
Runway 01 TODA 5,905ft, LDA 5,905ft
Runway 19 TODA 5,905ft, LDA 5,905ft

Radio:
Approach – 268.875 124.15 362.3
Director – 293.775 344.0 124.15
Talkdown – 379.65 123.3 385.4
Tower – 337.9 122.1 257.8
Ground – 336.35
Operations – 312.55

Notes:
Originally opened as a Royal Naval Air Service airfield (known as Narborough), RAF Marham was developed in the 1930s and became a Bomber Command airfield during World War Two, operating Wellingtons, Stirlings and Mosquitoes. Post-war, the site was developed further to accommodate B-29 Washingtons (both RAF and USAF models), followed by Valiant V–bomber squadrons. A long association with the Victor then began, until the type was withdrawn from RAF service in 1993. Marham is currently the home to Nos. 2 and 13 Squadrons which fly Tornado reconnaissance aircraft, and No. 39 (1 PRU) Squadron which flies the Canberra. Visiting aircraft can be seen, but most activity is provided by the resident units. Despite being a large base with huge runways, observation of activity is difficult as the surrounding roads are placed at some distance from the airfield. Good views can be achieved from the road overlooking the approach to Runway 06, although a closer view of the approach to Runway 24 is possible, but even this is less than ideal. The shorter Runway 01/19 is only used in emergency. Aircraft can sometimes be seen in the fire dump area close to the

MARHAM. One of just a handful of Canberras still operating with the Royal Air Force, with No. 39 (1PRU) Squadron.

southern shelter complex, and many Victors were dismantled on this site. Tornadoes can sometimes be seen taxiing within the shelter complexes, but in most respects Marham is a rather frustrating site for watching movements.

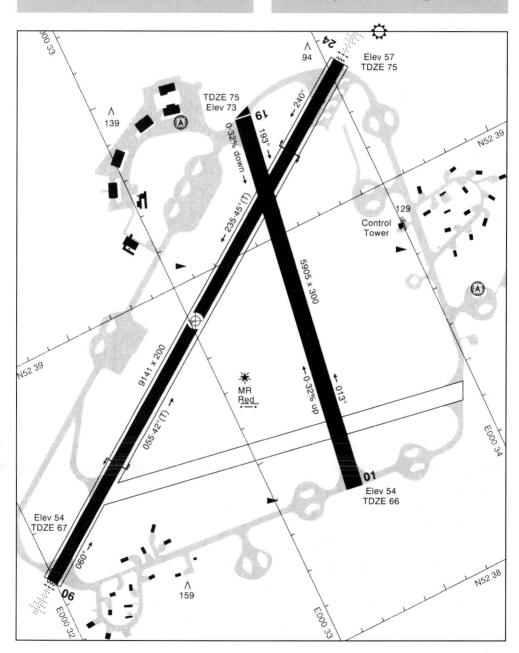

Middle Wallop

☺☺☺☺☺☺

Operator: Army
Location: N51 08.96 W001 34.22 (6nm SW of Andover off the A343)
Elevation: 297ft
Tel: 01980 674380
Hours:
0830–1700 Mon–Thu, 0830–1600 Fri

Runways:
08/26 (256T) 2,400ft (grass)
01/19 2,400ft (grass)
13/31 2,400ft (grass)

Radio:
Approach – 312.0 118.275
Director – 312.675
Talkdown – 364.825
Tower – 372.625 118.275

MIDDLE WALLOP is a busy Army helicopter training base, although a handful of fixed-wing types are also present, including aircraft belonging to the Army's Historical Flight.

Notes:
Unusual in that the site does not possess any concrete runways, Middle Wallop is a significant military airfield, closely associated with the Army Air Corps. Intensive helicopter flying keeps the airfield busy at most times, with Gazelles providing most of the activity. Some fixed-wing flying also takes place and visitors can occasionally be seen, usually helicopters. Observation of the airfield is easily achieved from the A343, and the nearby Museum of Army Aviation is well worth a visit. The base also regularly opens its gates to the public, and Middle Wallop's air shows have attracted some very unusual aircraft in the past, ranging from a variety of foreign helicopter types to modern fast jets, with even a Constellation landing at the airfield during 1988.

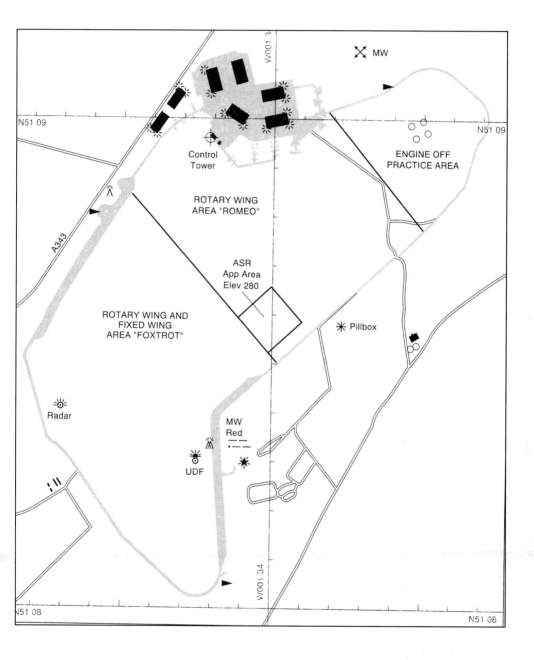

X MW

N51 09

ENGINE OFF
PRACTICE AREA

Control
Tower

ROTARY WING
AREA "ROMEO"

A343

ASR
App Area
Elev 280

ROTARY WING AND
FIXED WING
AREA "FOXTROT"

* Pillbox

Radar

MW
Red

* UDF

W001 34

N51 08

N51 08

Mildenhall

☺☺☺☺☺☺

Operator: United States Air Force
Location: N52 21.65 E000 29.30 (1nm NW of Mildenhall)
Elevation: 33ft
Tel: 01638 542251
Hours:
24 hrs

Runways:

11/29 (103.28T) 9,227ft
Runway 11 TODA 10,227ft, LDA 9,227ft
Runway 29 TODA 10,227ft, LDA 9,227ft

Radio:

Approach – 337.6
Departures – 242.075 137.2
Tower – 370.25 122.55
Ground – 278.15 142.275
Operations – 365.1 312.45

MILDENHALL is a fairly active transport and tanker base, best known for its annual two-day Air Fete.

Notes:
An historic Royal Air Force site, Mildenhall is most closely associated with the United States Air Force, which has operated from the airfield since World War Two. Little of the original Royal Air Force airfield remains other than the standard RAF hangars. The airfield's huge runway and numerous dispersal areas were built specifically for USAF operations, and the base has hosted a wide variety of aircraft transiting to and from the USA and Europe. Types such as the Globemaster and Cargomaster were once common sights, but Mildenhall's most familiar aircraft type has been the KC-135. Both refuelling tanker and reconnaissance variants of the aircraft have been based here. The C-130 Hercules has also been located at Mildenhall on detachment, but possibly the most famous resident was the SR-71 detachment, housed in a special hangar to the west of the runway. In view of the 'stop-start' nature of Blackbird operations, it's not impossible that the SR-71 may yet

return to its former home at Mildenhall. Currently, the base is home to a fleet of KC-135 tankers, and handles a daily routine of C-5, C-17 and C-141 transports moving to and from the USA. Observation of activities is best achieved from a viewing enclosure close to the Runway 29 threshold, although closer approach views can be found at each end of the runway, if approached on foot. Of course, the base hosts a large two-day 'open house' event every year, during which a large number of modern and historic aircraft are on view.

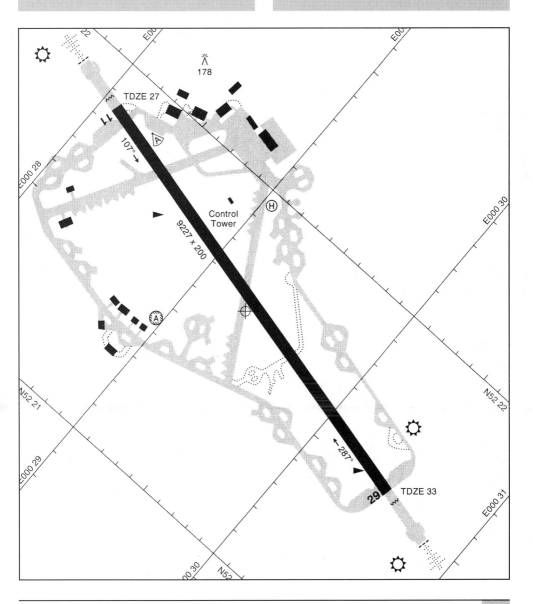

Newcastle (Woolsington)

☺☺☺☺☺☺

Operator: Civilian
Location: N55 02.25 W001 41.50 (3nm NW of Newcastle off the A696)
Elevation: 266ft
Tel: 0191 286 0966
Hours:
24hrs

Runways:
07/25 (065T slope 0.35% down) 7,641ft
Runway 07 TODA 7,887ft, LDA 7,247ft
Runway 25 TODA 7,828ft, LDA 6,972ft

Radio:
Approach – 124.375 284.6
Radar – 118.5 124.375 284.6
Tower – 119.7
Information – 114.25

NEWCASTLE currently provides a base for FR Aviation Falcons, which are employed on electronic warfare training with the RAF and Navy.

Notes:
First opened in 1935 after a long debate and search for a suitable airfield site, Woolsington's modest beginnings have led to a large and fully equipped regional airport, capable of handling aircraft of all sizes. Both scheduled and charter flights are part of the daily movements schedule (charters are predominantly in the summer months), and a variety of business and general aviation types use the airport. There is also a flying club based at the site. Military visitors are also quite common thanks largely to the airport's proximity to low flying areas and weapons ranges. FR Aviation operates a fleet of Falcon jets from the airport on detachment from its home base at Bournemouth. Viewing facilities are available within the terminal facility, and good approach views of Runway 07 are easily obtained. Activity is not on the scale of larger airports such as Manchester, but the range of medium-sized airliners, light aircraft and a handful of military types creates an interesting variety.

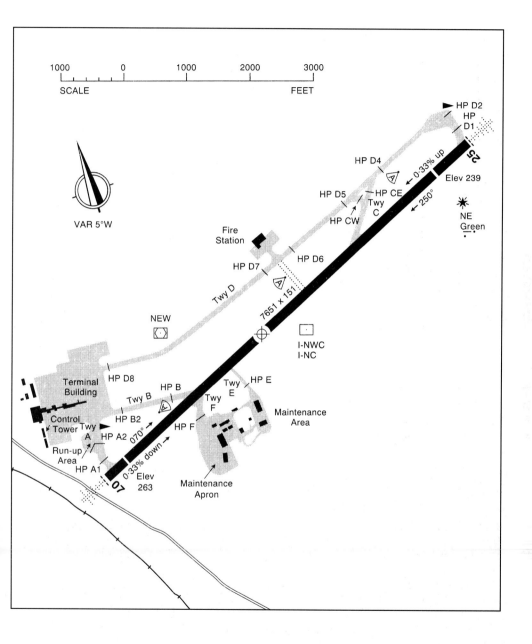

1000   0   1000   2000   3000

SCALE   FEET

VAR 5°W

HP D2
HP D1
25
HP D4
0·33% up
Elev 239
HP D5
HP CE
Twy C
HP CW
←250°
NE Green
Fire Station
HP D7
HP D6
Twy D
7651 x 151
NEW
I-NWC
I-NC
Terminal Building
HP D8
Twy B
HP B
Twy E
HP E
Control Tower
Twy A
HP B2
Twy F
Maintenance Area
Run-up Area
HP A2
070°
HP F
HP A1
0·33% down
Elev 263
Maintenance Apron
07
Elev 263

Northolt
☺☺☺☺☺

Operator: Royal Air Force
Location: N51 33.18 W000 25.09 (6nm NW of central London off the A40)
Elevation: 124ft
Tel: 020 8845 2300
Hours:
0800–2000 Mon–Sun

Runways:
07/25 (069.85T slope 0.18% up) 5,525ft
Runway 07 TODA 5,525ft, LDA 5,223ft
Runway 25 TODA 5,584ft, LDA 5,525ft

Radio:
Approach – 344.975 362.3 126.45
Director – 379.425 375.5 130.35
Talkdown – 375.5 385.4 125.875
Tower – 312.35 257.8 124.975
Departures – 120.32
Operations – 244.425

Notes:
A well-known Royal Air Force Fighter Command station during World War Two, Northolt hosted a total of forty-five different fighter squadrons at various stages through the war. Although remaining under RAF control in post-war years, the airfield was opened for civil use and became the site for London's main airport prior to the construction of Heathrow. Civilian operations gradually declined, however, and now only a few aircraft use Northolt's facilities. Military activity now occupies most of Northolt's flying schedule, and the airfield's location close to central London makes it ideal for transport and communication flights. Not surprisingly, virtually all of Northolt's movements are

NORTHOLT is associated with the BAe 146s operated by the Queen's Flight (now No. 32 Squadron). However, the Station Flight also operates a pair of Islander communications aircraft.

made by transport or VIP aircraft, and the station is home to No. 32 (The Royal) Squadron, with a fleet of BAe 125, BAe 146 and Twin Squirrel aircraft flown as required by members of the Royal Family, and Government VIPs. Observation of aircraft movements is very difficult, thanks to the airfield's location close to the very busy A40 (from where the airfield is obscured, sandwiched between housing complexes. A decent view is possible from the A4180, but most views are best achieved on foot. Despite the varied nature of the aircraft movements, however, activity is fairly low.

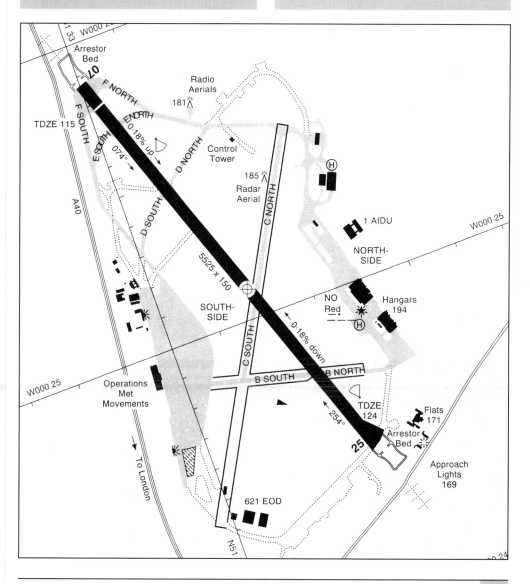

Odiham

☺☺☺☺☺

Operator: Royal Air Force
Location: N51 14.05 W000 56.57 (7nm W of Aldershot off the A32)
Elevation: 405ft
Tel: 01256 702134
Hours:
0800–1700 Mon–Fri

Runways:
10/28 (092.62T slope 0.07% down)
6,032ft
Runway 10 TODA 6,124ft, LDA 6,025ft
Runway 28 TODA 6,124ft, LDA 6,031ft

Radio:
Approach – 386.775 125.25
Talkdown – 300.45 385.4 123.3
Tower – 309.625 257.8 122.1
Information – 315.975 122.1

ODIHAM, currently home to the RAF's Chinook heavy-lift helicopter fleet.

Notes:
Originally the home to Army co-operation units (flying Lysanders, Mustangs and Tomahawks), Odiham's role has effectively turned full circle, with present-day operations mostly being in support of the Army. PR squadrons were based at Odiham later in World War Two, and Fighter Command arrived in 1946 with Tempests, Spitfires, Vampires, Meteors and Javelins. Odiham is still remembered for the RAF's huge Coronation Review, which included a series of mass fly-past formations and a huge static display of RAF aircraft which literally filled Odiham's disused runway and northern dispersals. Helicopters first arrived at the base in 1960, and types such as the Belvedere, Whirlwind and Wessex were based here, followed by the more recent Puma, and now the Chinook. Odiham is now an all-Chinook base (apart from a single Gazelle, the only one of its type remaining in RAF service) and the home to Nos. 7, 18 and 27 Squadrons. While Nos. 7 and 27 Squadrons utilise the main northern ramp area, the Chinooks of No.18 Squadron occupy the eastern dispersal, where a new hangar was built for the unit prior to its arrival from Laarbruch in 1997. Observing activity is difficult because of the local terrain, but approach views can be found at reasonable distances from both runway thresholds. Of course, there is no guarantee that the resident Chinooks will use the runway headings for arrival or departure, and visiting/fixed wing aircraft are fairly few in number. In addition, many of the Chinooks are regularly detached away from base in support of operations across the UK and around the world.

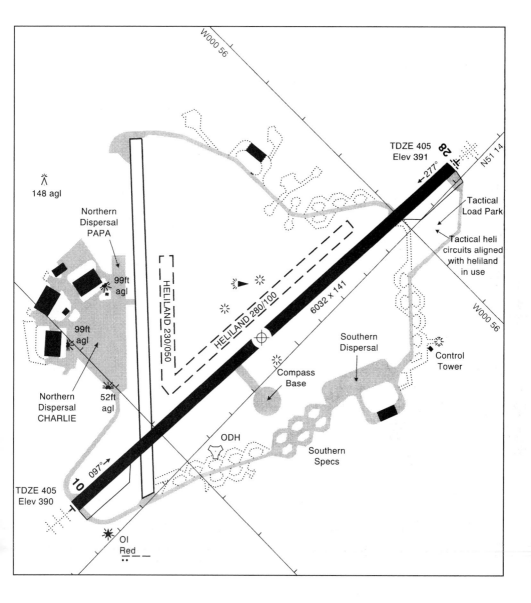

Plymouth
☺☺☺
Operator: Civilian
Location: N50 25.37 W004 06.37 (4nm N of Plymouth)
Elevation: 474ft
Tel: 01752 772752
Hours:
0630–2230 Mon-Fri, 0001–2359 Sat-Sun
Runways:
13/31 (123T slope 0.95% down) 3,839ft
Runway 13 TODA 3,839ft, LDA 3,406ft
Runway 31 TODA 3,806ft, LDA 3,461ft
06/21 (049T slope 0.57% up) 2,467ft
Runway 06 TODA 2,467ft, LDA 2,467ft
Runway 24 TODA 2,467ft, LDA 2,343ft

Radio:
Approach – 133.55
Tower – 122.6
Ground – 121.75

Notes:
Although regarded as one of the 'new breed' of city airports, Plymouth's airfield first opened in 1931. However, activity remained fairly low until the 1970s, when Brymon Airways began regular commuter flights. Services to destinations such as Heathrow, the Scillies and Newquay are still maintained. The Royal Navy also maintains a presence here, and their Grading Flight currently operates a fleet of Grob 115 basic trainers, following the retirement of their distinctively marked Chipmunks. The small but active airfield can be observed from various locations, including the main terminal complex.

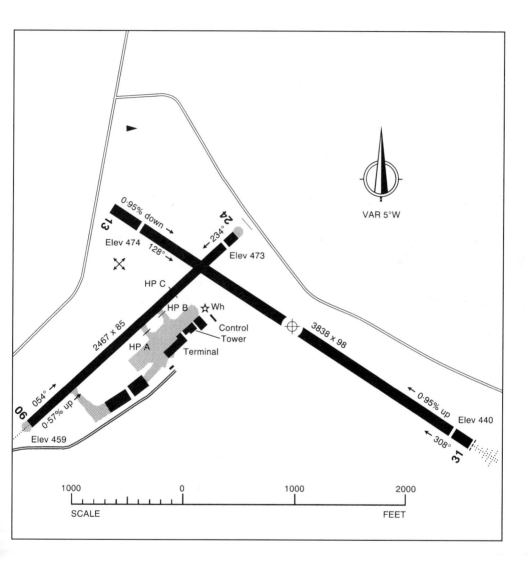

VAR 5°W

13

0.95% down →

24

Elev 474

128°

234°

Elev 473

HP C

HP B ☆ Wh

2467 x 85

Control Tower

HP A

Terminal

3838 x 98

054° →

0.57% up ↑

0.95% up ←

Elev 440

06

Elev 459

308° ←

31

1000   0   1000   2000

SCALE   FEET

Prestwick

☺☺☺☺☺☺

Operator: Civilian
Location: N55 30.47 W004 35.20 (1nm
NE of Prestwick off the A77)
Elevation: 66ft
Tel: 01292 479822
Hours:
0030–0230, 0300–2359 Mon–Sun

Runways:

13/31 (121T slope 0.29% up) 9,800ft
Runway 13 TODA 10,400ft, LDA 8,999ft
Runway 31 TODA 10,089ft, LDA 9,800ft
03/21 (024T slope 0.2% up) 6,000ft
Runway 03 TODA 6,302ft, LDA 6,000ft
Runway 21 TODA 6,640ft, LDA 6,000ft

Radio:

Approach – 120.55
Radar – 120.55 119.45
Tower – 118.15 121.8
Information – 127.125

Notes:
For either political or economic reasons, Prestwick was for many years designated as a 'gateway' airfield, which meant that all transatlantic flights to and from Scottish airports were obliged to pass through Prestwick. When this arrangement ended, it wasn't surprising that many operators moved to other airports, leaving Prestwick under-utilised. The gradual withdrawal of American forces from the UK and Europe also resulted in the countless transatlantic ferry flights which once used Prestwick slowly diminishing to almost zero. However, since 1992 the airport has been under private ownership, and operations are now on the increase again, with scheduled domestic services, steady cargo and charter traffic, and some general aviation. The British Aerospace Flying College is based here, together with two flying clubs. British Aerospace maintains a production and maintenance/overhaul facility here (the site is well known for Bulldog and Jetstream production), and the Royal Navy operates Sea Kings from HMS *Gannet*, a Fleet Air Arm enclave adjacent to the main terminal area. Viewing opportunities exist around the airfield, and although activity is sporadic, the occasional transatlantic ferry flight (many of which are military) still appears and British Airways Concordes fly circuit training at the airfield.

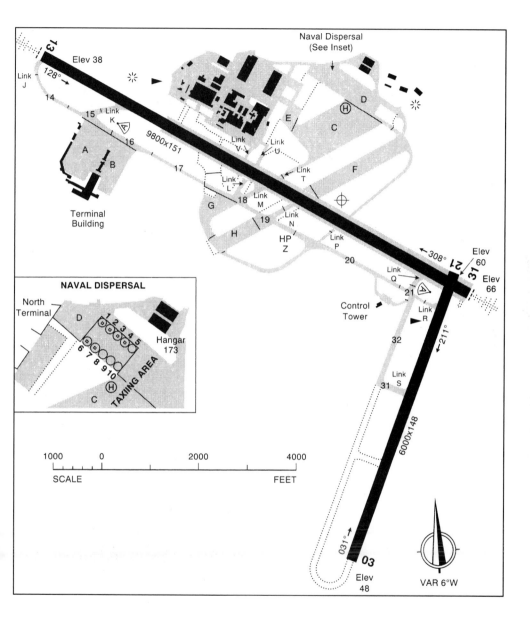

Naval Dispersal
(See Inset)

Elev 38

Link J
128°
14
15 Link K
16
9800x151
17
A
B
Terminal
Building
Link L
18 Link M
G
19 Link N
H
HP Z
20

E
Link V
Link U
C
D
F
Link T

308°
21
31
Elev 60
Elev 66
Link Q
21
Control Tower
Link R
32
211°
31 Link S
6000x148

031°
03
Elev 48

VAR 6°W

NAVAL DISPERSAL

North Terminal
D
1 2 3 4 5
6 7 8 9 10
C
Hangar 173
TAXIING AREA

SCALE   FEET
1000   0   2000   4000

St Athan
☺☺☺☺☺
Operator: Royal Air Force
Location: N51 24.29 W003 26.15 (10nm SW of Cardiff on the B4265)
Elevation: 163ft
Tel: 01446 798798
Hours:
0830–1700 Mon–Thu, 0830–1600 Fri

Runways:
08/26 (073.05T slope 0.45% down) 5,988ft
Runway 08 TODA 5,991ft, LDA 5,988ft
Runway 26 TODA 6,001ft, LDA 5,988ft

Radio:
Approach – 357.175 362.3 122.1
Talkdown – 340.1 372.375 123.3
Tower – 336.525 257.8 122.1
Ground – 386.5

Notes:
Opened during 1938 as a maintenance and storage facility, St Athan has remained active in this role ever since, and almost every Royal Air Force aircraft type has been handled by the station at some stage. Most notably, the base was responsible for the maintenance of Meteors and Canberras, and the V-Force. Many aircraft have been scrapped on the site, including types such as the Vulcan. St Athan is currently the home of the RAF's Centre of Engineering, responsible for types such as the Hawk, Harrier, Jaguar and Tornado, and also the Royal Navy's Sea Harriers. Larger aircraft such as the VC10 are also handled. Resident flying

ST ATHAN receives a wide variety of RAF aircraft for thorough servicing, ranging from front-line Tornadoes to the Battle of Britain Memorial Flight's Lancaster.

units comprise the University of Wales Air Squadron equipped with Bulldogs, No. 634 Volunteer Gliding School with Vikings, and the St Athan Station Flight with a pair of Tucanos. Hawk detachments from Valley are also common (using the nearby Pembrey weapons range), and various RAF types make test flights to and from the airfield. Viewing opportunities are plenty, with access to most parts of the airfield possible, including the runway approaches. Aircraft movements are sporadic, but varied, and some aircraft can be seen in semi-painted condition, whilst making test flights.

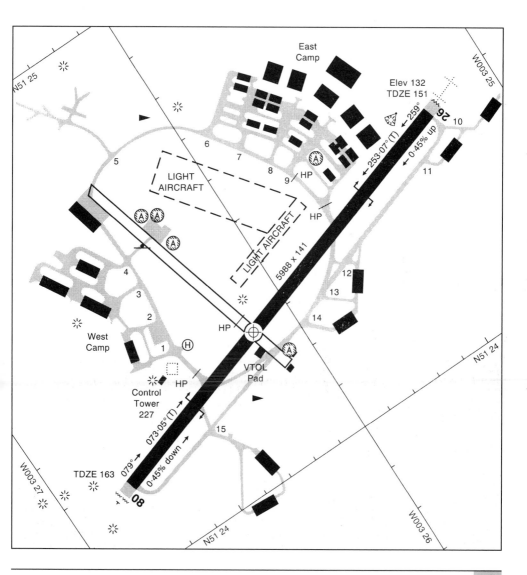

St Mawgan
☺ ☺ ☺ ☺ ☺ ☺

Operator: Royal Air Force
Location: N50 26.43 W004 59.72 (3nm NE of Newquay off the A3059)
Elevation: 390ft
Tel: 01637 872201
Hours:
0700–2359 Mon–Thu, 0650–2200 Fri–Sun

Runways:
13/31 (120.51T slope 0.93% up) 9,006ft
Runway 13 TODA 9,478ft, LDA 9,006ft
Runway 31 TODA 9,380ft, LDA 9,006ft

Radio:
Approach – 357.2 126.5 122.1
Director – 360.55 125.55 344.0 123.3
Talkdown – 387.45 123.3 385.4
Tower – 241.825 123.4 122.1
Ground – 376.625
Operations – 260.0

ST MAWGAN maintains a Shackleton as a gate guard, with a further example (illustrated) still intact on the airfield and used as a fire escape training airframe.

Notes:
Opening as a satellite to nearby RAF St Eval, St Mawgan was initially used by USAAF Liberator transports, and countless aircraft used the airfield for transatlantic ferry stopovers. Royal Air Force Coastal Command took over in 1951 and Lancaster maritime reconnaissance aircraft arrived, later replaced by Shackletons, then by Nimrods in 1969. Nimrod operations continued until 1992, when the aircraft were relocated to Kinloss, leaving St Mawgan virtually inactive, apart from helicopter operations performed by No. 203(R) Squadron, the RAF Sea King training unit. However, the base has more recently been earmarked as a site for numerous RAF and Nato exercises, and the airfield facilities (which include shelters constructed for Buccaneer detachments) look set to become more regularly utilised for frequent periods throughout the year. The station also holds a very popular open day every summer which attracts a variety of RAF, Navy and Nato aircraft. Civil aviation also shares St Mawgan's facilities, with a small airport facility located on the northern boundary of the airfield. A

small number of scheduled and business flights operate from here. Excellent views of the airfield are available under the approaches to both ends of the runway, and a viewing area is being constructed near the Runway 31 threshold. Aircraft movements are few, and even civil flights are infrequent, but the airfield is much busier during exercise periods.

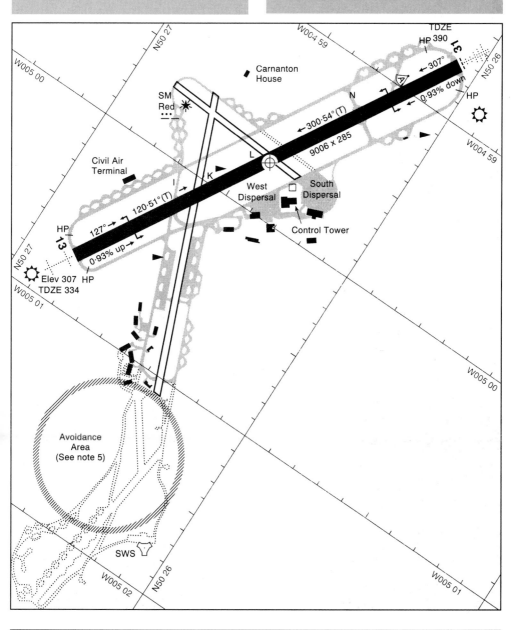

Scampton

☺☺☺☺☺

Operator: Royal Air Force
Location: N53 18.45 W000 32.95 (3nm N of Lincoln on the A15)
Elevation: 203ft
Tel: 01400 261201
Hours:
As required

Runways:

05/23 041.16T slope 0.31% down) 9,012ft
Runway 05 TODA 9,206ft, LDA 9,012ft
Runway 23 TODA 9,619ft, LDA 9,012ft

Radio:
Tower – 282.4   122.1

SCAMPTON is no longer a fully active RAF station, although it is still used for daily practice flights by the Red Arrows, based at nearby Cranwell.

Notes:
Perhaps the most famous of all Royal Air Force bases, Scampton was a major World War Two bomber base, and home to No. 617 Squadron – the famous Dambusters – whose legendary raids were mounted from this base. Post-war, the station operated Canberras prior to being extensively modernised before the first Vulcan V-bomber squadrons arrived. Scampton remained active as a Vulcan base (and for many years housed the Vulcan's Blue Steel stand-off bombs) into the 1980s, when the Vulcan was retired. The station then transferred to training operations, flying Bulldogs, Jet Provosts and Tucanos, and the Red Arrows aerobatic team moved here from Kemble. More recently the RAF vacated the airfield, but the Red Arrows (now located at Cranwell) use the airfield on

a daily basis for display practice flying. Some private flying now takes place at the airfield and a small number of jet warbirds have arrived, which may indicate the direction of Scampton's future.

Observation of the flying activities (mostly provided by the Red Arrows) can be made from locations at either end of the runway, and from various points along the northern airfield perimeter.

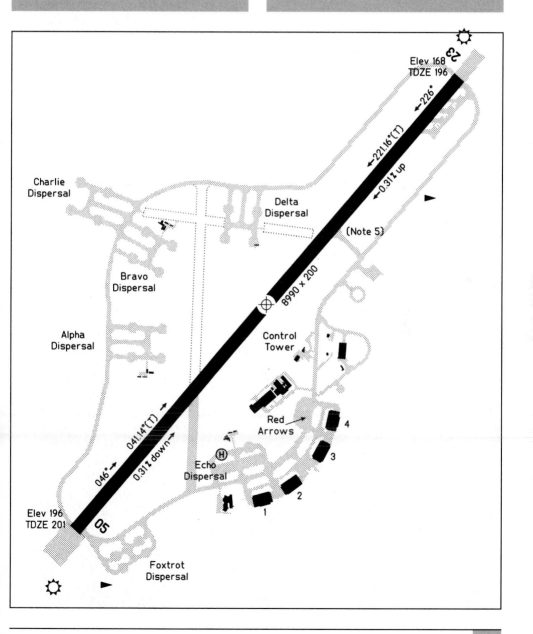

Shawbury

☺☺☺

Operator: Royal Air Force
Location: N52 47.89 W002 40.08 (8nm NE of Shrewsbury off the A53)
Elevation: 249ft
Tel: 01939 250351
Hours:
0800–1700 Mon–Fri

Runways:
18/36 (359.88T) 6,018ft
Runway 36 TODA 6,898ft, LDA 6,018ft
Runway 18 TODA 7,018ft, LDA 6,018ft
05/23 (224.78T) 4,523ft
Runway 05 TODA 4,523ft, LDA 4,523ft
Runway 23 TODA 4,523ft, LDA 4,523ft

Radio:
Radar – 362.475 120.775
Approach – 365.325
Director – 254.2 123.3
Talkdown – 356.975 376.675 123.3
Tower – 340.35 122.1
Ground – 337.9

Notes:
Traditionally a training airfield since it first opened in 1917, Shawbury has also been linked with Royal Air Force helicopter training operations for many years, the first rotary-wing inhabitants arriving in the early 1970s. After a long association with the Whirlwind, Gazelle and Wessex, these types have now been replaced in favour of the 'new generation' Squirrel and Griffin, which are operated (by FBS) on behalf of the tri-service Defence Helicopter Flying School. Nos. 660 Squadron (Army Air Corps) and 705 NAS (Fleet Air Arm) fly the Squirrels for all three services' requirements, while No. 60 (R) Squadron operates the Griffins, and the Central Flying School operates both

SHAWBURY, photographed in 1998 with some of the airfield's storage hangars visible in the distance.

types as required. Fixed-wing activity has now virtually ceased at Shawbury following the demise of the Jet Provosts used by the Central Air Traffic Control School (their 'real' training now being computer-orientated simulation). Visiting aircraft types are few, although some aircraft are occasionally flown in or out of storage from the base's extensive hangarage complex. Viewing operations at Shawbury is difficult, with only poor views from most roads, and helicopter approaches might not be on runway headings.

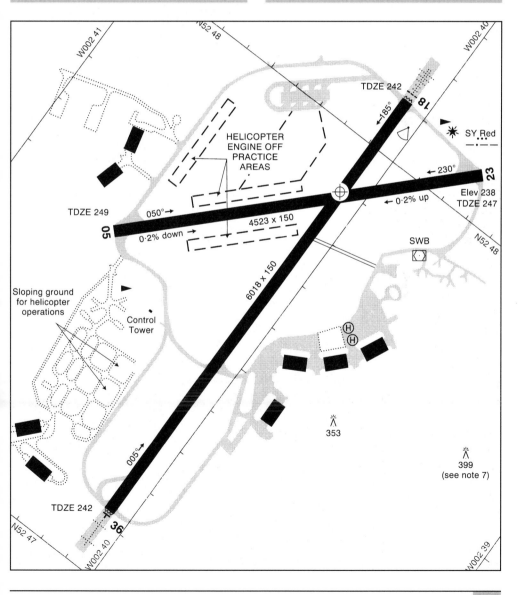

Southampton (Eastleigh)
☺☺☺☺

Operator: Civilian
Location: N50 57.02 W001 21.41 (3nm N of Southampton off the A335)
Elevation: 44ft
Tel: 023 8062 9600
Hours:
(winter)   0625–2100 Mon–Fri,
              0615–2000 Sat,
              0900–2100 Sun
(summer)   0525–2000 Mon–Fri,
              0525–1900 Sat,
              0800–2000 Sun

Runways:
02/20 (019T slope 0.23% up) 5,653ft
Runway 02 TODA 6,007ft, LDA 5,413ft
Runway 20 TODA 5,922ft, LDA 5,266ft

Radio:
Zone – 120.225
Approach – 128.85
Radar – 128.25
Tower – 118.2
Operations – 130.65

Notes:
Famous as the site from where the prototype Supermarine Spitfire made its first flight on 5 March 1936, one might expect to find a significant amount of reference to this historical event at Southampton Airport. In fact, there is little more than a commemorative plaque within the terminal building, and one is left to imagine the scene so many years ago when the graceful, blue-painted fighter took to the air from Eastleigh's grass field. Present-day operations take advantage of a concrete runway, enabling most aircraft types to use the facility, although most movements are confined to medium-sized turboprops, and only occasional jet visitors are seen. Resident flying schools use single- and twin-engined light aircraft, and the airfield circuit is usually fairly busy, even though there aren't too many surprises to be seen. Military aircraft are very rare. Views of the airport are best found within the terminal area, as the road crossing the approach to Runway 02 is the M27, and is consequently less than ideal for plane spotting.

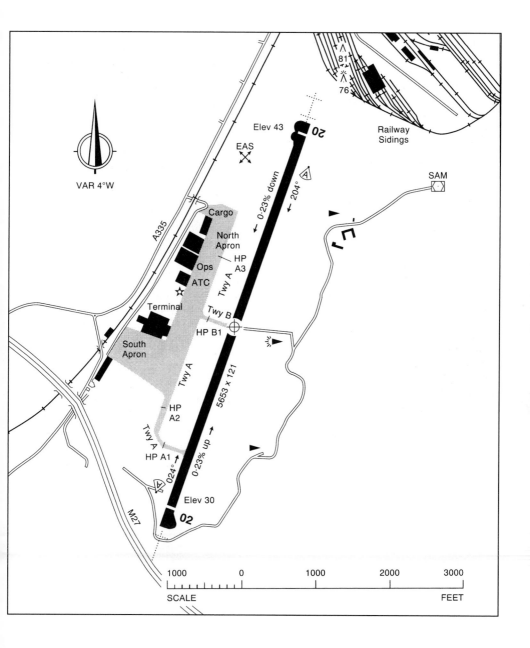

VAR 4°W

Elev 43

EAS

Railway
Sidings

SAM

81

76

0·23% down

204°

Cargo

North
Apron

A335

HP
A3

Ops

ATC

Twy A

Terminal

Twy B

HP B1

South
Apron

Twy A

5653 × 121

HP
A2

Twy A

HP A1

024°

0·23% up

Elev 30

M27

02

20

| 1000 | 0 | 1000 | 2000 | 3000 |

SCALE

FEET

Southend
☺☺☺☺☺

Operator: Civilian
Location: N51 34.28 E000 41.73 (1nm N
of Southend-on-Sea, off the A127)
Elevation: 48ft
Tel: 01702 340201
Hours:
0800–2000 Mon–Sun

Runways:
06/24 (055T slope 0.23% down) 5,265ft
Runway 06 TODA 5,167ft, LDA 4,508ft
Runway 24 TODA 5,266ft, LDA 4,770ft

Radio:
Approach – 128.95
Radar – 128.95 125.05
Tower – 127.725
Departures – 121.8

Notes:
A successful regional airport, Southend
has endured a difficult time in which
passenger levels have slumped in favour
of freight and other non-passenger
services. Even the airport's fascinating
aviation museum was closed, with many
of its exhibits destroyed, and the future
of the airfield became rather uncertain.
However, more recently the airport has
received some significant investment
and facilities have been improved, with
a completely new terminal facility

*SOUTHEND is a fairly active airport, and also
home to a Vulcan bomber, preserved in
near-flying condition, awaiting CAA
permission to fly.*

opened a couple of years ago. Southend hopes to encourage the return of more scheduled and charter services, effectively returning the airport to a more secure foundation. For the time being, most activity is provided by the various resident flying clubs, although a number of maintenance facilities are based at Southend, encouraging an interesting variety of unusual visitors, ranging from aged Boeings to the mighty Belfast. An historic site, Southend is best remembered as a car ferry base, from where bizarre Carvair transports operated cross-Channel services. At present,

Southend's most famous resident is Vulcan XL426, preserved in near-flying condition by a group of dedicated enthusiasts, who are still waiting for the happy day when the Civil Aviation Authority (CAA) will give permission for their Vulcan to fly again. Until then, visitors are treated to occasional opportunities to see the Vulcan roar down Southend's runway. Good views of the runway can be obtained from the road crossing the approach to Runway 06, and visitors are welcome in the general aviation area, where the Vulcan is positioned.

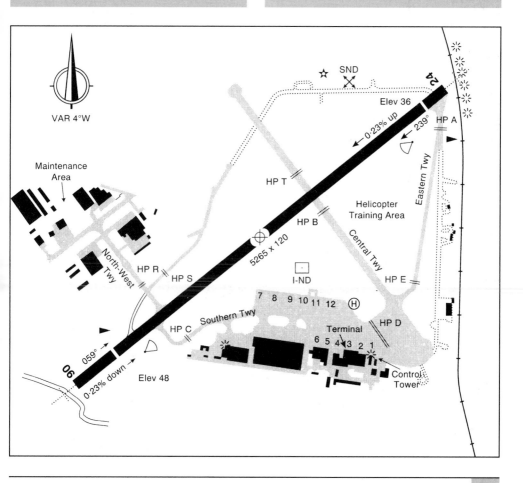

Swansea (Fairwood Common)

☺☺☺☺

Operator: Civilian
Location: N51 36.32 W004 04.07 (3nm W of Swansea off the A4118)
Elevation: 299ft
Tel: 01792 204063
Hours:
(winter) 0900–1700 Mon–Sun
(summer) 0800–1700 Mon–Sun

Runways:
04/22 (036T slope 0.79% up) 4,829ft
Runway 04 TODA 4,925ft, LDA 4,432ft
Runway 22 TODA 4,928ft, LDA 4,137ft
10/28 (096T) 3,492ft
Runway 10 TODA 3,104ft, LDA 2,940ft
Runway 28 TODA 3,337ft, LDA 2,713ft
15/33 (145T) 3,402ft
Runway 15 TODA 3,130ft, LDA 2,966ft
Runway 33 TODA 3,360ft, LDA 2,785ft

Radio:
Approach – 119.7
Tower – 119.7

Notes:
A former Royal Air Force airfield used for fighter operations during World War Two, Fairwood Common was transferred to civilian operations in 1957 and has remained active ever since. Although capable of accepting medium-sized airliners, Swansea rarely handles aircraft larger than typical business types, and light aircraft are the most common types seen at the airport. Two flying clubs are resident on the airfield and visitors are fairly common. Larger aircraft and military types are rare. Viewing is possible from a variety of locations, the general aviation sites being the most convenient.

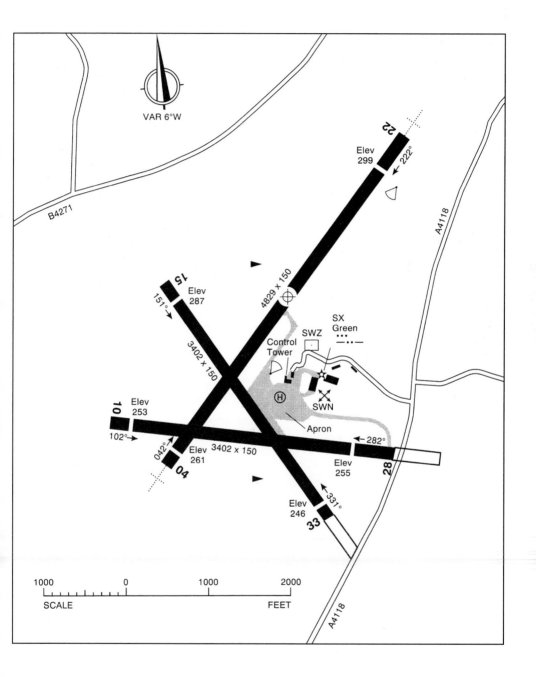

VAR 6°W

B4271

A4118

22
Elev
299
222°

15
151°
Elev
287

4829 x 150

3402 x 150

SX
Green
•••
—•—•—

SWZ

Control
Tower

(H)

SWN

Apron

10
Elev
253
102°

042°
04
Elev
261
3402 x 150

←282°
Elev
255
28

331°
Elev
246
33

A4118

1000   0   1000   2000

SCALE   FEET

169

Teesside
(Middleton St George)
☺ ☺ ☺ ☺ ☺

Operator: Civilian
Location: N54 30.55 W001 25.76 (3nm SE of Darlington on the A67)
Elevation: 120ft
Tel: 01325 332811
Hours:
0630–2200 Mon–Sat, 0645–2200 Sun

Runways:
05/23 (047T slope 0.01% up) 7,516ft
Runway 05 TODA 8,432ft, LDA 7,516ft
Runway 23 TODA 8,202ft, LDA 7,516ft
01/19 (183T) 2,428ft
Runway 01 TODA 2,428ft, LDA 2,428ft
Runway 19 TODA 2,428ft, LDA 2,428ft

Radio:
Approach – 118.85 296.725
Radar – 118.85 128.85 296.725
Tower – 119.8 379.8

Notes:
A famous former Royal Air Force station, Middleton St George was a major bomber base during World War Two and post-war became the home to Hunter and Javelin squadrons. Most notably, the station was home to Lightning interceptors and a single preserved example remains on the airfield today. Teesside Airport opened during the mid-1960s when the Royal Air Force vacated the site, and many reminders of the airfield's military past remains. The vast majority of buildings are original RAF constructions. The fighter readiness platforms are still adjacent to the runway thresholds and even the former V–bomber dispersal is still visible on the eastern edge of the airfield perimeter. Today the airfield is much less active,

TEESSIDE, illustrating much of the airport's RAF heritage.

and although there are some scheduled and charter services, the majority of activity is confined to general aviation. Flying clubs are based at the airport and visitors are welcome. Good views of the airfield are to be found at many loca-tions, and the airport occasionally hosts an air display at which a number of aircraft are displayed on the ground. Military types are rarely seen at the airport other than at air show week-ends.

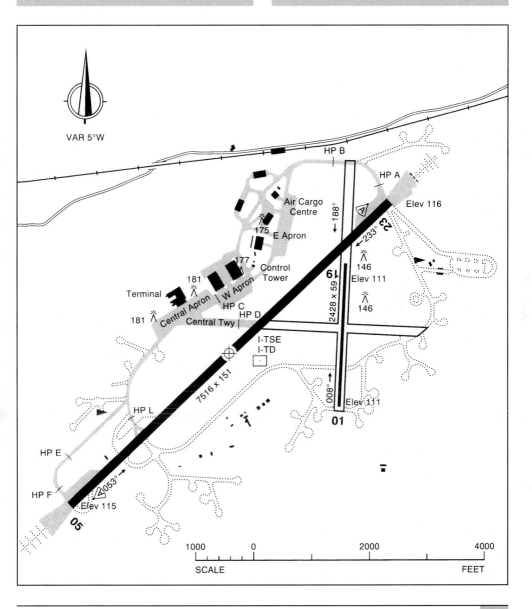

Topcliffe
☺☺☺☺

Operator: Royal Air Force
Location: N54 12.33 W001 22.93 (3nm SW of Thirsk off the A168)
Elevation: 92ft
Tel: 01748 875376
Hours:
0900–1615 Mon–Fri

Runways:
03/21 (021.74T slope 0.3% up) 6,027ft
Runway 03 TODA 5,951ft, LDA 4,704ft
Runway 21 TODA 5,951ft, LDA 5,065ft
13/31 (125.9T slope 0.10% down) 4,140ft
Runway 13 TODA 4,074ft, LDA 4,074ft
Runway 31 TODA 4,074ft, LDA 3,103ft

Radio:
Approach – 357.375 125.0 362.3 122.1
Director – 255.6 125.0 344.0 123.3
Talkdown – 344.35 385.4 123.3
Tower – 309.725 122.1 257.8
Ground – 387.45

Notes:
First opened as a Royal Air Force station in 1940, Topcliffe was home to the Whitleys. Canadian squadrons followed, and post-war the station became a transport base with Hastings before being transferred to Coastal Command, to operate Lockheed Neptunes. Finally, the station was home to an Air Navigation School with Varsities, before it was handed over to the Army in 1972. The RAF returned in 1993, however, when the Joint Elementary Flying Training School formed here with Slingsby Fireflies. They were then moved to Barkston Heath and the station became a satellite for RAF Linton-on-Ouse. Currently, no aircraft are actually based at Topcliffe, although numerous Tucanos can be seen on the ground or in the air on most days. The Central Flying School conducts its instructor training at Topcliffe and Tucanos from No. 1 Flying Training School use the airfield whenever Linton's circuit is overcrowded. Observation from outside the airfield perimeter is possible, although the runway thresholds are displaced, making photography difficult. Despite being fairly active, almost all of the airfield movements are provided by Tucanos, and other types are fairly rare.

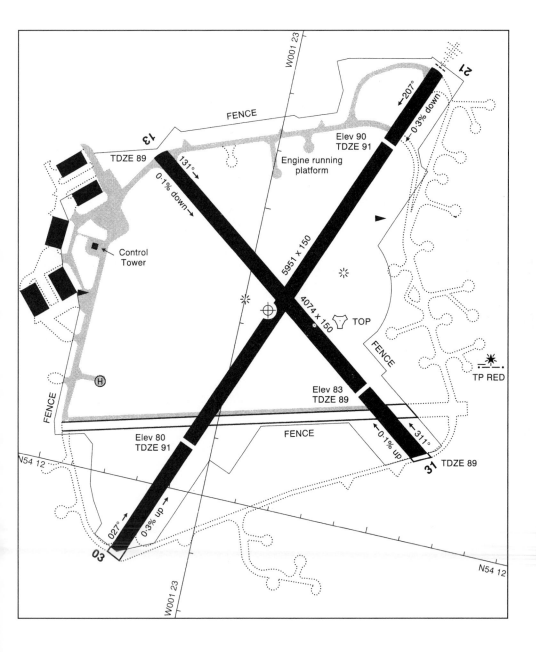

FENCE

13
TDZE 89

131°

0.1% down

W001 23

Elev 90
TDZE 91

Engine running
platform

21
←207°

0.3% down

Control
Tower

5951 x 150

4074 x 150

TOP

FENCE

TP RED

(H)

FENCE

Elev 83
TDZE 89

Elev 80
TDZE 91

FENCE

←311°

-0.1% up

31 TDZE 89

N54 12

027°→

0.3% up

03

W001 23

N54 12

Valley
☺☺☺☺☺☺☺☺

Operator: Royal Air Force
Location: N53 14.89 W004 32.12 (1nm
NW of Rhosneigr off the A5)
Elevation: 37ft
Tel: 01407 762241
Hours:
0800–2359 Mon–Thu, 0800–1800 Fri

Runways:
14/32 (130.41T slope 0.12% down)
7,513ft
Runway 14 TODA 7,530ft, LDA 7,513ft
Runway 32 TODA 7,530ft, LDA 7,513ft
01/19 (006.32T slope 0.22% up) 5,377ft
Runway 01 TODA 5,250ft, LDA 5,156ft
Runway 19 TODA 5,202ft, LDA 5,156ft
08/26 (069.89T slope 0.4% up) 4,200ft
Runway 08 TODA 4,675ft, LDA 3,497ft
Runway 26 TODA 4,199ft, LDA 3,799ft

Radio:
Approach – 372.325 362.3 134.35
Radar – 258.825 134.35
Director – 337.725 344.0 123.3 134.35
Talkdown – 358.675 385.4 123.3
Tower – 340.175 257.8 122.1
Ground – 356.75 122.1

Notes:
Opening in 1941 as a Royal Air Force
fighter base, Valley was also a vital ferry
flight staging point for USAAF operations
during World War Two. Following the
war, the airfield remained unused until
1951, when Training Command began
operations, and Valley has remained
active in the flying training role ever
since. Famous types such as the
Vampire, Gnat and Hunter were familiar
sights at Valley, and in 1976 the first
Hawks arrived at the base, beginning a
long and happy association with the
type which continues to this day. The
home of No. 4 Flying Training School
(FTS), Valley's Hawks are distributed
amongst the FTS component squadrons,
Nos. 19(R), 74(R) and 208(R) Squadrons.
Also based here is the Search and
Rescue Training Unit, part of No.
60(R) Squadron, equipped with Griffin
helicopters, together with No. 22
Squadron's C Flight detachment with
Sea Kings. Valley is a busy base, and
Hawk operations can sometimes require
the simultaneous use of two runways –

*VALLEY is the RAF's advanced flying training
base, and home to a large fleet of Hawks.*

something rarely seen at any other RAF station. Visiting aircraft are also very common, often connected with the nearby weapons ranges and low–flying areas. Viewing activity is easy, with a public viewing area close to the threshold of Runway 19. Excellent views of the approach to Runway 32 can be found on foot, as can views of Runway 14's threshold, although standing directly under the approach path is not recommended, as some aircraft can fly alarmingly low at this location!

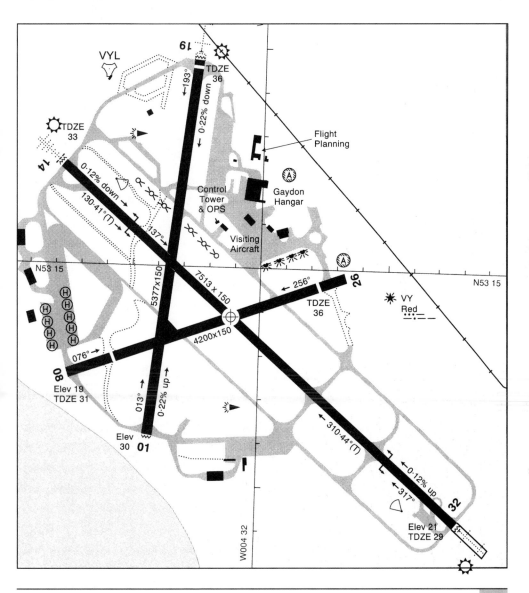

Waddington

☺☺☺☺☺☺☺☺☺

Operator: Royal Air Force
Location: N53 09.97 W000 31.43 (3nm S of Lincoln off the A15)
Elevation: 231ft
Tel: 01522 720271
Hours:
24hrs

Runways:
03/21 (021.69T slope 0.08% down) 9,000ft
Runway 03 TODA 9,164ft, LDA 9,000ft
Runway 21 TODA 9,000ft, LDA 9,000ft

Radio:
Approach – 312.5 362.3
Zone – 296.75 127.35 125.35
Director – 300.575 123.3 344.0
Departures – 249.85 123.3
Talkdown – 309.675 385.4
Tower – 388.225 257.8
Ground – 342.125
Operations – 244.275

Notes:
Originally opening in 1916, then closing in 1919, only to reopen in 1926, little remains of the original site of Waddington's operations, tucked away on the eastern airfield perimeter. The main site became the home to numerous bomber squadrons during World War Two, and resident types included the Hampden, Manchester and Lancaster. Post-war, the base became a Lincoln operator until the first Canberras arrived. Of course, Waddington is famous as the home of the Vulcan, and the first deliveries were made to this base. After a long and successful association with the type, the last Vulcans (which were operated in the tanker role) were withdrawn in preparation for the new Nimrod AEW3, and this aircraft was briefly based at Waddington on test duties. When the Nimrod programme was abandoned, Waddington's future looked uncertain. The only resident that remained was XH558, the RAF's last Vulcan retained for display flying. However, a major development programme paved the way for the Sentry AEW fleet, and Nos. 8 and 23 Squadrons now operate from Waddington, based in a huge purpose-built hangar on the former No. 44 Squadron Vulcan dispersal. More recently, No. 51 Squadron arrived with ELINT-configured Nimrods. Visiting aircraft types are very common, and many aircraft are from overseas

WADDINGTON was the Royal Air Force's first Vulcan base, and also the home to the RAF's very last active Vulcan, seen climbing in front of the base's hangar complex.

units, making use of the North Sea air combat range, which uses Waddington as a recovery base. Viewing activity is easy thanks to an excellent public car park, and a closer look at Runway 21 can be found on foot, although standing directly under the approach path is not recommended. More distant views of the approach to Runway 03 are also

possible, although the airfield is obscured from the adjacent road. Sadly, access to the famous 'Black Buck' Vulcan XM607 is no longer possible, and even more tragic is the destruction of its supporting Victor tanker. However, the Vulcan is placed on public display during Waddington's annual two-day air show.

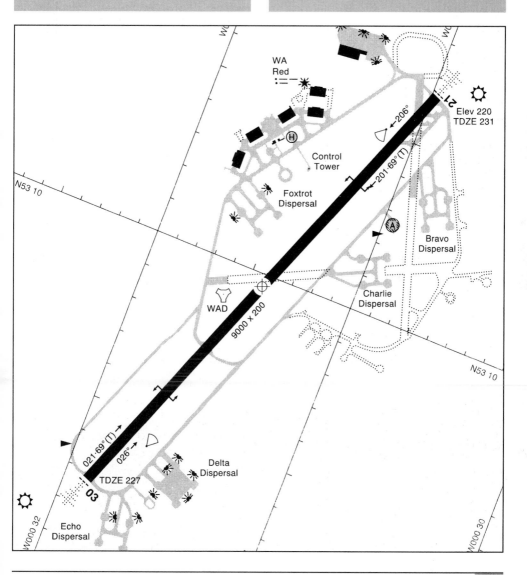

Warton

☺☺☺☺☺

Operator: Civilian
Location: N53 44.69 W002 53.03 (6nm W of Preston)
Elevation: 62ft
Tel: 01772 854150
Hours:
0800–1700 Mon–Fri

Runways:
08/26 (070T) 7,946ft
Runway 08 TODA 8,848ft, LDA 7,736ft
Runway 26 TODA 8,245ft, LDA 7,897ft
14/32 (132.66T) 4,190ft
Runway 14 TODA 4,324ft, LDA 3,671ft
Runway 32 TODA 4,386ft, LDA 3,832ft

Radio:
Approach – 124.45 336.475 130.8 311.3
Zone – 124.45 336.475 130.8 311.3
Radar – 129.725 343.7
Tower – 130.8 311.3

Notes:
Formerly the home of English Electric, Warton is famous as the manufacturing site for aircraft such as the Canberra, Lightning and (in part) the TSR2. More recently it was the British production base for the Tornado, and export versions of both the Tornado and Hawk can still be seen operating here. Of course, British Aerospace is now heavily committed to the Eurofighter Typhoon programme, and examples of this aircraft type regularly fly from Warton on test duties. Observing activity from the airfield perimeter is possible if approached on foot, but British Aerospace are naturally security sensitive, and caution is advised. Visiting aircraft are fairly rare, and normally confined to business and transport types associated with British Aerospace's activities.

WARTON is British Aerospace's main operating base for defence aircraft, and Tornadoes are regularly seen on test flights here. Eurofighter Typhoons are also increasingly common.

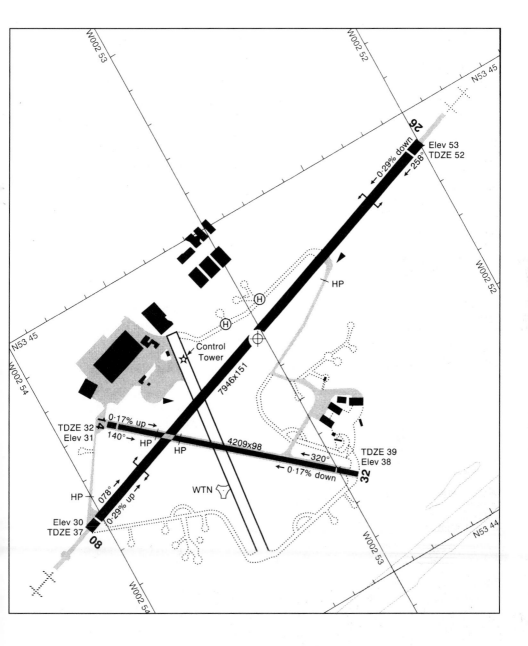

Elev 53
TDZE 52
←258°
0·29% down

HP

Control
Tower

7946x151

TDZE 32
Elev 31
0·17% up →
140° →
HP
HP
4209x98
←320°
TDZE 39
Elev 38
← 0·17% down

HP
078°
0·29% up
WTN

Elev 30
TDZE 37

Wattisham
☺

Operator: Army
Location: N52 07.64 E000 57.36 (8nm NW of Ipswich off the A1078)
Elevation: 284ft
Tel: 01449 728234
Hours:
0800–1700 Mon–Fri

Runways:
05/23 (047.88T slope 0.07% down) 7,490ft
Runway 05 TODA 7,988ft, LDA 7,493ft
Runway 23 TODA 7,968ft, LDA 7,945ft

Radio:
Approach – 291.125 125.8 123.3
Director – 283.575 123.3
Talkdown – 356.175 359.825 123.3
Tower – 358.6 122.1

Notes:
A famous Royal Air Force fighter station, Wattisham opened in 1939, initially operating Blenheim bombers, but later becoming a base for USAAF P–38 and P–51 aircraft. Post-war, the RAF operated Meteors, Hunters, Javelins and Lightnings from Wattisham, and the famous Firebirds aerobatic team was based here with red-trimmed Lightning F1s. Phantoms arrived in the 1970s and remained at Wattisham, joined by a new fleet of refurbished F-4Js, operated

WATTISHAM was for many years associated with the Phantom, but following the withdrawal of the RAF's F-4 squadrons, the RAF vacated the base and Wattisham is now an Army helicopter base.

by No. 74 Squadron The airfield was transferred to Army control in 1993 following the departure of the last Phantoms, and the only remaining Royal Air Force presence is No. 22 Squadron's B Flight, with a pair of Sea King helicopters. The extensive shelter complex remains mostly empty, and Army helicopter operations now provide the bulk of the airfield's daily movements, with fixed–wing activity fairly low. Visiting types are few, and although good views of the approach areas and taxiway can be found, there is little to see or photograph. The sensitive nature of Army operations would suggest that viewing and/or photography may be discouraged in any case.

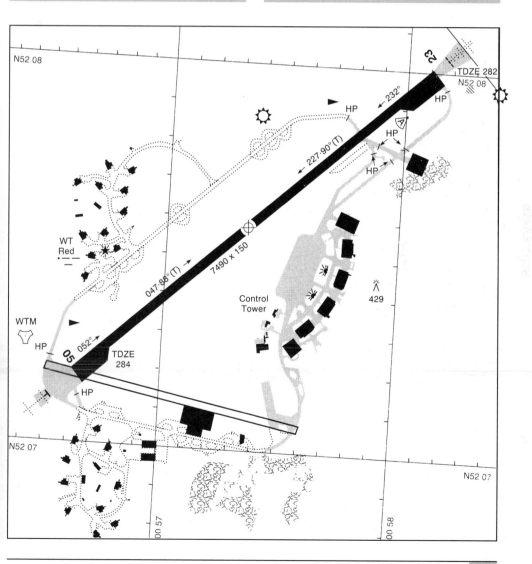

West Freugh

☺

Operator: Ministry of Defence
Location: N54 51.07 W004 56.87 (6nm
SE of Stranraer)
Elevation: 57ft
Tel: 01776 888791
Hours:
0845–1200, 1300–1615 Mon–Thu,
0845–1200, 1300–1545 Fri

Runways:
06/24 (055T slope 0.36% down) 6,040ft
Runway 06 TODA 6,075ft, LDA 6,040ft
Runway 24 TODA 6,122ft, LDA 6,040ft
12/30 (290.1T slope 0.16% down) 2,858ft
Runway 12 TODA 2,995ft, LDA 2,858ft
Runway 30 TODA 2,995ft, LDA 2,858ft

Radio:
Approach – 260.025 130.05
Radar – 260.025 130.05
Talkdown – 259.0 130.725
Tower – 337.925 122.55

Notes:
One of only a few remaining airfields owned and operated by the Ministry of Defence's Procurement Executive, West Freugh remains active as a base for aircraft engaged on test duties in the adjacent Luce Bay weapons range. For many years the airfield hosted a pair of Buccaneers and a pair of Dakotas (one of which continues to fly with the Battle of Britain Memorial Flight), but at present there are no resident aircraft, and the airfield is only used as and when required by the MoD. Consequently, there is little activity and virtually no movements other than those associated with the weapons range. Observation is possible but discouraged, in view of the sensitive nature of the MoD's operations at the airfield. In view of the very expensive nature of the Defence Research Agency's test programmes, there must be some doubt as to whether West Freugh's operations will continue for much longer, or whether the airfield might be offered to civilian operators, in much the same way that Farnborough has recently been developed.

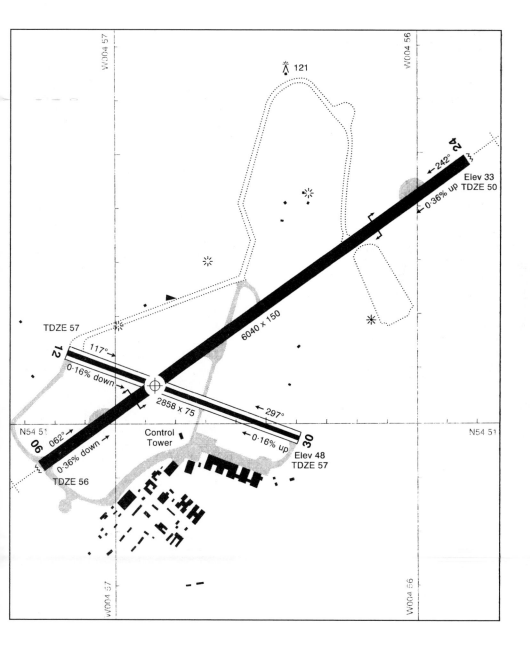

121

242°

Elev 33
TDZE 50

0·36% up

TDZE 57

6040 x 150

117°

12

0·16% down

2858 x 75

297°

N54 51

062°

06

0·36% down

0·16% up

30

Control
Tower

Elev 48
TDZE 57

TDZE 56

N54 51

W004 57

W004 56

W004 57

W004 56

Wittering
☺☺☺☺☺☺

Operator: Royal Air Force
Location: N52 36.75 W000 28.60 (2nm S of Stamford on the A1)
Elevation: 273ft
Tel: 01780 783838
Hours:
(winter) 0800–1700 Mon–Fri
(summer) 0700–1630 Mon–Fri

Runways:
08/26 (073.2T slope 0.32% down) 9,050ft
Runway 08 TODA 9,181ft, LDA 8,930ft
Runway 26 TODA 9,191ft, LDA 9,050ft

Radio:
Approach – 388.525 130.2 362.3
Departures – 376.575 344.0
Talkdown – 396.85 337.95 123.3
Tower – 357.15 118.15 257.8
Ground – 311.95

Notes:
A combination of two airfield sites, dating from World War One, Royal Air Force Wittering opened in 1924 as the home of the Central Flying School. Hurricanes, Spitfires and Havocs were based here during World War Two and post-war the airfield was developed into a huge V-bomber base, operating Valiants and eventually Victors, equipped with Blue Steel missiles. When the Victor bombers were withdrawn, Wittering became the home of the RAF's first Harriers, and the base's association with the type has continued ever since (Hunters also being based here during the 1970s). Currently, the base is home to Nos. 20(R) Squadron (the Harrier Operational Conversion Unit) and No.1 Squadron, operating the Harrier GR5 and the twin-seat Harrier T10. During 1999 No. 1 Squadron will move to nearby Cottesmore, leaving the Harrier OCU at Wittering as part of a new 'twin-base' concept. It is likely that the new Joint Force 2000 Harrier unit will be based at Wittering, however, and may well see the Fleet Air Arm's Harrier move here from Yeovilton. Observation of Wittering's activities is very difficult, with no easy road access. The A1 crosses the approach to Runway 26 but parking (and walking) is naturally very difficult. Most of the airfield is obscured from this vantage point too, and it is hoped that the base will eventually provide some sort of public viewing facility. Harrier operations keep the base busy and night operations do take place, but thanks to the Harrier's night vision capability, the airfield lights may well remain switched off! Visitors are few, although overshoots by other RAF types are fairly common.

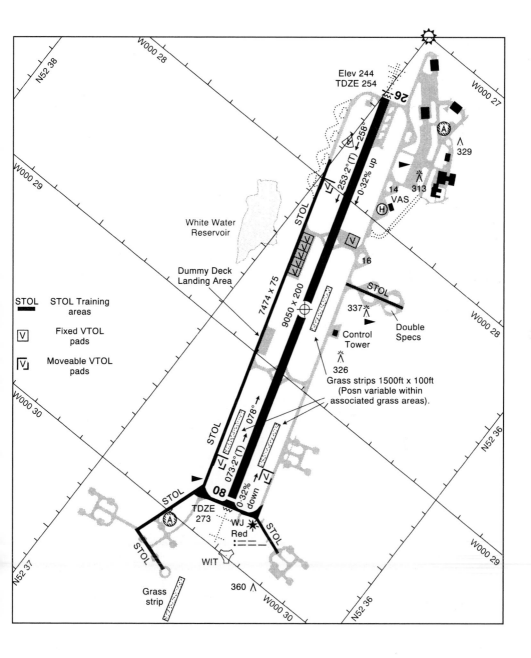

Elev 244
TDZE 254

White Water
Reservoir

Dummy Deck
Landing Area

STOL   STOL Training
      areas

V   Fixed VTOL
      pads

V⌋   Moveable VTOL
      pads

329

313
14
VAS

16

Control
Tower

337

326

Double
Specs

Grass strips 1500ft x 100ft
(Posn variable within
associated grass areas).

7474 x 75

9050 x 200

253·2°(T) → 258°
0·32% up

078° →
073·2°(T)

0·32%
down

08

TDZE
273

WJ
Red

WIT

360

STOL

Grass
strip

Woodford
☺☺

Operator: Civilian
Location: N53 20.28 W002 08.93 (3nm NE of Wilmslow)
Elevation: 298ft
Tel: 0161 439 5050
Hours:
0800–2000 Mon–Sun

Runways:
07/25 (066.6T) 7,520ft
Runway 07 TODA 7,602ft, LDA 6,762ft
Runway 25 TODA 7,766ft, LDA 6,795ft

Radio:
Approach – 269.125 130.75 358.575
126.925
Radar – 358.575 130.05 269.125
Tower – 358.575 126.925 269.125
130.05

Notes:
Situated close to Manchester Airport, Woodford is famous as the home and manufacturing base of Avro since the World War One era. Many outstanding aircraft have been constructed and flown for the first time at Woodford, including the Anson, Manchester, Lancaster, Lincoln, Shackleton and of course the Vulcan. Victor tanker conversions were undertaken here too, and the Nimrod was developed at the site. Currently the airfield remains under the control of Avro (part of British Aerospace), and most activity is connected with the continued production of the BAe146 business jet (now the RJ85

WOODFORD viewed from the south, the huge assembly hangar and BAe office complex dominating the picture.

family). Variants of this aircraft can often be seen operating on test flights from Woodford. Other activity is fairly rare although some general aviation flying takes place at the airfield. Military visitors are now rather unusual, but the airfield regularly hosts an excellent air display, with a good selection of aircraft on show, both on the ground and in the air. Observation of more mundane day-to-day flying is possible from the airfield perimeter, although activity is fairly low.

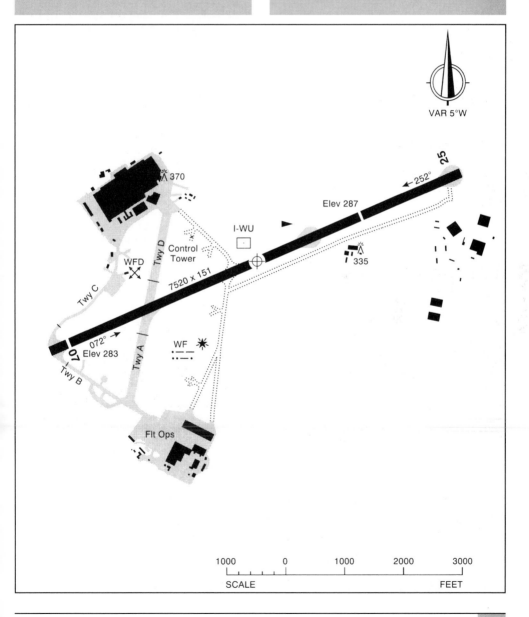

Woodvale

☺☺

Operator: Royal Air Force
Location: N53 34.89 W003 03.33 (3nm S of Southport off the A565)
Elevation: 37ft
Tel: 01704 872287
Hours:
0900–1715 Wed–Sun

Runways:

04/22 (030.37T) 5,410ft
Runway 04 TODA 6,001ft, LDA 5,394ft
Runway 22 TODA 5,899ft, LDA 5,394ft
09/27 (260.45T slope 0.25% down) 3,463ft
Runway 09 TODA 3,463ft, LDA 2,330ft
Runway 27 TODA 3,463ft, LDA 3,013ft

Radio:

Approach – 312.8 121.0
Tower – 259.95 119.75

Notes:
Opened during 1941 for Royal Air Force operations, Woodvale was home to Beaufighter, Spitfire and Mosquito squadrons engaged in the defence of Liverpool's docks and Irish Sea shipping convoys. Post-war, Woodvale's operations gradually wound down, and after a period of operations with Meteors, the station has become a base for the Liverpool University Air Squadron, together with the Manchester & Salford University Air Squadron/No.10 Air Experience Flight. Together, these units operate a fleet of around a dozen Bulldogs and share the airfield with a couple of flying clubs. Virtually all of the flying is confined to these resident units, although some light aircraft visitors can occasionally be seen, usually connected with the nearby golf course. Observation from the flying club site is easy, although activity is fairly low.

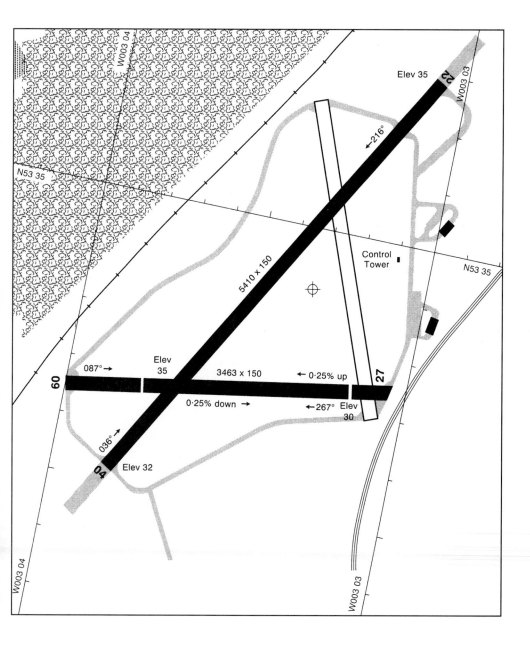

W003 04

Elev 35

W003 03

22

←216°

N53 35

5410 x 150

Control
Tower

N53 35

087° →

Elev
35

3463 x 150

← 0·25% up

27

60

0·25% down →

←267° Elev
30

036° ↑

04

Elev 32

W003 04

W003 03

Yeovilton

☺☺☺☺☺☺

Operator: Royal Navy
Location: N51 00.56 W002 38.33 (4nm N of Yeovil)
Elevation: 75ft
Tel: 01935 840551
Hours:
0830–1700 Mon–Thu, 0830–1600 Fri

Runways:
09/27 (083.01T slope 0.22% up) 7,580ft
Runway 09 TODA 7,861ft, LDA 7,580ft
Runway 27 TODA 7,608ft, LDA 7,503ft
04/22 (217T slope 0.12% down) 4,797ft
Runway 04 TODA 4,796ft, LDA 4,796ft
Runway 22 TODA 4,796ft, LDA 4,796ft

Radio:
Approach – 369.875 127.35 362.3
Radar – 369.875 127.35
Director – 338.875 362.3 123.3
Talkdown – 339.975 123.3 344.35
Tower – 372.65 122.1
Ground – 311.325

Notes:
An historic and busy Fleet Air Arm base, most Naval aircraft types have been based at Yeovilton at some stage. Currently, the base is home to the Navy's Lynx squadrons and Sea Harrier units, combined with Sea King commando operations. Consequently, the airfield is fairly active, but with much of the activity rotary-winged, there is little to see from the runway approach areas. The best vantage point is the threshold of Runway 09, which is accessible by road, but fixed-wing types are fairly few in numbers. However, the base is more active during exercises and exotic types such as A-7 Corsairs and F-8 Crusaders can be seen occasionally. The station also holds an excellent annual air show

YEOVILTON, with the Harrier 'ski jump' visible adjacent to the runway threshold.

which features extensive air and ground displays by Nato aircraft. Yeovilton is also the home of the Fleet Air Arm Museum, which contains an outstanding collection of naval aircraft dating from World War One through to the present day. Despite the museum and an excellent café and shop facility, there is no suitable public viewing area from where airfield activities can be observed easily, and the unique Harrier ski jump remains tantalisingly in the far distance.

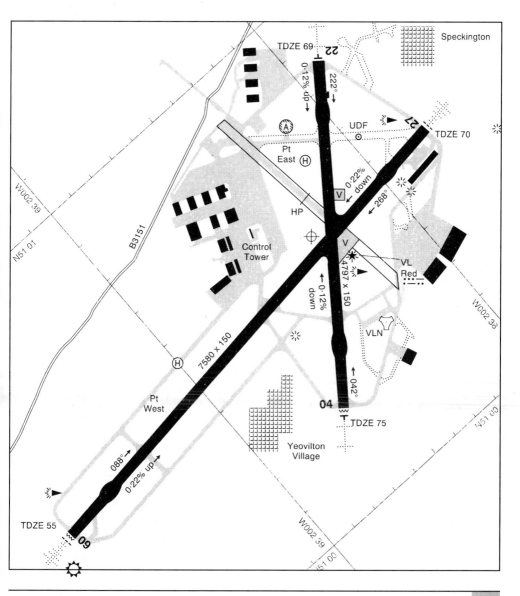

MINOR AIRFIELDS

Aberporth
☺☺

Operator: Ministry of Defence
Location: N52 06.70 W004 33.41 (4nm NE of Cardigan)
Tel: 01239 813090

Runways:
08/26 3,002ft
04/22 1,775ft (grass)

Radio:
259.0 122.15

Notes:
A small Defence Research Agency airfield, Aberporth has very few movements, mostly confined to communications aircraft associated with the nearby weapons range. The only resident unit is No. 636 Volunteer Gliding School, which is equipped with Vikings.

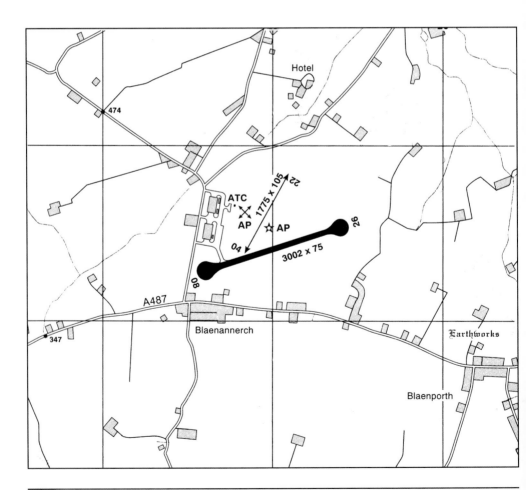

Andrewsfield
☺

Location: N51 53.70 E000 26.95 (4nm NW of Braintree)
Tel: 01371 856744

Runways:
09L/27R 2,621ft (grass)
09R/27L 2,621ft (grass)

Radio:
125.55 130.55

Notes:
A former USAAF base, Andrewsfield was a major World War Two airfield operating B-17s, Marauders and P-51 Mustangs. No. 616 Squadron also operated Meteors here. Some remnants of the wartime airfield remain, but present-day activity is confined to general aviation, on a small portion of the original airfield site.

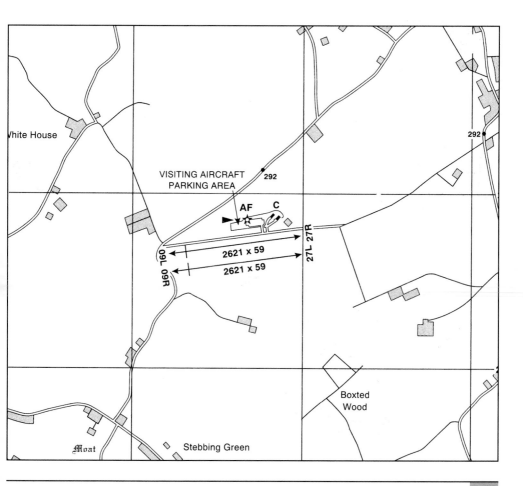

Ashcroft
☺

Location: N53 09.85 W002 32.29 (2nm SW of Winsford)
Tel: 01270 528378

Runways:
06/24 1,312ft (grass)
09/27 1,805ft (grass)
15/33 1,312ft (grass)

Radio:
122.525

Notes:
Ashcroft is a small, privately owned airfield. The three landing strips are available to visitors but the site is fairly inactive and used only as required.

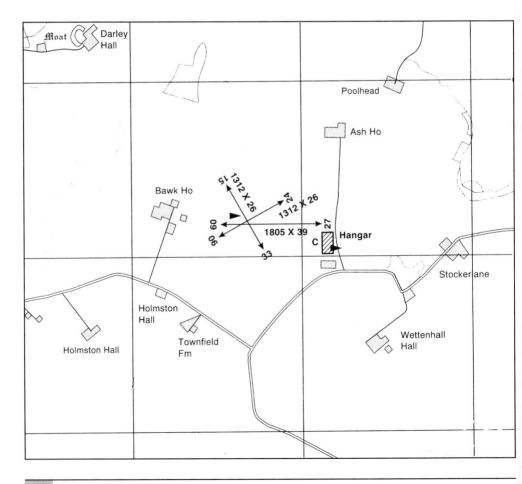

Ballykelly
☺

Location: N55 03.69 W007 00.89 (2nm W of Limavady)
Tel: 01504 763221

Runways:
02/20 6,020ft
08/26 5,500ft

Radio:
123.625

Notes:
The former site of Royal Air Force Ballykelly, the airfield is now used by the Army. Movements are few, mostly confined to helicopters. The huge airfield complex remains visible, including the active railway line which crosses what is now a disused portion of the former main runway. The old V-bomber operational readiness platform is also still present, together with the huge Shackleton hangar. Although easily visible, close scrutiny or photography of the site is not recommended.

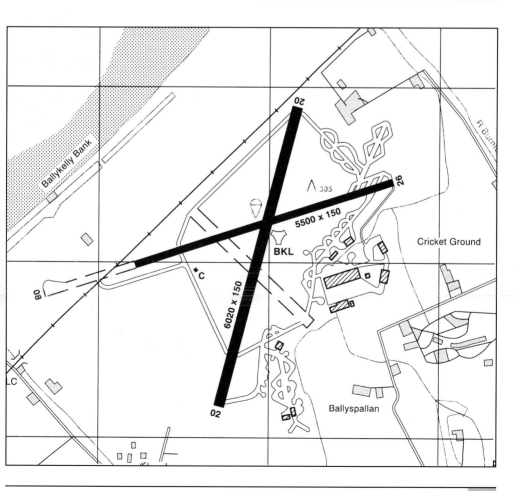

Barra

☺

Location: N57 01.62 W007 26.25 (4nm NE of Castlebay)

Tel: 01871 890212

Runways:
07/25 4,921ft (sand)
11/29 2,188ft (sand)
15/33 2,776ft (sand)

Radio:
118.075 130.65

Notes:
Uniquely built on a beach, Barra's runways are open only when the tide is out! Handling only delivery flights, a small scheduled service and a few visitors, there are, not surprisingly, few support facilities at this airfield. However, access to the whole area is simple and operating times are somewhat predictable, based on the local tides.

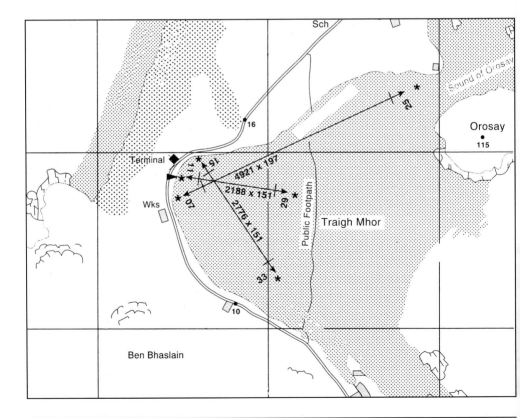

Barrow/Walney Island

☺

Location: N54 07.87 W003 15.81 (1nm NW of Barrow-in-Furness)
Tel: 01229 471147

Runways:
06/24 3,438ft
17/35 3,227ft

Radio:
123.1

Notes:
Using only part of a former wartime site where Lysanders and Ansons were once based, Barrow is operated by Vickers Shipbuilding, and the majority of the (few) aircraft movements are business aircraft connected with the company. Visitors are sometimes present but there is little activity other than gliding.

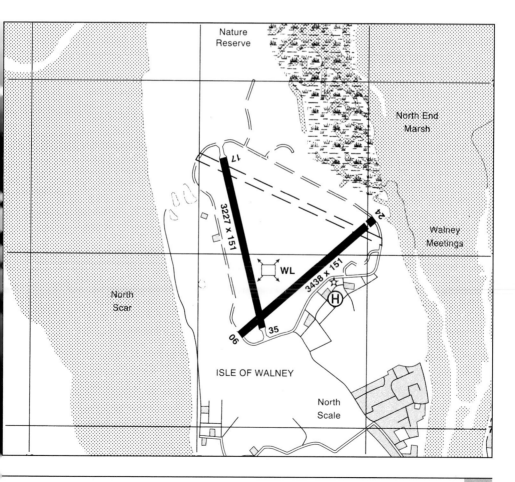

Beccles
☺

Location: N52 26.10 E001 36.97 (2nm SE of Beccles)

Tel: 01502 475124

Runway:
09/27 1,637ft

Radio:
134.6

Notes:
Beccles is a small, infrequently used air strip, with a (more active) adjacent helicopter facility. The airfield uses a small portion of a much larger World War Two aerodrome site.

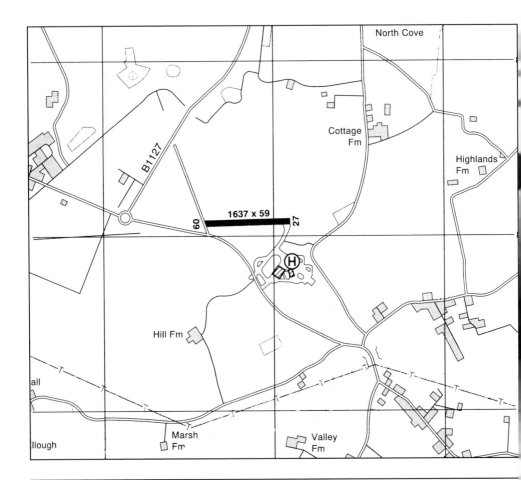

EGHJ

Bembridge
☺☺

Location: N50 40.68 W001 06.55 (2nm NE of Sandown)
Tel: 01983 873331

Runway:
12/30 2,746ft

Radio:
123.250

Notes:
Although a relatively unknown airfield, Bembridge is the home of Britten-Norman (now part of Pilatus), manufacturer of the famous Islander and Trislander. Assembly and test flying of PBN aircraft continues at this site. There are also some visiting aircraft, pleasure flights and gliding.

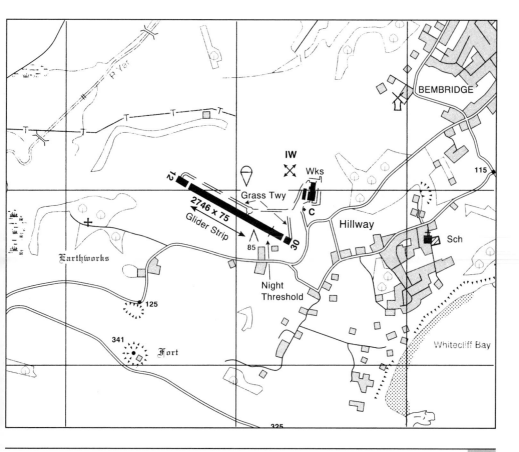

Beverley/Linley Hill
☺

Location: N53 53.92 W000 21.72 (4nm
NE of Beverley)
Tel: 01964 544994

Runway:
12/30 2,362ft (grass)

Radio:
123.05

Notes:
Beverley is a former farm strip which
has been upgraded following the relocation of the Hull Aero Club from
Brough. The resident light aircraft are
occasionally joined by a few visitors, but
activity is fairly low.

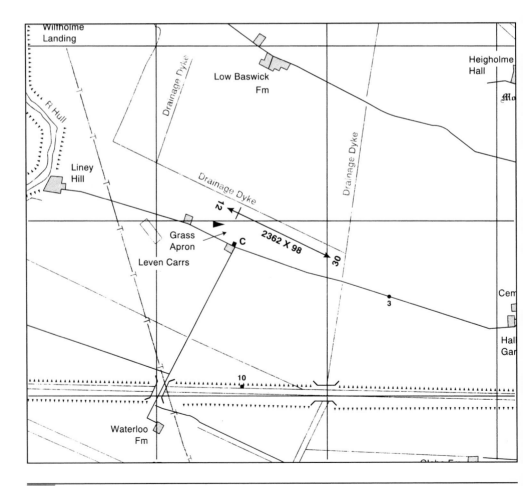

Bodmin
☺☺

Location: N50 29.98 W004 39.95 (3nm NE of Bodmin)
Tel: 01208 821419

Runways:
03/21 1,575ft (grass)
14/32 2,001ft (grass)

Radio:
122.7

Notes:
Although adjacent to the busy A30, Bodmin is a small and sleepy airfield, hosting a number of light aircraft belonging to the Cornwall Flying Club and a variety of visitors. The short, hump-backed runways are connected by an equally unusual taxiway which runs down a slope. Perched on top of the very bleak Bodmin moor, the airfield is prone to some very severe weather.

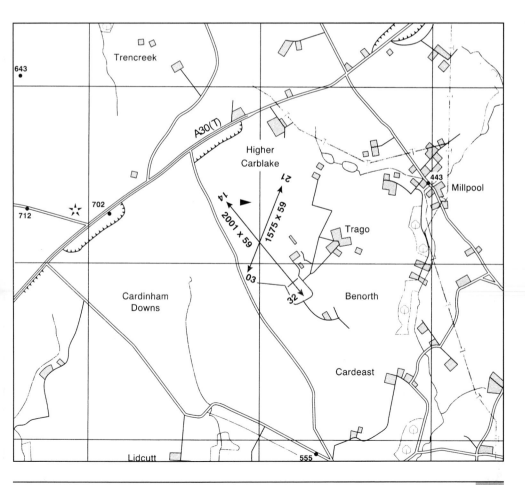

Bourn
☺

Location: N52 12.62 W000 02.57 (7nm W of Cambridge)
Tel: 01954 719602

Runway:
01/19 2,077ft

Radio:
129.8

Notes:
Nestled in the corner of a former Royal Air Force bomber airfield where Stirlings, Wellingtons, Mosquitoes and Lancasters were once based, Bourn is now the home of the Rural Flying Corps, a small private flying group with a variety of light aircraft. Visiting types are also welcome and many remnants of the former RAF base are still visible.

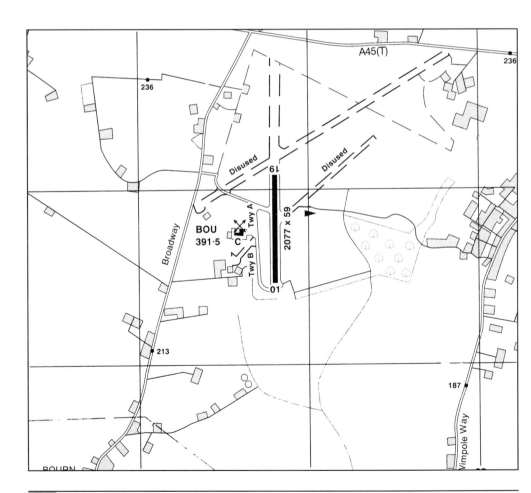

Brough
☺

Location: N53 43.25 W000 33.83 (8nm W of Hull)
Tel: 01482 667121

Runways:
06/24 2,070ft (grass)
12/30 3,458ft

Radio:
130.550

Notes:
Part of the British Aerospace factory site, Brough is rarely used, other than for company aircraft, and a few light aircraft operated by the Blackburn Flying Club and the Humberside Police Flying Club. Huge Beverley transports once made test flights from the field, but present-day activity is virtually nil. The adjacent factory is the former Blackburn works, and remnants of the slipway from where many famous seaplanes were flown can still be seen.

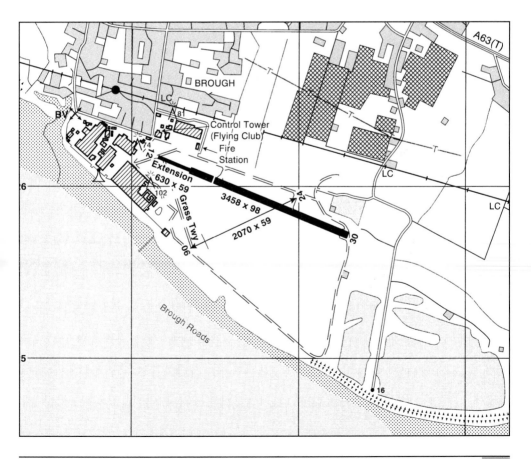

Bruntingthorpe

☺☺☺☺☺

Location: N52 29.22 W001 07.84 (6nm S of Leicester)

Tel: 0116 247 8030

Runway:
06/24 9,847ft

Radio:
122.825

Notes:
The site of a former USAF bomber base, Bruntingthorpe's huge runway remains intact. Although the airfield is now primarily used for motor industry storage and proving work, some aviation activity remains, thanks to the presence of a growing number of privately owned airworthy jet warbirds, including Vampires, Canberras, and the Royal Air Force's last flying Vulcan, at present confined to ground running. On certain days each year the Vulcan (as well as the resident Victor, Buccaneer, Lightnings and others) make fast taxi 'take-off' runs down the runway, much to the delight of nostalgia-filled onlookers.

BRUNTINGTHORPE is home to a variety of preserved aircraft: some in non-flying status, others airworthy and some (such as this Comet) potentially flyable if CAA approval can be obtained.

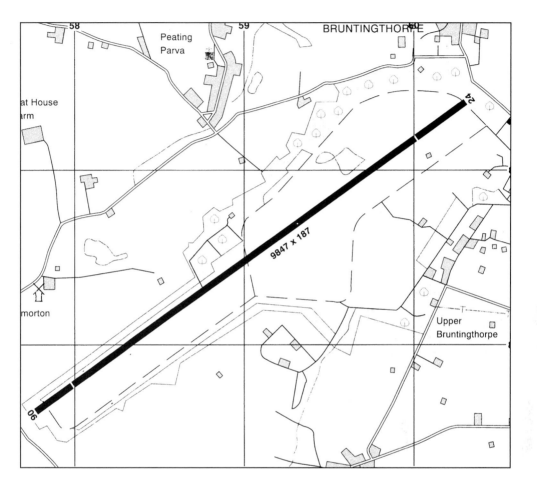

Caernarfon
☺

Location: N53 06.11 W004 20.23 (3nm SW of Caernarfon)
Tel: 01286 830800

Runway:
08/26 3,018ft

Radio:
122.25

Notes:
Using part of the former Royal Air Force Llandwrog airfield, this small air strip is now home to a flying school and an air taxi company. Visiting light aircraft are welcome and pleasure flights are operated from the airfield, usually in a vintage Rapide aircraft.

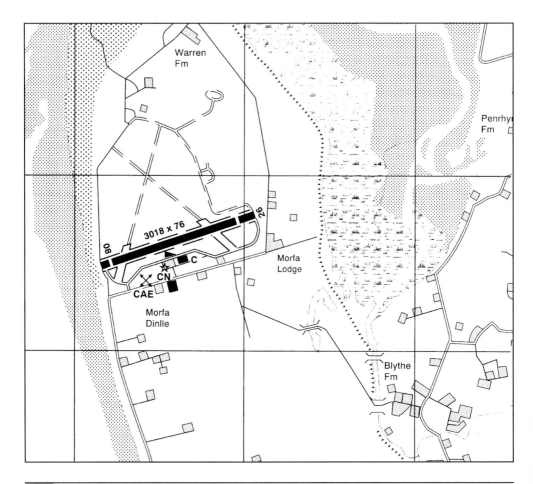

Campbeltown

☺☺

Location: N55 26.17 W005 40,79 (3nm
W of Campbeltown)
Tel: 01586 553797

Runway:
11/29 10,003ft

Radio:
125.9

Notes:
Using facilities of the former Royal Air
Force Machrihanish airfield, there can
be few regional airports which can
boast a 10,000-foot runway! Once used
by visiting Nato aircraft, particularly
maritime types such as the P-3 Orion,
Machrihanish has now been abandoned
as a Nato operating base. The massive
airfield is now largely disused, leaving
behind only rumours of strange and
exotic aircraft which (supposedly) made
secret night flights from the base. Other
than a few light aircraft, the airfield is
used very little, and whether there will
be a more productive future for such a
large site remains to be seen.

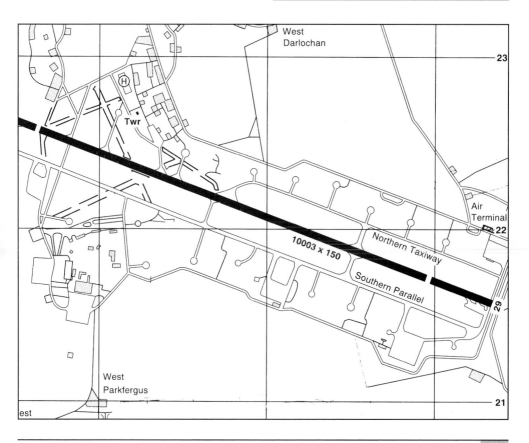

Chatteris
☺

Location: N52 29.24 E000 05.25 (2nm S of March)
Tel: 01354 740810

Runways:
03/21 1,722ft (grass)
06/24 1,575ft (grass)
11/29 1,394ft (grass)
16/34 1,575ft (grass)

Radio:
129.90

Notes:
A small airfield comprising no fewer than four air strips, Chatteris is used mainly for parachute drops and microlight flying, although some light aircraft do visit the site. Situated in a very busy low flying area, movements are consequently few.

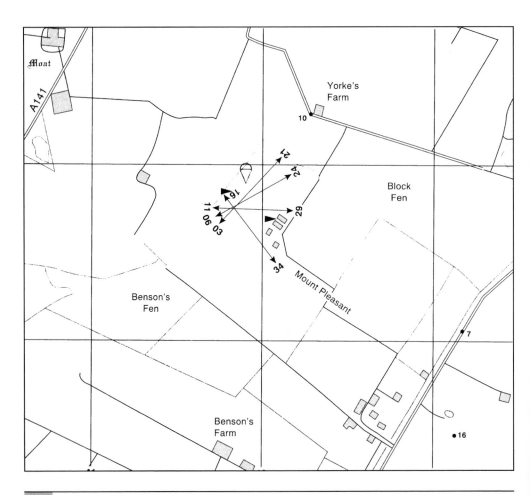

Chichester/Goodwood
☺

Location: N50 51.55 W000 45.55 (1nm NE of Chichester)

Tel: 01243 774261

Runways:
06/24 2,779fƀt (grass)
10/28 2,011ft (grass)
14R/32L 4,222ft (grass)

Radio:
122.45

Notes:
Once the home of Spitfires and Typhoons during World War Two, Goodwood still houses a number of historic aircraft types ranging from Tiger Moths and Harvards to a Spitfire. However, most of the resident aircraft and visitors are more traditional light types. With a resident flying school and also offering pleasure flights, Chichester is a relatively active general aviation site.

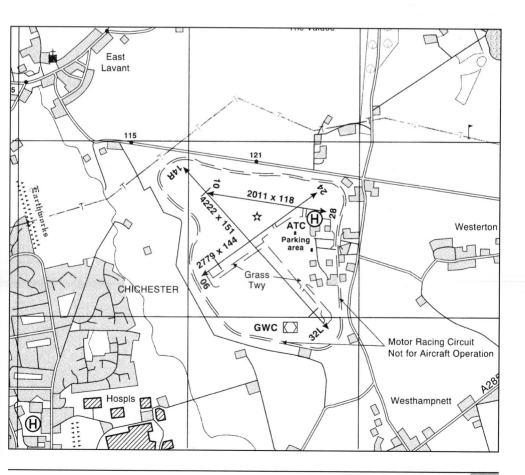

Clacton

☺

Location: N51 47.10 E001 07.73 (1nm W of Clacton)

Tel: 01255 424671

Runway:
18/36 2,001ft (grass)

Radio:
135.40

Notes:
Home of the Clacton Aero Club, this small airfield is devoted to light aircraft operations, enlivened by the occasional historic aircraft such as a Tiger Moth or DH Dragon Rapide. Visitors are welcome and spectators are particularly well catered for, with a footpath running across the runway. (Pedestrians are advised to give way to aircraft!)

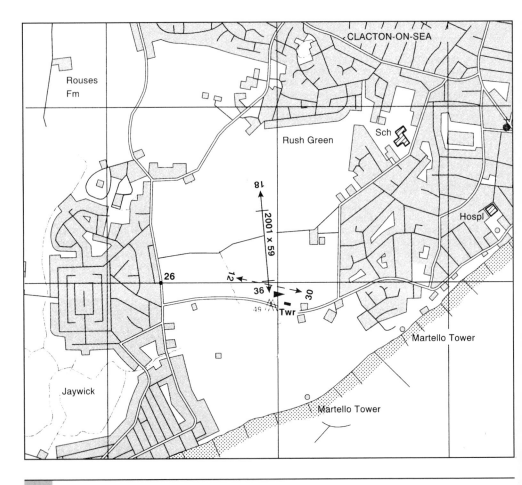

Compton Abbas

☺

Location: N50 58.03 W002 09.22
Tel: 01747 811767

Runway:
08/26 2,635ft (grass)

Radio:
122.7

Notes:
One of the most picturesque airfields in Britain, Compton Abbas is a small site which caters for general aviation, with just a small number of resident aircraft. Visiting aircraft are welcome and a varied selection can usually be seen. Spectators are also well catered for at this airfield.

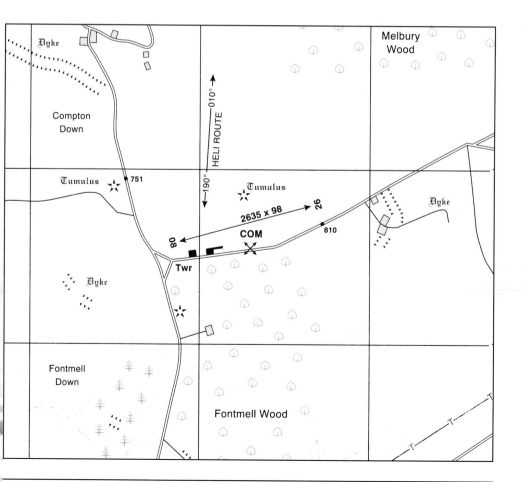

Crowfield

☺

Location: N52 10.27 E001 06.66 (4nm SE of Stowmarket)

Tel: 01449 711017

Runway:
13/31 2,520ft (grass)

Radio:
122.775

Notes:
Developed from a small farm strip, despite strong local opposition, this relatively new aerodrome welcomes visitors, and currently provides a home for the Crowfield Flying School. Few facilities are available and activity is fairly low, but the site is now established for general aviation.

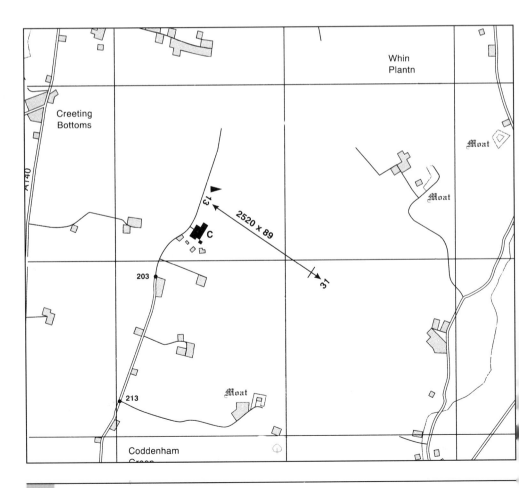

Cumbernauld

☺

Location: N55 58.50 W003 58.47 (16nm NE of Glasgow)
Tel: 01236 722100

Runway:
08/26 2,690ft

Radio:
120.6

Notes:
A fairly recent development, Cumbernauld is situated in an industrial area. It is currently the home of the West of Scotland Flying Club and Dollar Helicopters. Caledonian Seaplanes owns the airfield and operates aircraft from a nearby loch, so float-equipped aircraft are sometimes seen at the airfield. Although not very busy, activity can be observed from the airport restaurant in comfort.

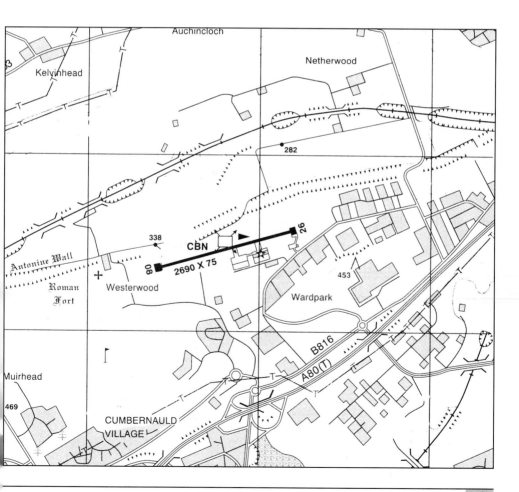

Defford/Croft Farm
☺

Location   N52 05.13 W002 08.15 (3nm W of Pershore)
Tel: 01386 750400

Runway:
10/28 1,870ft (grass)

Radio:
119.10

Notes:
Although the airfield name may seem familiar, this unlicensed air strip should not be confused with the former Ministry of Defence airfield which is now a satcom base, and unsuitable for flying. Available to visiting light aircraft, Defford is a relatively quiet strip situated between the historic former Royal Signals & Radar Establishment airfields at Defford and Pershore, both of which are now disused.

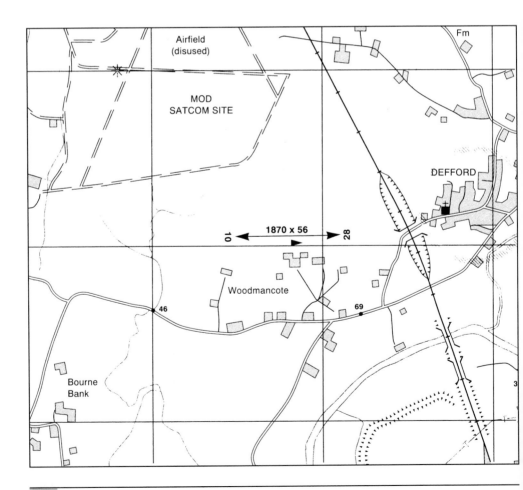

Denham

☺☺☺

Location: N51 35.30 W000 30.78 (1nm E of Gerrards Cross)

Tel: 01895 832161

Runways:
06/24 2,556ft
12/30 1,850ft (grass)

Radio:
130.725

Notes:
Although only small, Denham has an interesting history, as it was used as a pre-flying training ground school in World War One and as a base for Martin-Baker in the 1920s. During World War Two the site was a Relief Landing Ground for Booker. Now the home of a couple of flying schools and numerous privately-owned aircraft, Denham is a fairly active airfield open to general aviation visitors.

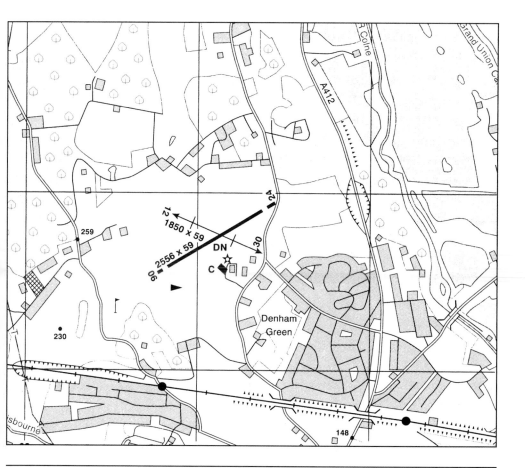

Derby

☺

Location: N52 51.58 W001 37.05 (6nm SW of Derby)
Tel: 01283 733803

Runways:
05/23 1,732ft (grass)
10/28 1,496ft (grass)
17/35 1,975ft (grass)

Radio:
118.35

Notes:
This new site was first opened in 1993 after the closure of nearby Burnaston. A huge car factory development forced the closure of the latter airfield, leaving the Derby Aero Club without a home. Following some vigorous campaigning a new airfield site was located, enabling the Club to relocate. The new airfield is certainly small, but it is perhaps a miracle that it exists at all, in the face of opposition from a giant car manufacturer. Visitors at Derby are welcome and the site is gradually becoming busier.

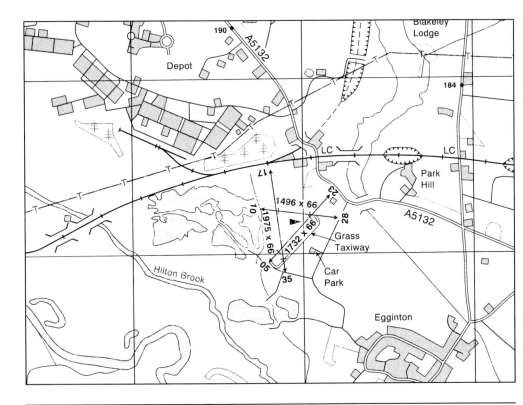

Derry/Eglinton
☺

Location: N55 02.57 W007 09.67 (7nm NE of Londonderry)
Tel: 01504 810784

Runways:
03/21 4,068ft
08/26 5,486ft

Radio:
134.15 123.625

Notes:
Opened in 1941 as a base for Hurricanes and Hudsons, USAAF squadrons arrived later in the war, and military flying continued at the airfield until 1966, when the base was transferred to civilian control. With a few scheduled services and a flying club based on the site, Londonderry Airport is slowly developing into a more ambitious facility. General aviation flying is encouraged and visitors are quite common.

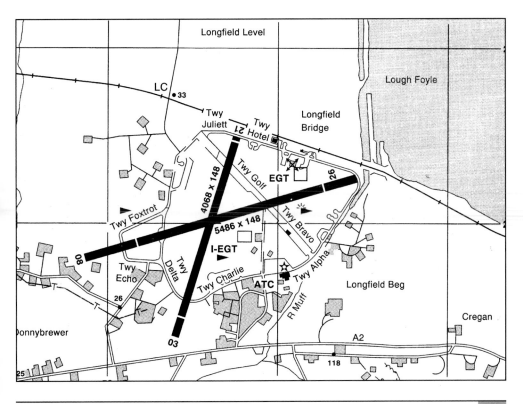

Dornoch
☺

Location: N57 52.14 W004 01.32 (1nm S of Dornoch)

Runway:
10/28 2,543ft (grass)

Radio:
—

Notes:
A very small, unlicensed aerodrome, Dornoch is available only to light aircraft. The grass strip is positioned neatly on a small headland between Dornoch Sands and Gizzen Briggs, providing a very suitable and un-cluttered area. However, flying can be complicated by the proximity of the Tain Weapons range, where RAF and Nato ground attack aircraft regularly plant practice bombs.

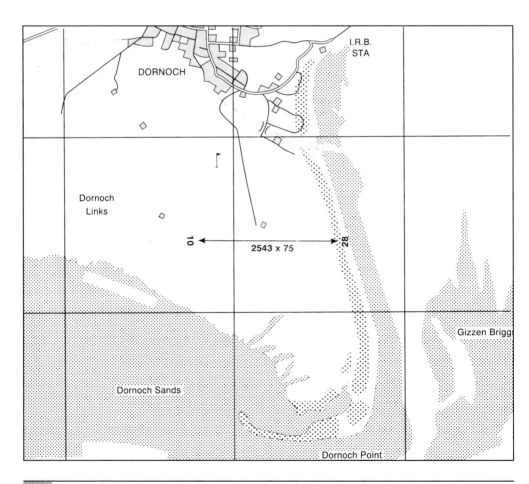

Duxford

☺☺☺☺☺☺☺☺

Location: N52 05.45 E000 07.92 (8nm S of Cambridge)
Tel: 01223 833376

Runways:
06/24 4,931ft
06/24 2,920ft (grass)

Radio:
122.075

Notes:
A famous former Royal Air Force station, Duxford is well remembered for its association with the Spitfire, the Battle of Britain, Sir Douglas Bader and the motion picture *The Battle of Britain*, much of which was filmed at Duxford. Post-war, the station hosted Hunters and Javelins, but after the RAF vacated the site, Duxford was disused for many years until the Imperial War Museum arrived, creating the beginnings of the large and hugely popular museum now based at the site. The adjacent M11 required a section of runway to be removed (without any compensation at the other end), but flying from Duxford has continued regardless, and even a B-52 safely landed here. Numerous warbirds (including jets) are based here and regularly fly during summer months.

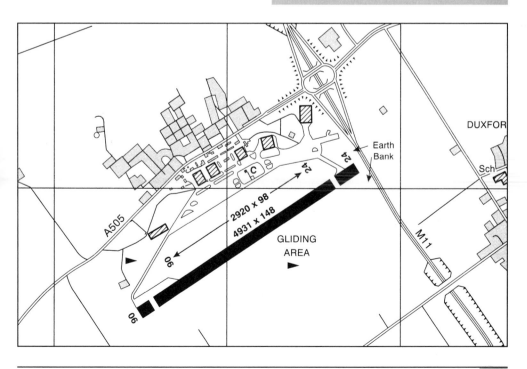

Eaglescott
☺

Location: N50 55.70 W003 59.37 (6nm SE of Torrington)
Tel: 01769 520404

Runway:
08/26 1,969ft (grass)

Radio:
123.0

Notes:
Although small and fairly quiet, Eaglescott handles a variety of light aircraft in addition to numerous microlights and gliders. Visitors are welcome and its rural setting provides an interesting location for spotters. Parachuting also takes place north of the runway.

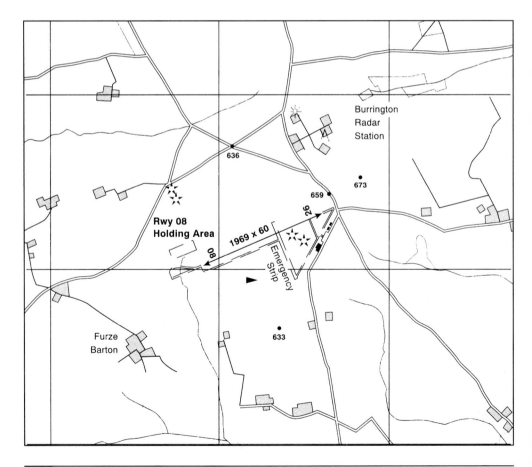

Earls Colne

☺☺

Location: N51 54.83 E000 40.97 (3nm SE of Halstead

Tel: 01787 223943

Runways:
06/24 3,080ft (grass)

Notes:
Once used by the USAAF for B-17 and B-26 operations, Earls Colne was subsequently transferred to Royal Air Force Bomber Command, and Halifaxes were based here prior to the station's closure in 1946. After a period of disuse, parts of the airfield have now been redeveloped and a grass strip is available to handle light aircraft. In addition to the resident Essex Flying School, a variety of warbirds are reconstructed and maintained at the airfield, making for a very interesting range of aircraft. Visiting types are also welcome.

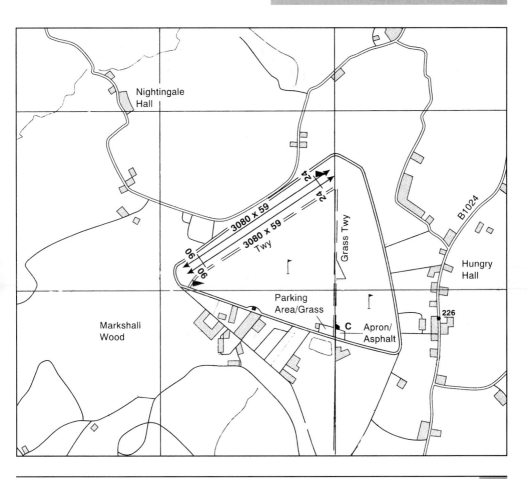

Elmsett
☺

Location: N52 04.52 E000 58.68 (3nm S
of Wattisham airfield)
Tel: 01473 824116

Runway:
05/23 2,789ft (grass)

Radio:
125.80 130.425

Notes:
A small, light aircraft strip, Elmsett
handles only a small number of general
aviation types. Flying is often dependent upon the operational status of
nearby Wattisham airfield, as even
without the presence of the Royal Air
Force's Phantom squadrons, the Army
Air Corps keeps the local airspace very
busy.

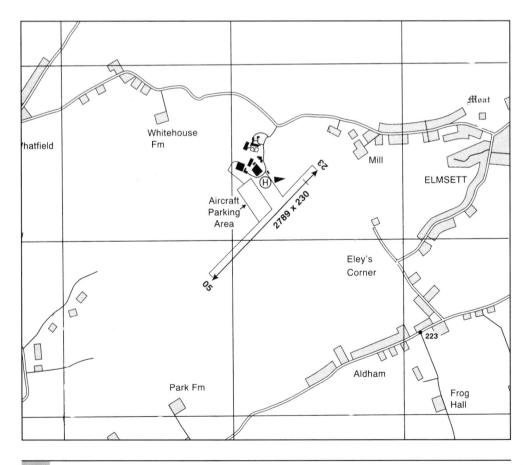

Elstree

☺☺☺

Location: N51 39.35 W000 19.55 (2nm E of Watford)
Tel: 020 8953 7480

Runway:
08/26 2,152ft

Radio:
122.4

Notes:
Despite its relatively small size, Elstree has been in business for a long time, and even Halifax freighters operated from the strip back in 1946. Today the airfield is home to various flying clubs and a number of privately owned aircraft, with a variety of visiting types positioned on either side of the runway. With the loss of nearby Leavesden, Elstree's importance to the local area has grown considerably.

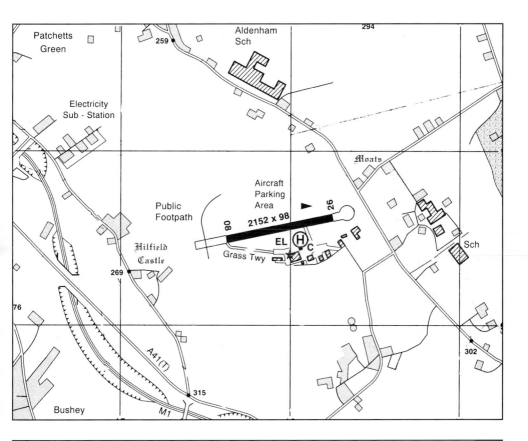

Enniskillen/St Angelo
☺

Location: N54 23.93 W007 39.12 (4nm N
of Enniskillen)
Tel: 01365 328282

Runway:
15/33 4,350ft

Radio:
123.2

Notes:
Situated in an area of beautiful countryside, this former wartime airfield is now
largely disused, with only one of the two
runways now available for aircraft. No
flying units are resident on the site but
visiting general aviation and business
aircraft are welcome. A public road
intersects the airfield and the eastern
portion of the airfield is now used by
Army helicopters.

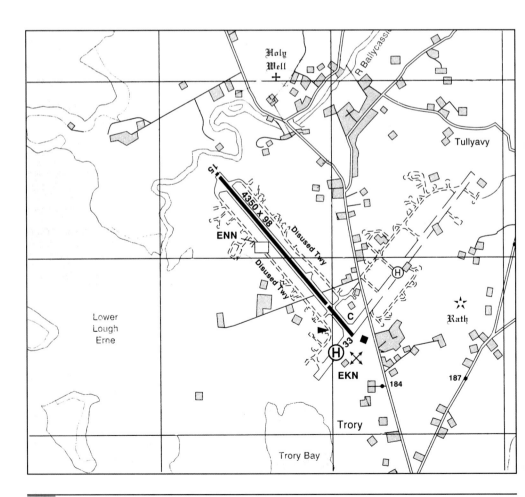

Fair Isle
☺

Location: N59 32.15 W001 37.68 (24nm SW of Sumburgh Head)
Tel: 01595 760224

Runway:
06/24 1,594ft (gravel)

Notes:
Perched on a bleak hill, this small strip is available to light aircraft. The runway surface is somewhat unusual in that it is gravel rather than grass. Prone to moss growth, landings can sometimes be tricky on the runway!

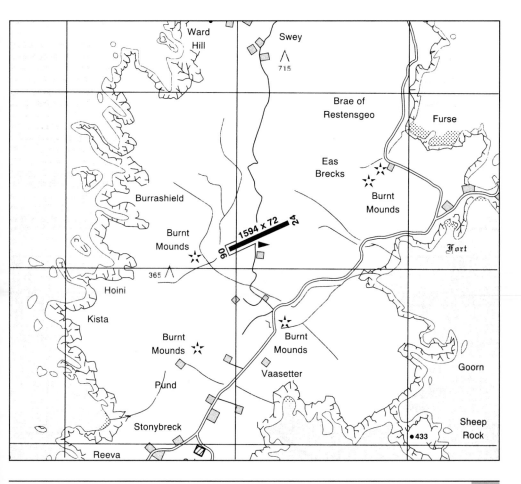

Fairoaks

☺☺☺

Location: N51 20.88 W000 33.53 (2nm N of Woking)
Tel: 01276 857700

Runway:
06/24 2,667ft

Radio:
123.425

Notes:
Opened in 1931 as a private aerodrome, Fairoaks was developed by the RAF and became a training base with Tiger Moths during World War Two. Long since vacated by the Royal Air Force, the airfield is now the home of flying clubs and a number of privately owned aircraft. Owned by Alan Mann Helicopters, rotary-wing activity is consequently fairly high. The airfield also sees a varied selection of light aircraft visitors.

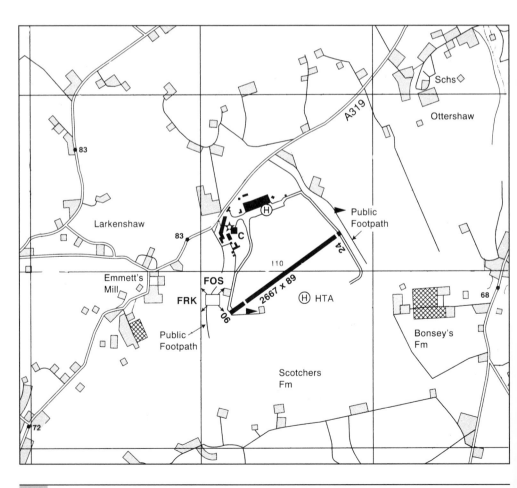

Fenland

☺☺

Location: N52 44.35 W000 01.78 (6nm SE of Spalding)
Tel: 01945 582891

Runways:
08/26 1,093ft (grass)
18/36 2,047ft (grass)

Radio:
122.925

Notes:
A small and relatively quiet airfield, Fenland attracts a variety of sports and home-built aircraft. A flying school and helicopter centre are also based here. Visitors are very welcome and the airfield can be quite active at weekends.

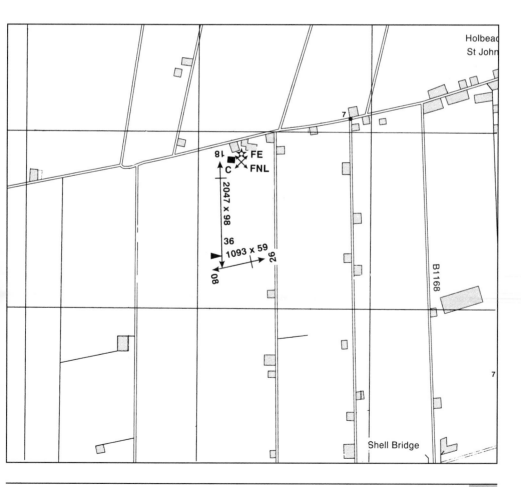

Fife
☺

Location: N56 11.00 W003 13.22 (2nm W of Glenrothes)
Tel: 01592 753792

Runway:
07/25 2,296ft

Radio:
130.45

Notes:
A relatively new airfield, little development at the site has taken place so far, although a flying club is now resident at the site. Fife handles most light aircraft types, from both the general aviation and the business community. Visitors are very welcome and the airport is likely to become somewhat busier in the future.

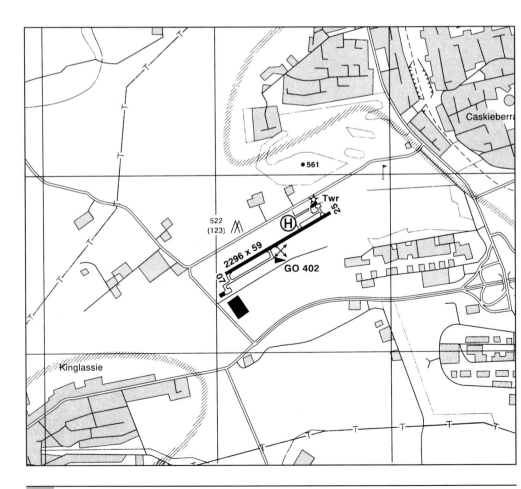

Finmere

☺☺

Location: N51 59.126 W001 03.362
(2nm SW of Buckingham)
Tel: 01280 860207

Runway:
10/28 2,300ft

Radio:
—

Notes:
Using just a fraction of a fairly extensive disused wartime airfield, Finmere is a relatively quiet general aviation site, open to light aircraft visitors. Positioned in an active military low flying area, operations can sometimes be difficult. However, the airfield is used by the Vintage Aircraft Club at specific times each year.

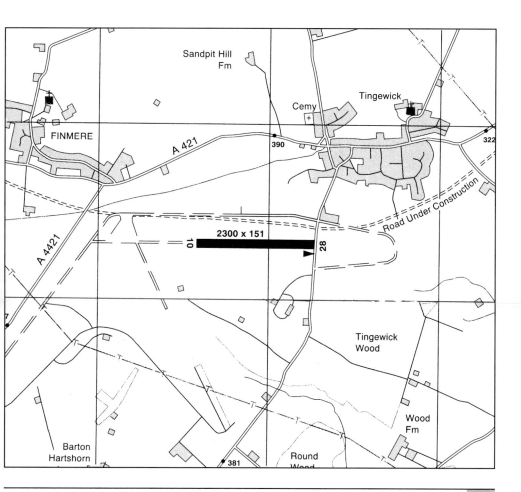

Flotta

☺

Location: N58 49.58 W003 08.53 (9nm SE of Stromness)

Tel: 01856 884000

Runway:
16/34 2,490ft

Radio:
122.15

Notes:
Another modern business airport, Flotta is relatively quiet but available to general aviation visitors. The site is positioned in open land close to Weddel Sound and has few facilities.

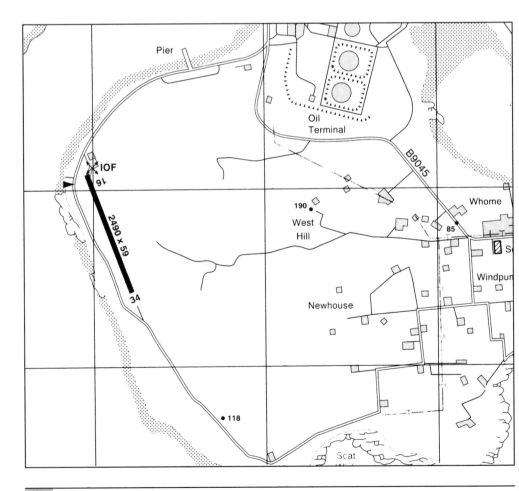

Fowlmere

☺

Location: N52 04.65 E000 03.70 (7nm SW of Cambridge)
Tel: 01763 208281

Runway:
07/25 2,310ft (grass)

Radio:
120.925 122.075

Notes:
Built on the second of two airfield sites (the first opened in 1918), Fowlmere was developed in 1940 as a base for Spitfire and Hurricane fighters, and USAAF Mustangs. Sadly, most of the wartime airfield has long since disappeared and only a single grass strip remains, together with a handful of resident light aircraft. Visitors can be seen but activity is fairly low, possibly due to the proximity of the much larger airfield at Duxford.

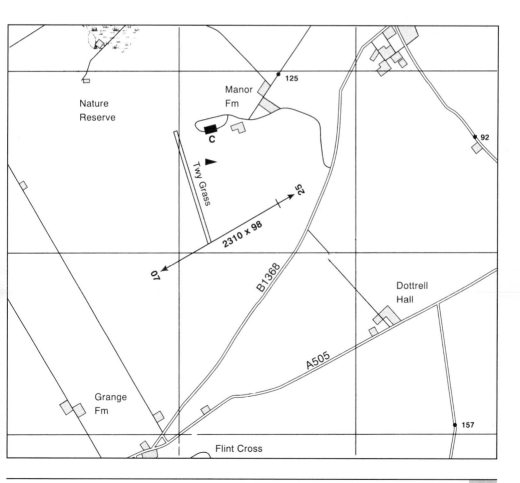

Full Sutton
☺

Location: N53 58.83 W000 51.85 (7nm E of York)
Tel: 01759 372717

Runways:
04/22 2,533ft (grass)
16/34 2,297ft

Radio:
132.325

Notes:
A former World War Two Royal Air Force base operating Halifaxes, Dakotas and Lancasters, Full Sutton was vacated in 1963 and eventually developed as a prison. However, part of the former airfield reopened in 1995 and a flying club is now resident. Visiting aircraft are appearing in steadily increasing numbers and the airfield looks set to enjoy a successful future. Perhaps the only unusual aspect of the airfield is the fact that Runway 34 (paved) can't be used, thanks to the proximity of the prison, which cannot be overflown.

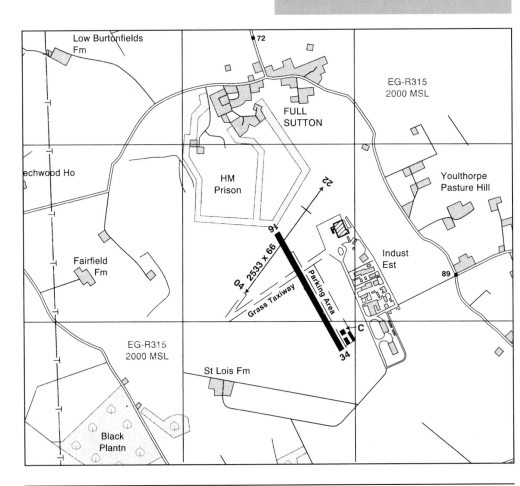

Glenforsa
☺

Location: N56 31.04 W005 54.85 (1nm E of Salen)

Tel: 01680 300402

Runway:
17/25 2,598ft (grass)

Radio:
—

Notes:
Located in an area of beautiful scenery, Glenforsa is a relatively unused site, open to light aircraft of all types. Planned arrivals are normally booked in advance so that grazing sheep can be cleared off the runway! Some ground services are available, but in view of the airfield's location, Glenforsa is never likely to be very busy.

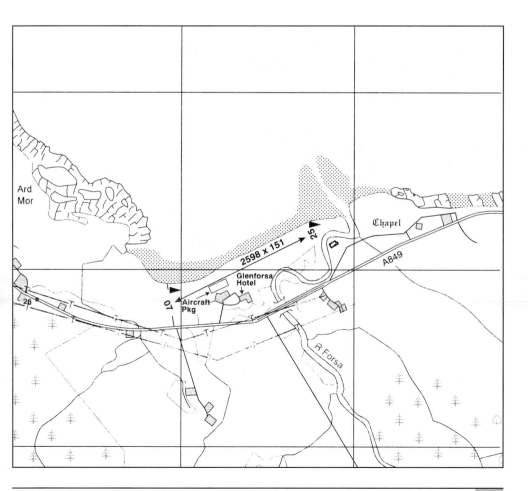

Halfpenny Green

☺☺☺

Location: N52 31.05 W002 15.58 (5nm SE of Bridgnorth)
Tel: 01384 221350

Runways:
04/22 2,100ft
10/28 2,543ft
16/34 3,921ft

Radio:
123.0

Notes:
Formerly known as Royal Air Force Bobbington (a World War Two training airfield) Halfpenny Green is now home to a number of flying schools and a police helicopter unit, but retains much of its former RAF construction and 'feel'. Visiting light aircraft are common and an airship is also resident at certain times. Spectators are welcome at this fairly busy airfield.

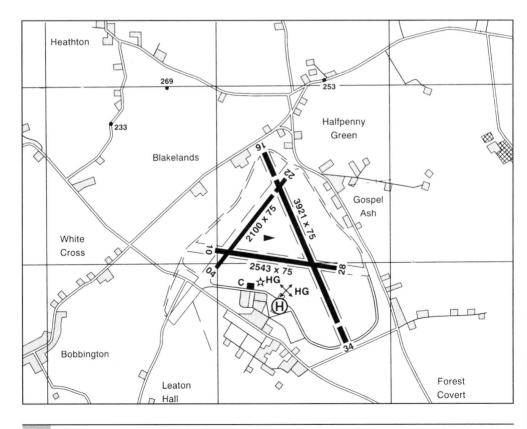

Halton

☺

Location: N51 47.55 W000 44.27 (3nm SE of Aylesbury)
Tel: 01296 623535

Runways:
02/20 3,707ft (grass)
08/26 2,710ft (grass)

Radio:
130.425

Notes:
Although an active Royal Air Force station, most of the activity at Halton is concerned with ground training. The airfield is therefore relatively quiet, except at weekends. No. 613 Volunteer Gliding School is based here with Vigilants, and other light aircraft and gliders also use the site, including RAF Halton's flying club. A variety of RAF aircraft have made delivery flights to the airfield before ending their days in the ground school, and even larger types such as a Vulcan have safely landed here. However, such flights have been much less common in recent years.

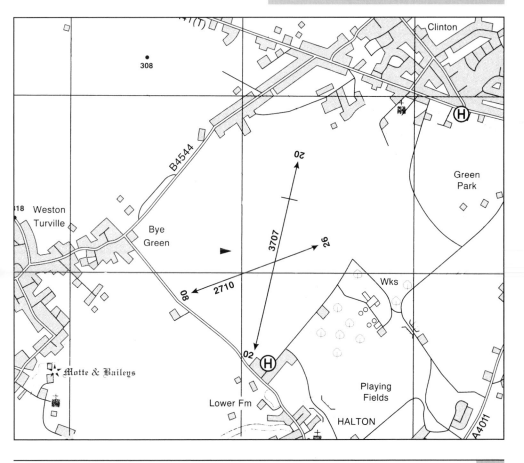

Haverfordwest
☺

Location: N51 50.02 W004 57.63 (2nm N of Haverfordwest)
Tel: 01437 765283

Runways:
04/22 4,006ft
09/27 3,412ft

Radio:
122.2

Notes:
Another former Royal Air Force airfield used for bomber training during World War Two, Haverfordwest was closed in 1945, only to reopen for general aviation operations in 1955. Only part of the original airfield is now used, but the site is open to most aircraft types and a flying school is resident at the airfield. Following the closure of nearby RAF Brawdy, Haverfordwest is now the only significant aerodrome in the area.

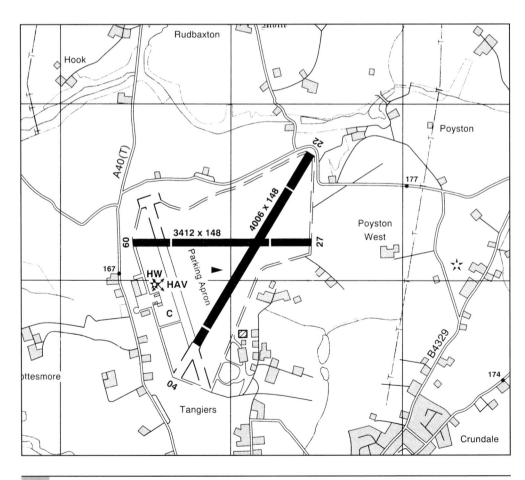

Henlow
☺

Location: N52 01.17 W000 18.10 (9nm SE of Bedford)
Tel: 01462 851515

Runways:
02/20 3,145ft (grass)
09/27 3,170ft (grass)
13/31 2,624ft (grass)

Radio:
121.1

Notes:
A small grass airfield, Henlow's resident unit is No. 616 Volunteer Gliding School, which is equipped with Vigilants. Other light aircraft are also present, and some aircraft can occasionally be seen on RAF or British Aerospace business. Parachuting also takes place over the airfield.

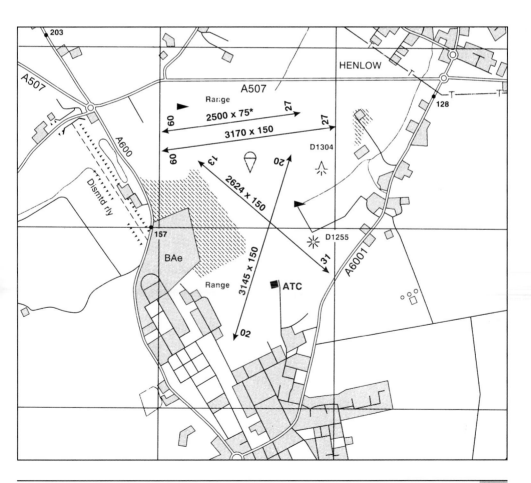

Hucknall
☺

Location: N53 00.85 W001 13.10 (5nm NW of Nottingham)
Tel: 0115 9642539

Runways:
04/22 2,395ft (grass)
11/29 2,838ft (grass)

Radio:
130.8

Notes:
A well-known airfield where Rolls-Royce has maintained a presence for many years, Hucknall is perhaps best known for the wartime tests with a P-51 Mustang which was experimentally fitted with a Rolls-Royce engine. The rest, as they say, is history. Despite a significant concrete runway, present-day flying is limited to general aviation operations from an adjacent grass area. Types such as a Spey-powered Vulcan, RB.211-powered VC10 and even exotic visitors such as the US Navy's Blue Angels Phantoms are now little more than memories.

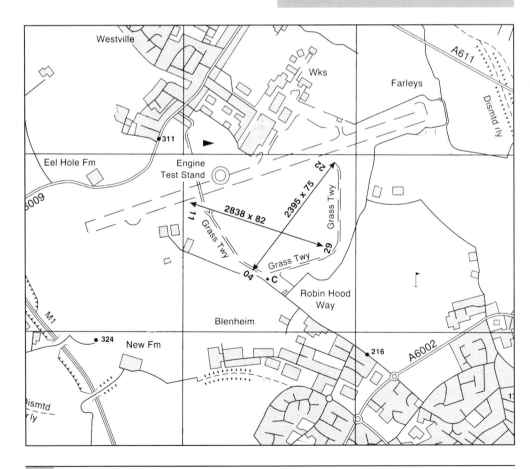

Islay
☺

Location: N55 40.92 W006 15.40 (4nm NW of Port Ellen)
Tel: 01496 302361

Runways:
08/26 2,083ft
13/31 5,069ft

Radio:
123.15

Notes:
Utilising just part of a fairly large wartime airfield, Islay is certainly remote and very quiet. Activity is restricted to sporadic general aviation and business visitors, combined with the regular scheduled British Airways service. Visitors and spectators are welcome, but the airfield's location in the Western Isles ensures that the airfield is never likely to be very busy.

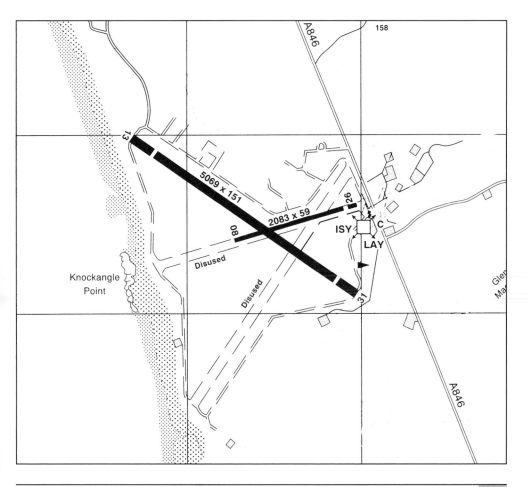

Isle of Skye/Broadford

☺

Location: N57 15.19 W005 49.68 (2nm NE of Broadford)
Tel: 01478 612727

Runway:
07/25 2,530ft

Radio:
130.65

Notes:
A small and quiet strip with few facilities and just a small 'terminal' building, Broadford is a community airfield providing a handling facility for both business and general aviation visitors. Access and observation is easy but activity at this bleak and windswept site is low.

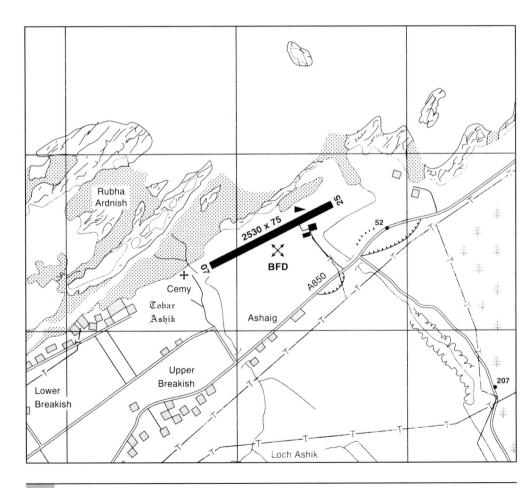

Isle of Wight/Sandown
☺

Location: N50 39.13 W001 10.83 (1nm W of Sandown)

Tel: 01983 405125

Runway:
05/23 2,900ft (grass)

Radio:
123.5

Notes:
Originally opened as Lea Farm in the 1930s, this small airfield closed during World War Two, only to reopen in 1948. Scheduled services used the airfield and general aviation activity was present until 1974, when the airfield closed again in anticipation of housing development. However, the site was saved once again and NDN built and tested the Firecracker trainer from this airfield, together with other designs. The company remains there to this day. Light aircraft keep the airfield fairly active and movements can be observed around the perimeter of the site.

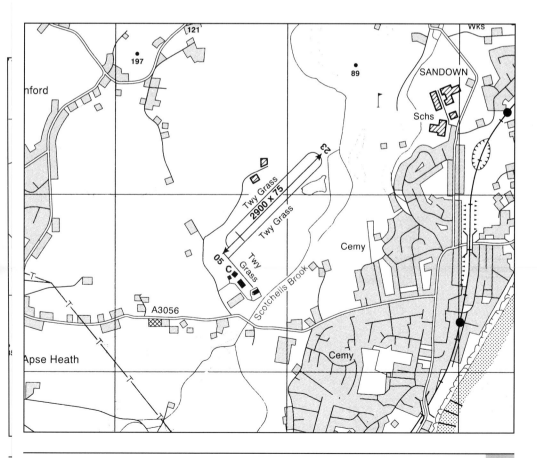

Lashenden/Headcorn
☺☺

Location: N51 09.41 E000 38.50 (8nm SE of Maidstone)

Tel: 01622 890226

Runways:
04/22 (grass)
11/29 2,612ft (grass)

Radio:
122.0

Notes:
Although often referred to as Headcorn, the latter site actually lies a few miles to the north, and Lashenden is another former wartime site where Spitfires and Mustangs were based. The small airfield houses a variety of aircraft, ranging from typical light types to Tiger Moths and aerobatic aircraft, together with a small museum. Parachuting is also popular at the site and visitors are welcome. Good views can be found from surrounding roads.

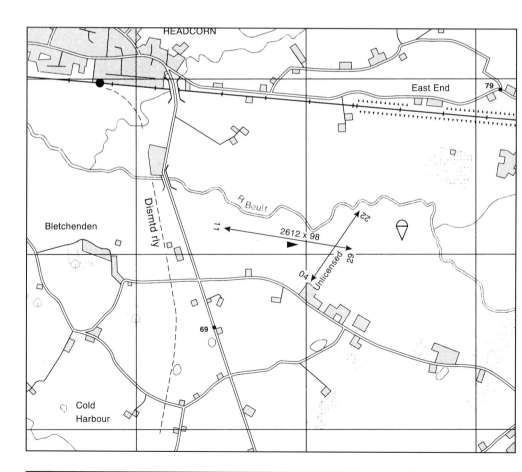

Lee-on-Solent
☺

Location: N50 48.91 W001 12.42 (2nm NW of Gosport)
Tel: 01705 551714

Runway:
05/23 4,294ft

Radio:
120.225

Notes:
A former Fleet Air Arm base, Lee-on-Solent is now inactive. Almost all movements are now confined to helicopter operations conducted by the police and Bristow Helicopters. Some light aircraft and glider flying does take place, but most of the airfield is now disused.

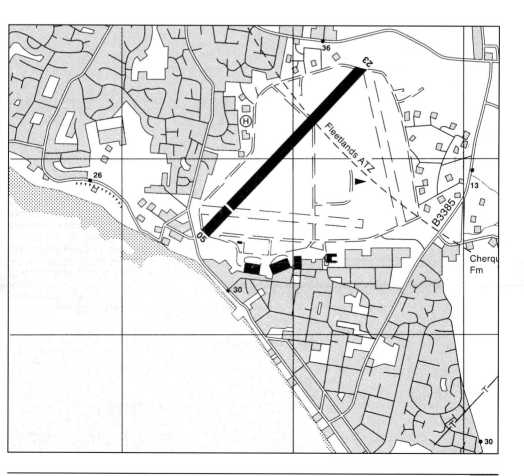

Leicester
☺☺

Location: N52 36.46 W001 01.92 (4nm SE of Leicester)
Tel: 0116 259 2360

Runways:
04/22 1,607ft
06/24 1,099ft (grass)
10/28 3,084ft
15/33 1,624ft
16/34 1,371ft (grass)

Radio:
122.125

Notes:
Although Leicester Airport is built on a former World War Two site, only part of the original airfield is now used, and light aircraft types keep the airfield fairly busy. A flying club is located at the airfield and visitors are common. A number of successful annual air shows have also been held here, attracting exotic exhibits such as a Starfighter and the Red Arrows. However, day-to-day activity is normally confined to general aviation.

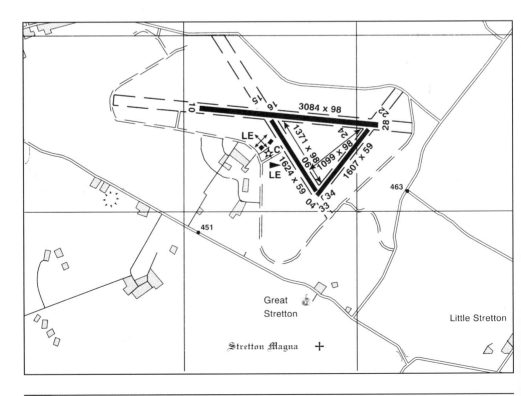

Lerwick/Tingwall

☺

Location: N60 11.53 W001 14.62 (4nm NW of Lerwick)

Tel: 01595 840306

Runway:
02/20 2,506ft

Radio:
122.6

Notes:
A small and exposed airfield, most flying at Lerwick is limited to occasional general aviation movements although there is a scheduled service connecting the airport with the mainland. Observation of the limited amount of activity is possible but the airfield is usually quiet.

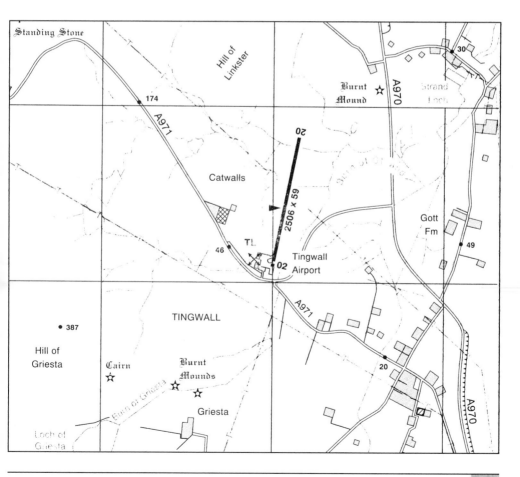

Little Gransden

☺

Location: N52 10.00 W000 09.23 (5nm SE of St Neots)
Tel: 01767 651950

Runways:
10/28 1,870ft (grass)
12/30 2,133ft (grass)
03/21 1,411ft (grass)

Radio:
130.850

Notes:
Little Gransden is a small grass airfield located a few miles from the former wartime base at Gransden Lodge. Movements can be observed from a picnic area on the airfield. Yak UK, which imports the famous Yak 'warbird', is based here. Consequently, some unusual and interesting aircraft can sometimes be seen amongst the typical Cessnas and Pipers.

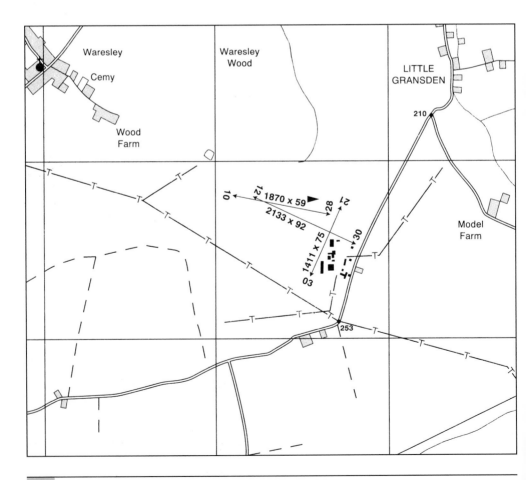

Lydd
☺

Location: N50 57.37 E000 56.35 (1nm E
of Lydd)
Tel: 01797 320401

Runway:
04/22 4,935ft

Radio:
120.70

Notes:
Once the home of the unique and rather romantic Bristol Freighters and Carvairs assigned to cross-channel ferrying, Lydd was developed specifically to cater for channel crossings. Sadly, with the prospect of more sea ferry services, the tunnel and even hovercraft, the aerial ferry option became unattractive and the last flight was made from Lydd in 1978. Since then the airfield has been promoted as a general aviation site with particular emphasis on cross-channel movements, and many of the light aircraft seen at the airport are registered abroad. Spectators are welcome and movements can be observed from the airport cafeteria.

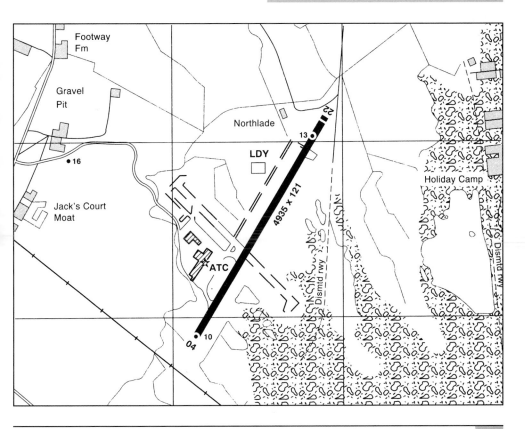

Manchester/Barton

☺☺

Location: N53 28.28 W002 23.35 (5nm W of Manchester)

Tel: 0161 787 7326

Runways:

02/20 1,739ft (grass)
06/24 1,854ft (grass)
09/27 2,054ft (grass)
14/32 1,345ft (grass)

Radio:

122.70 119.4 125.1

Notes:
Opened as Manchester's main airport in 1930, Barton was eventually abandoned in favour of Ringway, thanks to the site's poor drainage and very short runways. However, Proctors were produced here during the Second World War and general aviation has remained at Barton ever since. The airfield is busy, particularly at weekends, and air shows are often held, attracting displays from all types of aircraft, including modern fast jets. There are also tentative plans to build a tarmac runway.

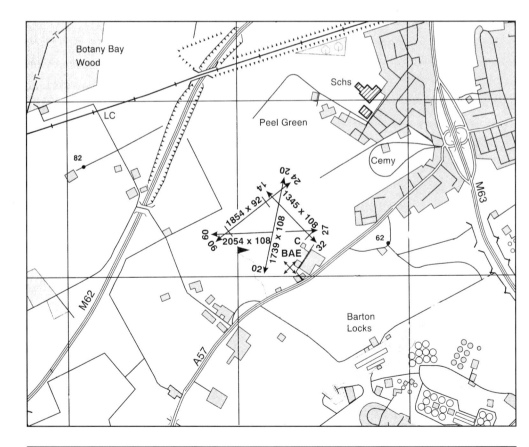

Mona
☺

Location: N53 15.55 W004 22.38 (2nm W of Llangefni)
Tel: 01407 762241

Runway:
04/22 5,285ft

Radio:
122.0 379.7 372.325 358.75

Notes:
Opened as an airship base during World War One, during World War Two Mona was used as an air gunnery base, equipped with Ansons and Bothas amongst others. Currently the airfield is home to the Mona Flying Club, but most activity is provided by RAF Hawks, as the airfield is designated as a Relief Landing Ground for nearby RAF Valley. Hawks can be seen in Mona's circuits at most times of the day, whereas private flying is a more likely sight at weekends. Good views can be obtained at each end of the main runway.

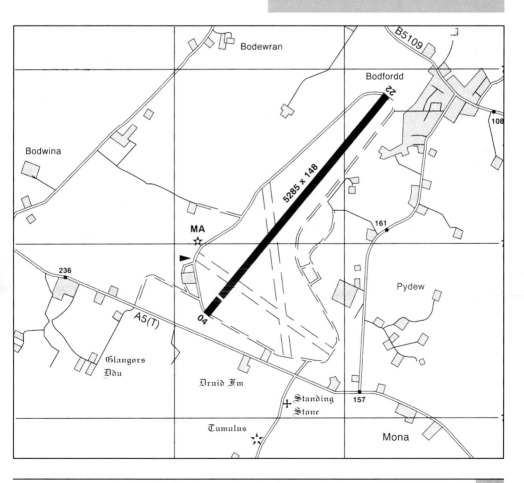

Netherthorpe
☺☺
Location: N53 19.02 W001 11.77 (2nm NW of Worksop)
Tel: 01909 475233

Runways:
06/24 1,476ft (grass)
18/36 1,253ft (grass)

Radio:
123.275

Notes:
Home to the Sheffield Aero Club, flying at Netherthorpe is restricted to light aircraft thanks to the short runways. Active since 1935, Netherthorpe still attracts plenty of visitors and can be fairly active, particularly at weekends. Viewing from surrounding roadside vantage points is possible.

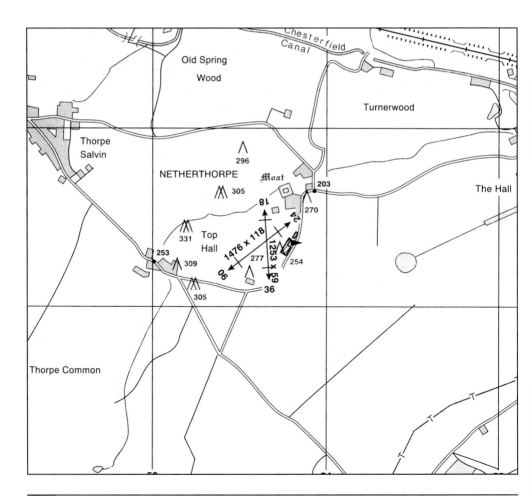

Newtownards

☺

Location: N54 34.87 W005 41.53 (8nm E of Belfast

Tel: 01247 813327

Runways:
04/22 2,496ft
08/26 2,031ft
16/34 1,814ft

Radio:
123.5

Notes:
Opened in 1934, Newtownards was for many years the main airport serving the Belfast area. With the development of Aldergrove and Belfast City airports, Newtownards has concentrated on general aviation, and the airfield is now the home of the Ulster Flying Club and a number of privately owned aircraft. Plenty of visitors keep the airfield fairly busy and observation is easy from the airfield perimeter.

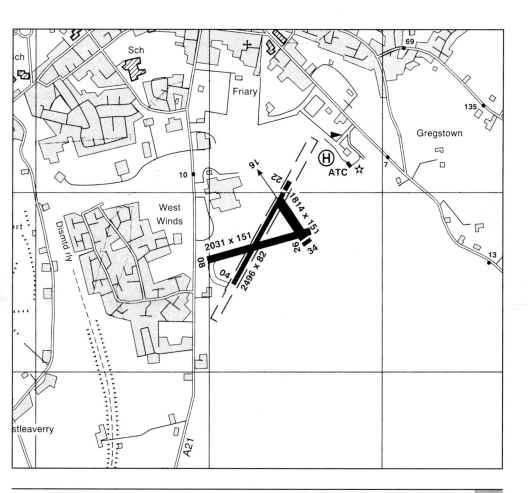

Northampton/Sywell

☺☺☺

Location: N52 18.29 W000 47.48 (5nm NE of Northampton)
Tel: 01604 491112

Runways:
03/21 2,982ft (grass)
07/25 2,297ft (grass)
15/33 1,732ft (grass)

Radio:
122.7

Notes:
Opened in 1928, Sywell was a World War Two Royal Air Force training base operating Tiger Moths and Ansons, while Wellingtons were serviced here. Civilian operations resumed in 1947. A busy general aviation site, there is a resident flying club, and many private aircraft are based here. Visitors are common and there is even a small hotel on the airfield, making spotting particularly comfortable!

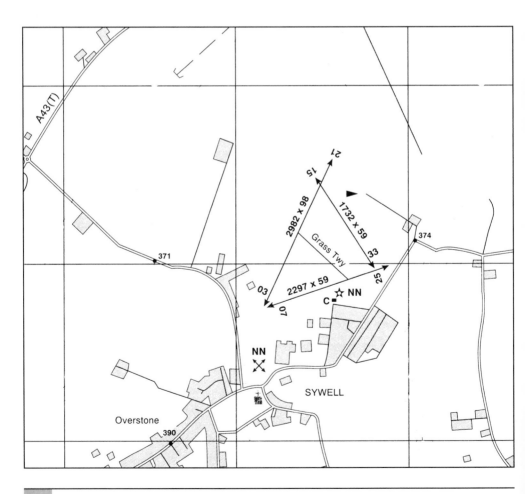

North Weald

☺☺☺☺

Location: N51 43.30 E000 09.25 (3nm SE of Harlow)
Tel: 01992 524500

Runways:
02/20 6,332ft
13/31 3,005ft

Radio:
123.525 129.975

Notes:
A famous Battle of Britain airfield, much of the eponymously titled motion picture was filmed here. Post-war, North Weald was the home of No. 111 Squadron's

Hunters, which formed the famous Black Arrows aerobatic team. The Royal Air Force vacated the site in 1960, but civilian flying has gradually been developed here and a number of warbirds are now housed on the airfield. Visiting light aircraft can also be seen along with the resident types, and some outstanding air shows have been held at the airfield in recent years, attracting both warbirds and modern military types. The first International Air Tattoo was also held here, before moving to Greenham Common. With continual pressure to close the airfield for housing and commercial development, however, North Weald's future seems less than secure.

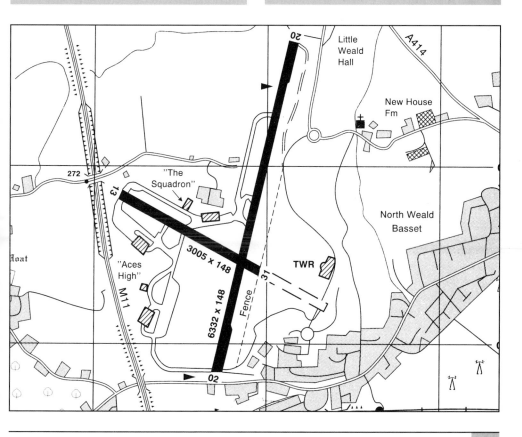

Nottingham/Tollerton

☺☺

Location: N52 55.20 W001 04.75 (3nm SE of Nottingham)
Tel: 0115 981 1327

Runways:
03/21 2,694ft
09/27 3,251ft

Radio:
122.8

Notes:
Opened in 1930, Tollerton was used from 1937 as a Royal Air Force training base utilising Magisters and Ansons. Fields Aviation Services maintained Lancasters, Liberators, Halifaxes and Hampdens at the site, and numerous Lancasters were dismantled and scrapped at Tollerton after the war. Today the airfield is a busy general aviation site, the home of a flying club, and various privately owned aircraft.

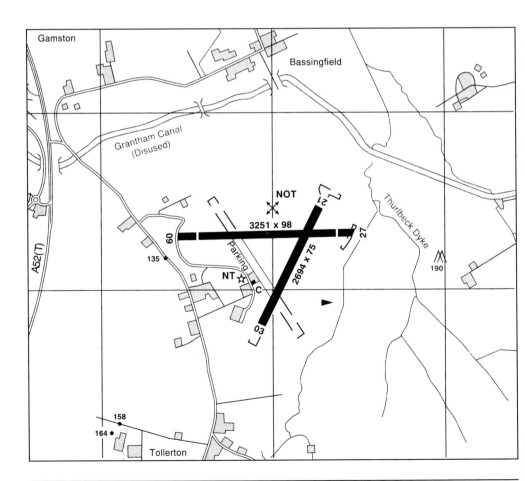

Oban/North Connel
☺

Location: N56 27.66 W005 24.17 (3nm NE of Oban)
Tel: 01631 710384

Runway:
02/20 3,700ft

Radio:
130.1 129.825

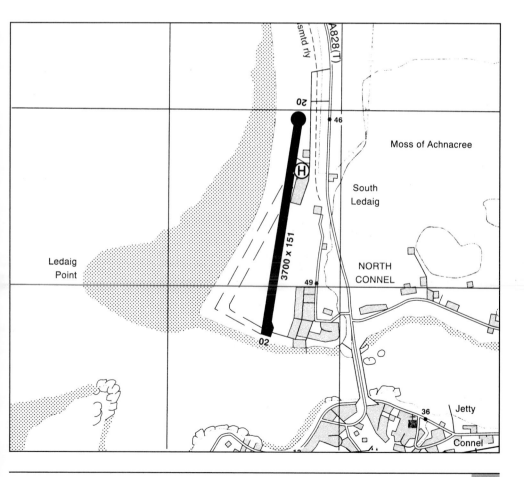

Old Sarum
☺☺

Location: N51 05.93 W001 47.05 (2nm NE of Salisbury)
Tel: 01722 322525

Runway:
06/24 2,562ft (grass)

Radio:
123.2 126.70

Notes:
An historic aviation site, Old Sarum dates back to 1915. The station's wooden hangars were constructed in 1917 and are now officially Listed buildings. A variety of privately owned aircraft are housed at the airfield and visiting types are common. Spectators are catered for with a café overlooking the airfield.

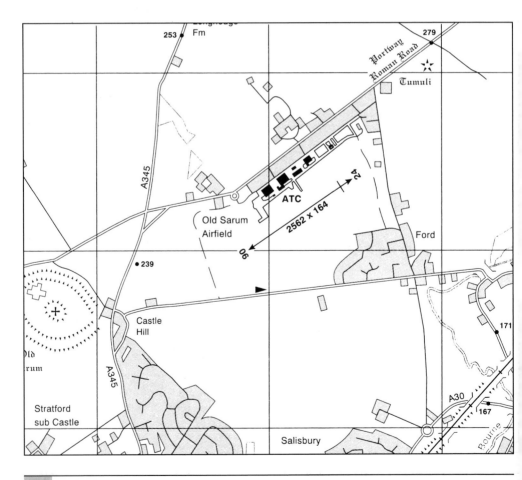

Old Warden/Biggleswade

☺☺☺☺☺

Location: N52 05.33 W000 19.09 (6nm SE of Bedford)

Tel: 01767 627563

Runways:
04/22 2,011ft (grass)
12/30 2,405ft (grass)

Radio:
123.05

Notes:
Possibly the most famous grass airfield in the country, Old Warden is of course the home of the Shuttleworth Collection, a unique line-up of fully airworthy pre-war and World-War-One-era aircraft. Although visiting light aircraft are common, it is the museum aircraft which attract the most attention, and examples can be seen outside on most days. Various air shows are also held each year, most concentrating on historic types, but often including modern aircraft such as the Tornado or even the Red Arrows. Although light aircraft use Old Warden's small runway strips with ease, even larger aircraft have made occasional appearances. Duxford's Varsity made an impressive touch-and-go during one show.

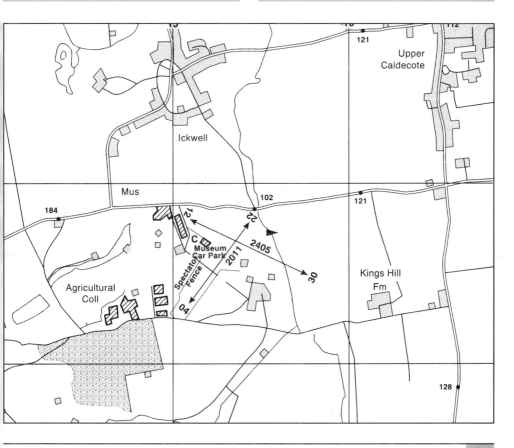

Oxford/Kidlington

☺☺☺

Location: N51 50.20 W001 19.18 (6nm NW of Oxford)

Tel: 01865 841234

Runways:

02/20 3,937ft
03/21 2,493ft
09/27 2,822ft (grass)
12/30 2,493ft (grass)

Radio:

125.325 118.875 121.95

Notes:

Opening in 1938 as a training base, Kidlington was primarily used during World War Two as a Relief Landing Ground for Abingdon, Little Rissington and Brize Norton. Harvards (over a hundred at one stage) were common at the airfield, and post-war Kidlington has remained active as a training base, albeit under civilian control. The Oxford Air Training School is the main resident, together with a handful of other schools and various privately owned aircraft. Visitors are common too, keeping the airfield busy at most times. Access is restricted but views from outside the airfield can be found.

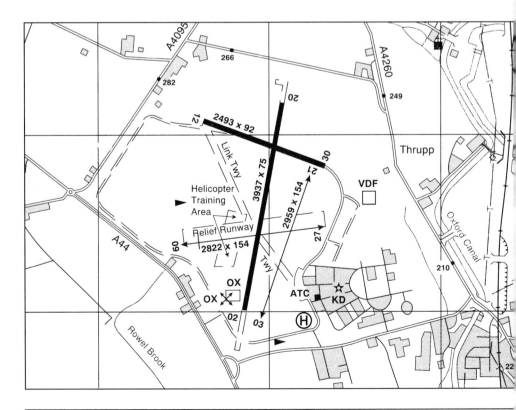

Panshanger

☺

Location: N51 48.15 W000 09.48 (2nm W of Hertford)

Tel: 01707 391791

Runway:
11/29 2,339ft (grass)

Radio:
120.25

Notes:
Once used as an Elementary Flying Training base with Tiger Moths and (later) Chipmunks, Panshanger is a general aviation site which was gradually fading into obscurity, The airfield has enjoyed a renovation in recent years, and there is now more activity at the airfield. A flying school is resident, together with privately owned types including Pitts aerobatic aircraft. Visitors can be seen too. Panshanger is now encroached upon by housing, with some gardens literally backing onto the airfield boundary. Observation is easy from most parts of the airfield boundary.

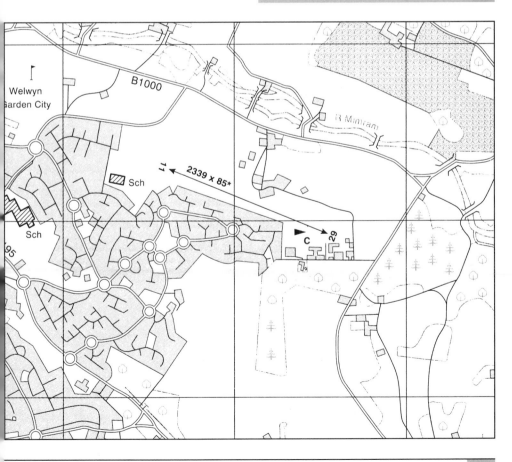

Perranporth
☺

Location: N50 19.90 W005 10.66 (1nm SW of Perranporth)
Tel: 01872 553310

Runways:
01/19 1,969ft
05/23 2,822ft
09/27 2,028ft

Radio:
119.75

Notes:
Spitfires, Avengers and Swordfish were based at this former wartime Royal Air Force base, although the airfield was effectively a satellite for nearby RAF Portreath. Largely because of the airfield's small runways and poor weather record, the RAF vacated the station in 1946. The airfield reopened for civil operations in 1951, albeit with little success. Today the airfield is used for light aircraft flying and gliding, using part of what was originally a small airfield. However, the airfield's cliff-top location is certainly impressive.

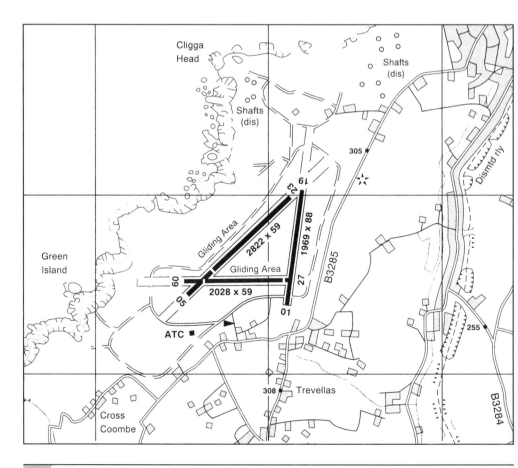

Perth/Scone
☺

Location: N56 26.35 W003 22.33 (3nm NE of Perth)
Tel: 01738 553357

Runways:
03/21 2,799ft
10/28 1,998ft
16/34 2,034ft (grass)

Radio:
119.8

Notes:
Used as a flying training base with Tiger Moths until 1954, Perth is now used for civilian flying training. A large number of light aircraft are based at the airfield, although some visiting types can often be seen. The airfield is fairly active, thanks to the flying training which is often in progress, and observation from the airfield perimeter can easily be achieved.

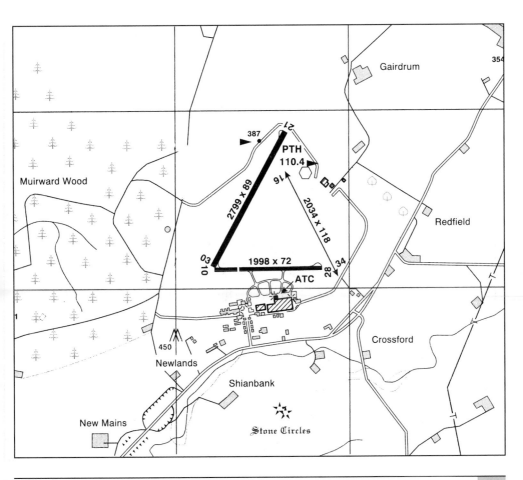

Peterborough/Conington
☺

Location: N52 28.08 W000 15.07 (6nm S of Peterborough)
Tel: 01487 832022

Runways:
10/28 3,238ft
16/34 2,625ft

Radio:
129.725

Notes:
Now known as Peterborough or Conington, this site was known as Glatton when the USAAF operated B-17s and Liberators here during World War Two. Using just part of the fairly large wartime airfield, Conington now hosts a small number of private aircraft and attracts a small number of visiting types, mostly for recreational or (occasionally) business purposes. Activity is fairly light but the airfield is certainly interesting, retaining much of its wartime ancestry.

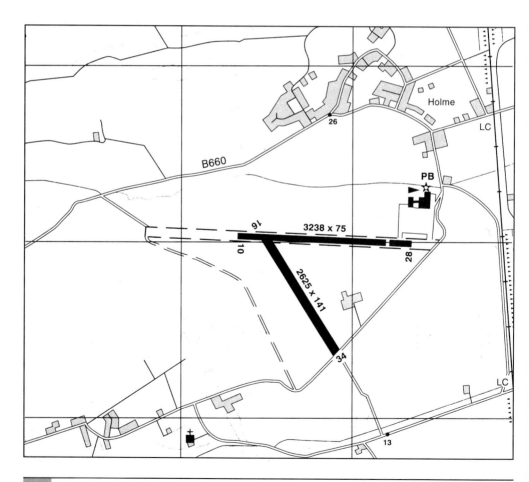

Peterborough/Sibson

☺

Location: N52 33.35 W000 23.18 (6nm W of Peterborough)
Tel: 01832 280289

Runways:
07/25 2,306ft (grass)
15/33 1,808ft (grass)

Radio:
122.3

Notes:
Opened as a Royal Air Force training base in 1941, Sibson was home to Oxfords, Magisters, Tutors and even a few Hurricanes. Today the airfield hosts a number of private aircraft, many associated with the airfield's key role as a parachute base. Types such as the Turbo Porter and Skyvan can often be seen amongst the usual smaller light aircraft. For some years a couple of former RAF Varsities were left to slowly deteriorate on the airfield, although one was eventually saved for preservation at Brooklands. Nearby RAF Wittering often affects operations from Sibson, but the airfield is usually fairly active.

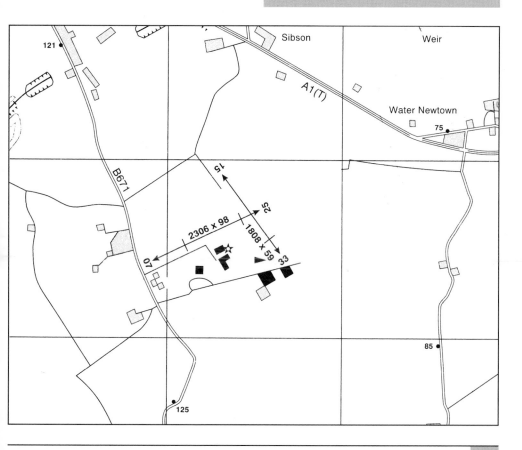

Plockton
☺

Location: N57 20.12 W005 40.32 (3nm
NE of Kyle of Lochalsh)
Tel: 0378 478542

Runway:
02/20 1,959ft

Radio:
122.375

Notes:
A small 'commuter' airfield, Plockton
is fairly inactive, with few facilities
(although hangarage is available) in a
very exposed location. Most movements
are light aircraft or helicopters.
Observation is possible, but normally
only a few aircraft can be seen.

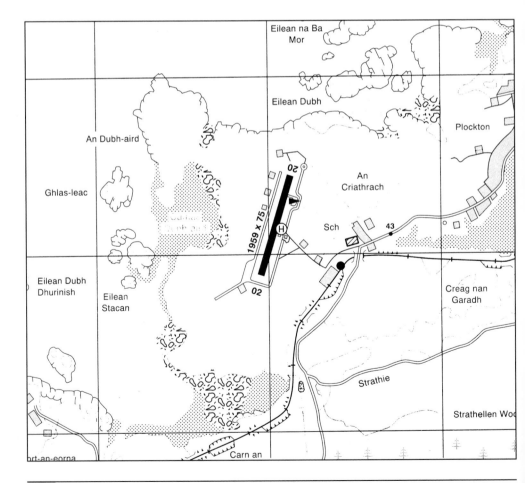

Popham

☺☺☺

Location: N51 11.66 W001 14.17 (8nm NE of Winchester)

Tel: 01256 397733

Runways:
03/21 2,952ft (grass)
08/26 2,999ft (grass)

Radio:
129.8

Notes:
Although Popham is owned by Charles Church (Spitfires) Ltd, the latter types are not to be seen here. The airfield is largely devoted to privately owned light aircraft, and a wide variety of types are visible, particularly at weekends, when the circuit can be quite busy. Adjacent to a very busy road and surrounded by some beautiful countryside, Popham is certainly an interesting airfield, with plenty of aircraft to observe.

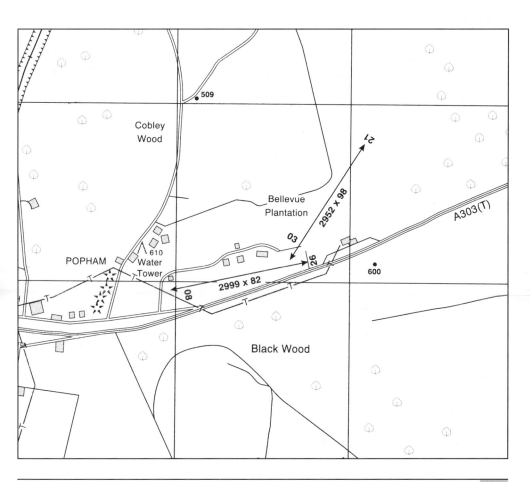

Redhill
☺☺

Location: N51 12.82 W000 08.32 (1nm SE of Redhill)
Tel: 01737 823377

Runways:
01/19 2,789ft (grass)
08L/26R 2,224ft (grass)
08R/26L 2,943ft (grass)

Radio:
120.275

Notes:
Formerly a wartime Spitfire base, Redhill is now a general aviation site and the home of Bristow Helicopters. Apart from flying clubs, microlights and helicopters, many visiting light aircraft are often present. Permission to develop the airfield into a commuter airfield feeding Gatwick was not granted and now the airfield is being promoted as a general aviation site.

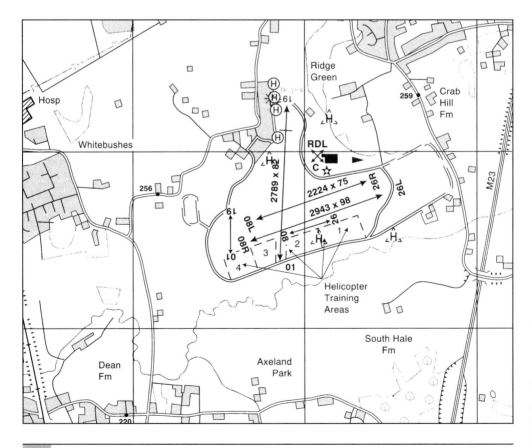

Retford/Gamston
☺

Location: N53 16.83 W000 57.08 (2nm S of East Retford)
Tel: 01777 838593

Runway:
03/21 4,035ft

Radio:
130.475

Notes:
The Royal Air Force did not vacate Gamston until the 1950s, but little remains of their presence, although the airfield is still largely intact. Gamston currently occupies a small part of the former RAF base, using just one runway, with a secondary runway reserved for glider launches and recovery. Microlights are also present, but most activity is provided by privately owned aircraft, and a variety of visitors. The airfield can be fairly active, especially at weekends.

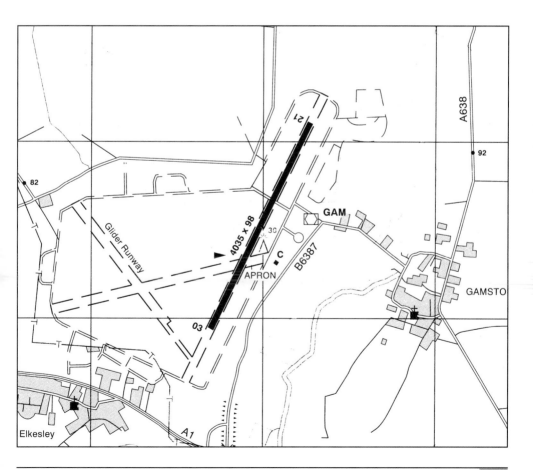

Rochester
☺

Location: N51 21.12 E000 30.20 (1nm S of Rochester)
Tel: 01634 816127

Runways:
02/20 2,713ft (grass)
02/20 (relief) 2,264ft (grass)
16/34 3,169ft (grass)

Radio:
122.25

Notes:
Despite the airfield's small size, Short Stirling bombers were built and flown from Rochester during World War Two. Rochester currently hosts much smaller aircraft, as it is the home of the Cherokee Flying Club and a variety of other organisations. Various privately owned aircraft are present at the airfield, and visitors are common, keeping the airfield fairly busy. The A229 offers an excellent view of the airfield.

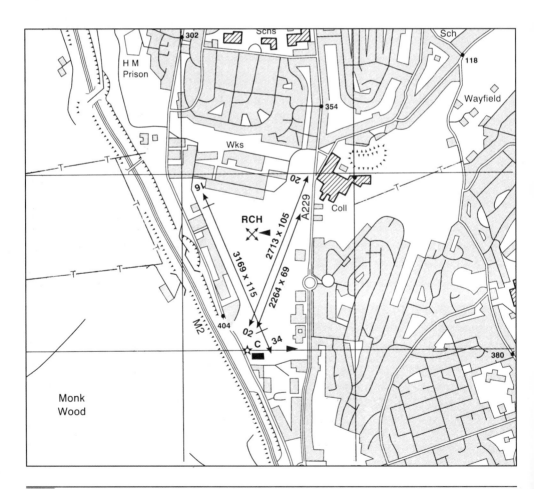

Sandtoft

☺☺

Location: N53 33.58 W000 51.50 (7nm SW of Scunthorpe)
Tel: 01427 873676

Runway:
05/23 2,907ft

Radio:
130.425

Notes:
Formerly a Royal Air Force bomber base during World War Two, Sandtoft was earmarked for development as a post-war USAF jet fighter base, but the airfield was eventually abandoned and left to decay. Most of the airfield is derelict, but a small part of the original site is now used as a thriving general aviation base. There is a variety of resident aircraft, including a Gannet and a couple of Jet Provosts. There is also a Hawker Tempest undergoing restoration in one of the hangars. Although a very small airfield, the residents and visiting types keep activity fairly high.

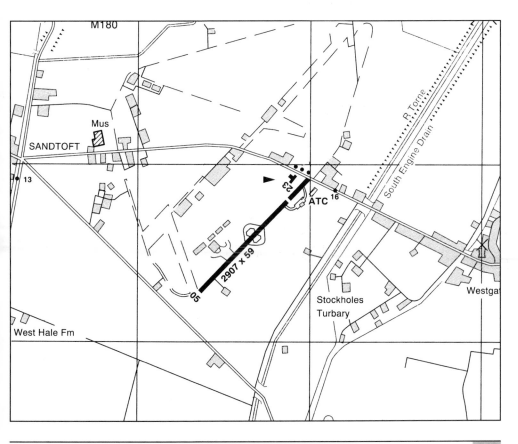

Scatsta

☺

Location: N60 25.92 W001 17.88 (17nm N of Lerwick)
Tel: 01806 242791

Runway:
06/24 3,150ft

Radio:
123.6 122.4 121.6

Notes:
Scatsta is a thriving general aviation and business airfield, although the vast majority of movements are directly related to the oil industry, thanks to the proximity of Sullom Voe, Europe's largest oil terminal. The airfield is moderately busy, and with the B9076 running parallel to the runway, observing movements is very easy.

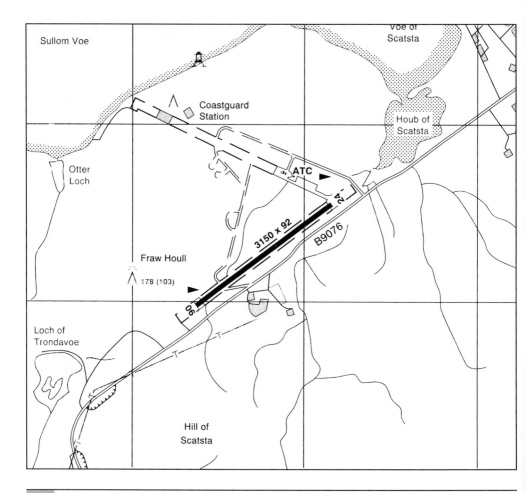

Scilly Isles/St Mary's
☺☺

Location: N49 54.80 W006 17.52 (1nm E of Hugh Town)
Tel: 01720 422677

Runways:
01/19 (grass) helicopter only
09/27 1,716ft (grass/asphalt)
15/33 1,968ft

Radio:
123.15

Notes:
Scheduled services from the UK (Land's End) began here in 1937, and these links continue today, providing the bulk of St Mary's activity. The famous helicopter link to Penzance also lands here, and visiting light aircraft combine with a handful of resident types to keep the airfield fairly active, despite a tranquil and picturesque location.

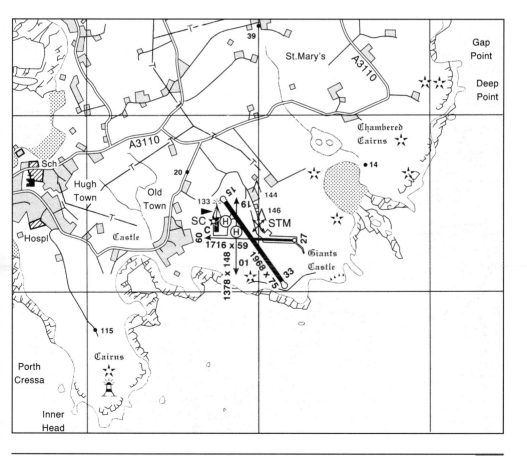

Seething
☺

Location: N52 30.65 E001 25.03 (9nm SE of Norwich)
Tel: 01502 711852

Runway:
06/24 2,625ft

Radio:
122.6

Notes:
Once the home of the USAAF's 448th Bomber Group and countless examples of the Liberator, Seething is now a tranquil airfield, occupying just part of the once-huge bomber base. Seething is only utilised for general aviation these days, and with only a few visitors, activity is fairly moderate. Observation from surrounding roads can be achieved easily.

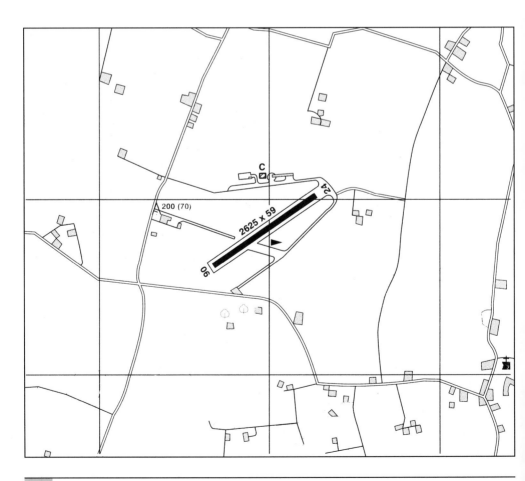

Sheffield City
☺

Location: N53 23.65 W001 23.31 (3nm NE of Sheffield)
Tel: 0114 244 4888

Runway:
10/28 3,934ft

Radio:
128.525 121.70

Notes:
The most recent 'city airport' to be completed, Sheffield City is neatly sandwiched between industrial areas. It has a moderate-sized runway which is (rather perversely) only available to multi-engine types. Most activity is provided by a handful of scheduled services, although some business aircraft also visit. A police helicopter and traffic monitoring aircraft are the only residents, but occasional unusual visitors can be seen either on the ground or overshooting, including a few military types.

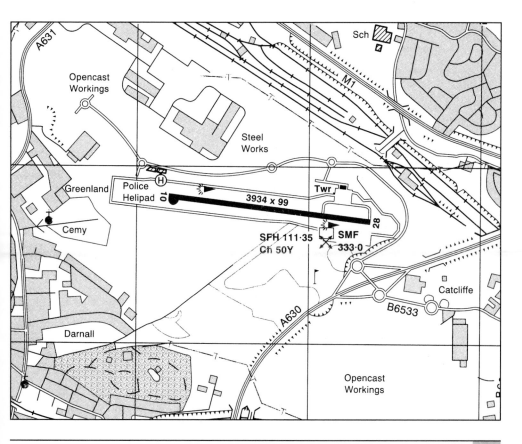

Sherburn-in-Elmet

☺☺

Location: N53 47.28 W001 13.10 (5nm W of Selby)
Tel: 01977 682674

Runways:
01/19 1,814ft (grass)
06/24 2,395ft (grass)
11/29 2,021ft (grass)

Radio:
122.6

Notes:
Sherburn-in-Elmet was formerly the home of a Blackburn factory (where countless Swordfish were completed). Hurricanes were based here during World War Two. Post-war, the airfield became a general aviation site, and various privately owned aircraft are now based here, together with the Sherburn Aero Club. Visitors are quite common. Although the original tarmac runway is still visible, this is only used for vehicle testing, and (rather oddly) flying takes place from a series of grass strips adjacent to the old runway. Viewing is possible from the B1222.

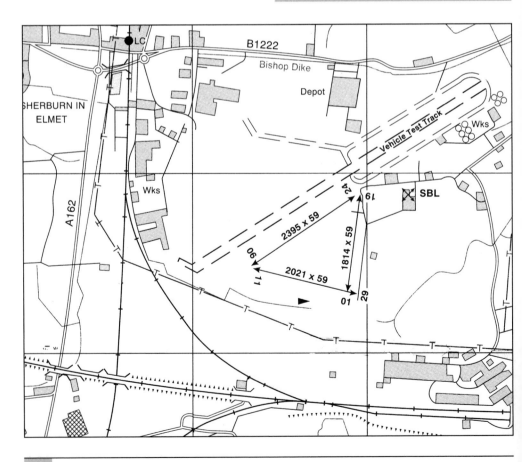

Shipdham
☺

Location: N52 37.77 E000 55.68 (3nm S of Dereham)
Tel: 01362 820337

Runway:
02/20 2,828ft

Radio:
119.55

Notes:
Formerly a USAAF B-24 Liberator base, Shipdham closed shortly after the Second World War and remained inactive until the 1970s, when part of the airfield was reopened for use by light aircraft. A flying club is now resident at the airfield and a few aircraft are based here. Visiting aircraft keep the airfield moderately busy. Much remains of the former wartime site, not least the original runways and taxiways.

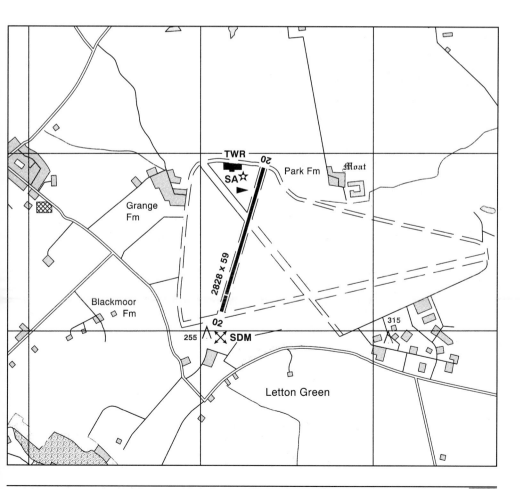

Shobdon

☺

Location: N52 14.48 W002 52.88 (8nm W of Leominster)
Tel: 01568 708723

Runway:
09/27 2,762ft

Radio:
123.5

Notes:
Built for glider training, Shobdon was originally known as Pembridge Landing Ground. Today, gliding is still popular at the site, together with microlight flying, helicopters and general aviation. There is an aero club and flying school, so the airfield is always fairly busy. A variety of aircraft can often be seen in the various maintenance facilities on the airfield.

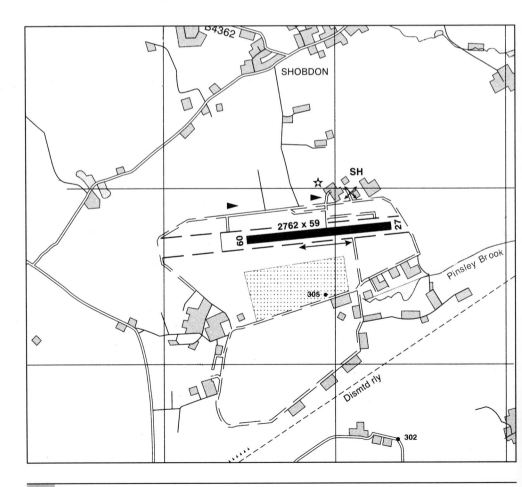

Shoreham

☺☺

Location: N50 50.07 W000 17.67 (1nm W of Shoreham-by-Sea)

Tel: 01273 296888

Runways:
03/21 2,703ft
07/25 2,982ft (grass)
13/31 1,394ft (grass)

Radio:
123.15   125.40   132.40

Notes:
The oldest licensed aerodrome in the UK, Shoreham first opened in 1910, and a variety of airlines operated from the base prior to World War Two. After the war the airfield was leased to Miles Aircraft and later Beagle Aircraft, who produced the Pup and Basset here. Today the airfield is a significant general aviation site, with numerous aircraft based there (including a Harvard and Tiger Moth). There are plenty of visitors, a number of flying clubs, and it is the headquarters of the Popular Flying Association.

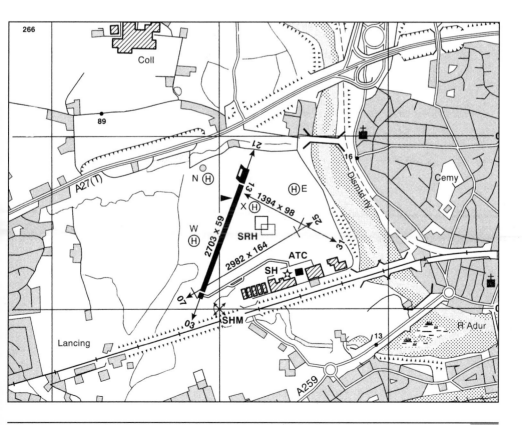

Sleap
☺

Location: N52 50.03 W002 46.30 (10nm N of Shrewsbury)
Tel: 01939 232882

Runways:
01/19 2,543ft
05/23 2,631ft

Radio:
122.45 120.775

Notes:
Sleap was originally a Royal Air Force Whitley base. Horsa gliders were also operated from the airfield and it was used for training operations until after the end of World War Two. Now used as a general aviation site, the airfield is often closed during weekdays, but activity is fairly moderate at weekends. Some reminders of the airfield's wartime connections remain, including the control tower which was demolished twice by runaway Whitley bombers!

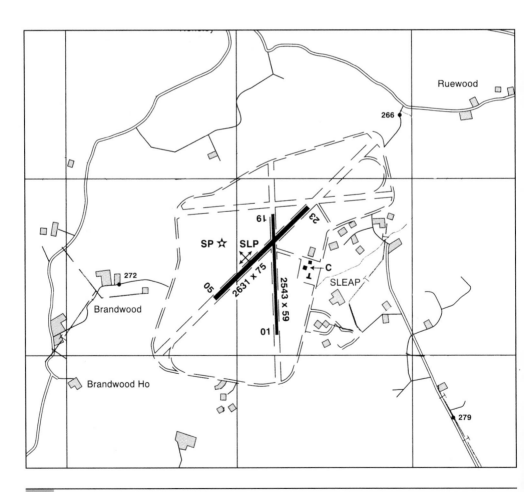

Stapleford
☺

Location: N51 39.15 E000 09.35 (4nm N of Romford)
Tel: 01708 688380

Runways:
04/22 3,533ft (grass/asphalt)
10/28 2,346ft (grass)

Radio:
122.8

Notes:
A former Battle of Britain Hurricane base, Stapleford is now primarily utilised for civilian flying training, courtesy of the Stapleford Flight Centre. Various light aircraft are also resident at the airfield, and visitors are common, keeping the airfield fairly busy. Observation is possible from the A113.

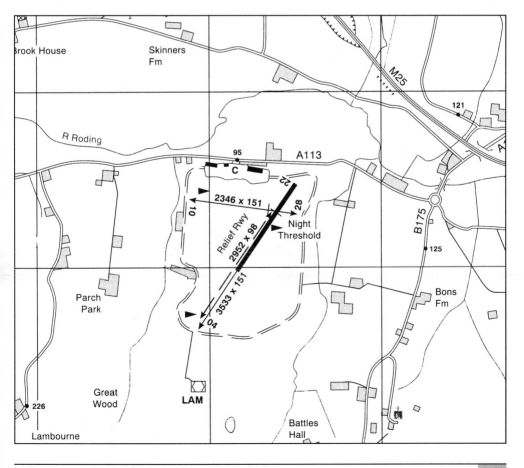

Sturgate
☺

Location: N53 22,87 W000 41.12 (4nm SE of Gainsborough)
Tel: 01427 838280

Runways:
09/27 2,690ft
14/32 1,509ft

Radio:
130.3

Notes:
Built late during World War Two, Sturgate was not completed in time to house any operational bomber squadrons. Post-war, the base was handed over to USAF control, and F-84 jets were based here. Today just a small part of the airfield remains in use as a general aviation site. A few resident aircraft and a few visitors provide a moderate amount of activity. The neighbouring airspace is fairly busy, with Scampton and Waddington nearby, so movements are often dependent upon surrounding activity.

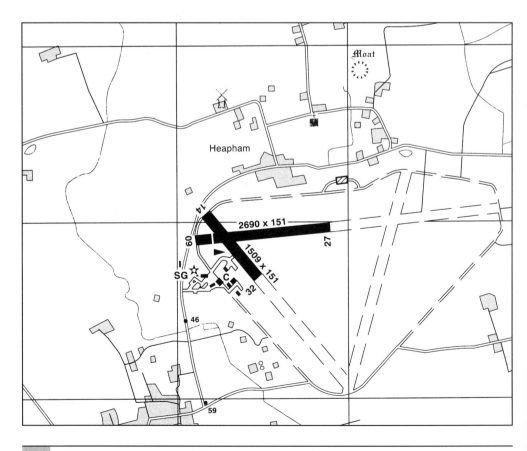

Tatenhill
☺

Location: N52 48.85 W001 45.67 (4nm W of Burton-on-Trent)
Tel: 01283 575650

Runway:
08/26 2,297ft

Radio:
124.075

Notes:
Using just part of a former wartime airfield, Tatenhill is a small general aviation site with limited hangarage and maintenance facilities. Flying activity is fairly low and only a few visitors are usually seen here.

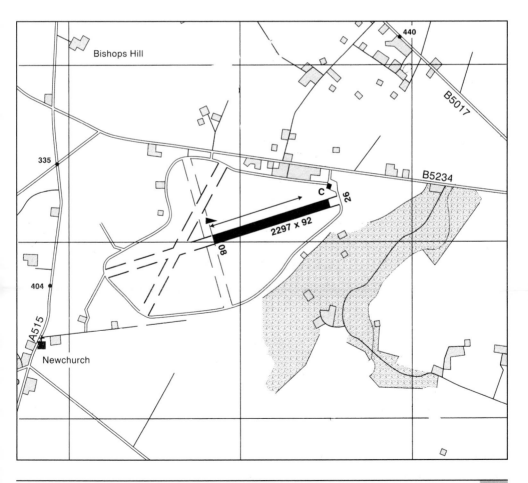

Thruxton
☺☺

Location: N51 12.62 W001 35.90 (4nm W of Andover)
Tel: 01264 772352

Runways:
07/25 2,526ft
13/31 2,460 (grass)

Radio:
130.45

Notes:
Formerly a World War Two Royal Air Force station, Thruxton is now more closely associated with motor racing. However, general aviation remains present at this site, with light aircraft, helicopters, gliders and parachuting keeping the airfield busy, particularly during race meetings. Visitors are also quite common, providing plenty to see.

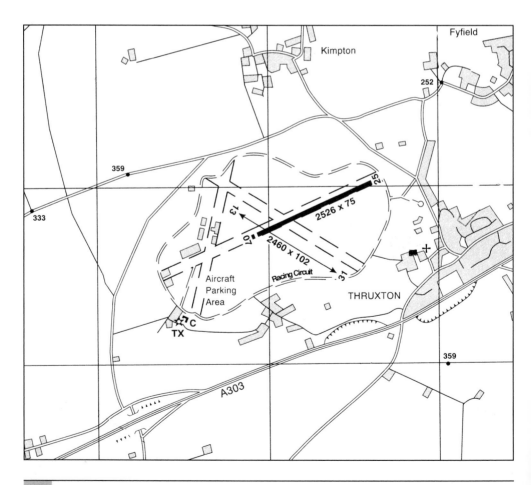

Tiree
☺

Location: N56 29.93 W006 52.20 (2nm
NE of Balemartine)
Tel: 01879 220456

Runways:
06/24 4,829ft
12/30 2,690ft

Radio:
122.7

Notes:
Opened in 1934, Tiree is a fairly large
airfield, although only part of the
original site is now used. A daily scheduled service to Glasgow provides the
main activity for the airport. Despite the
excellent condition of the facility, very
few aircraft use the airfield, probably
because of its rather remote location.
Observing the small amount of aerial
activity is, not surprisingly, fairly easy.

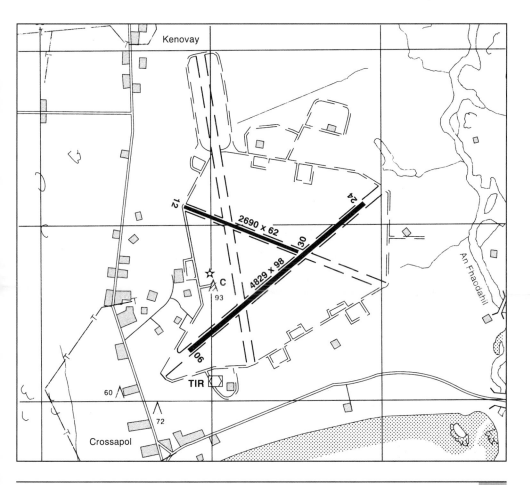

Turweston
☺

Location: N52 02.45 W001 05.73 (2nm E of Brackley)
Tel: 01280 701167

Runway:
09/27 3,002ft

Radio:
122.17

Notes:
Turweston was formerly a Royal Air Force station primarily used as a relief landing ground. Types such as the Wellington, Mitchell and Boston were seen here during World War Two. The airfield was closed in 1946. More recently a small part of the base has been opened for general aviation, and a small number of aircraft are based here. Home of the India Mike Charlie flying club, visitors are fairly few, but the site may well expand as the airfield becomes more familiar to private flyers.

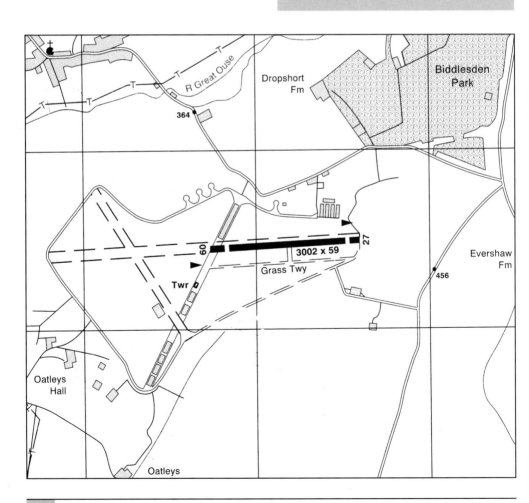

Unst

☺

Location: N60 44.82 W000 51.23 (S of Baltasound)

Tel: 01957 711887

Runway:
12/30 2,100ft

Radio:
130.35

Notes:
Out in the wilds of the Shetlands, Unst is a particularly remote and windswept airfield. With just two scheduled services to Lerwick and Sumburgh, flying activity is very low. Most flights are made by prior arrangements and the airfield can often be closed at various times. Observation of the limited activity is certainly possible, but Unst is certainly never busy.

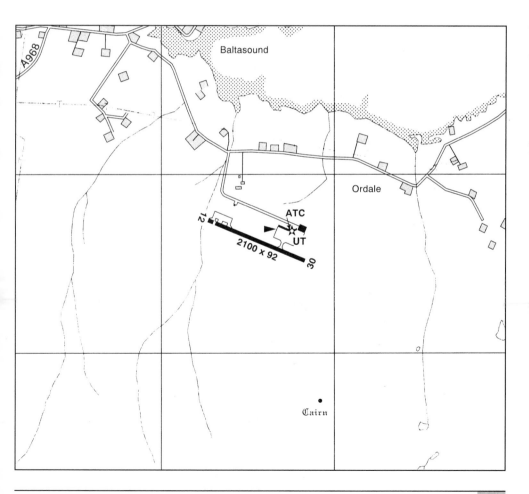

Upavon
☺

Location: N51 17.17 W001 46.92 (1nm E of Upavon)
Tel: 01980 615066

Runways:
05/23 3,500ft (grass)
08/26 3,200ft (grass)

Radio:
275.8

Notes:
An historic site of military aviation, Upavon is now operated by the Army, although the Royal Air Force maintains a non-flying presence at the station. No. 622 Volunteer Gliding Squadron is based here with Vikings, but little activity takes place apart from occasional Army fixed-wing and helicopter flights, or occasional exercises which may see Hercules aircraft performing low-level drops over the airfield. The A342 offers an excellent view of this windswept and rather moody site.

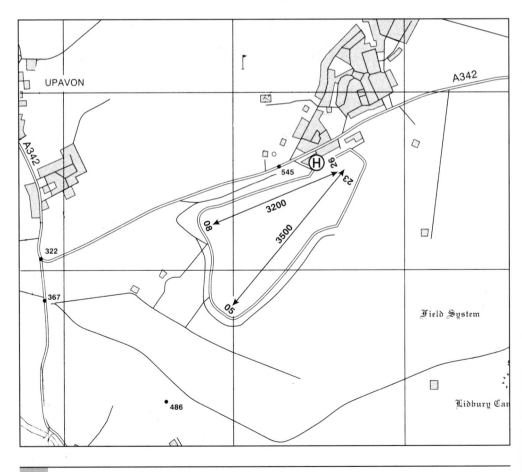

Wellesbourne Mountford

☺☺

Location: N52 11.53 W001 36.87 (3nm E of Stratford-upon-Avon)

Tel: 01789 842007

Runways:
05/23 1,932ft
18/36 2,992ft

Radio:
124.025

Notes:
A former World War Two Royal Air Force bomber training station, Wellesbourne was closed in 1964. The airfield is now largely used for vehicle storage and as an industrial estate. However, part of the airfield provides a base for a very active general aviation community. Various private aircraft are based here, and visitors are quite common. Also based here is a preserved Vulcan which occasionally makes very impressive (and noisy) runs along the runway.

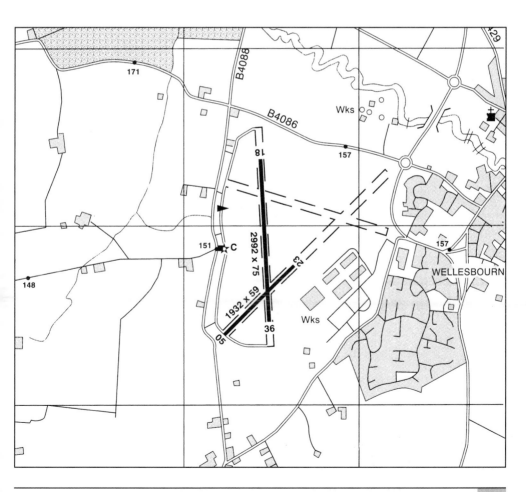

Welshpool
☺

Location: N52 37.75 W003 09.18 (2nm S of Welshpool)
Tel: 01938 555062

Runway:
04/22 2,723ft

Radio:
123.25

Notes:
Developed from a small grass strip, Welshpool is now the home of a thriving general aviation community, and a variety of private aircraft are based at this picturesque airfield. Visitors are also very common, keeping the airfield fairly busy, particularly at weekends. Spectators are welcome, and outdoor viewing and eating facilities are available.

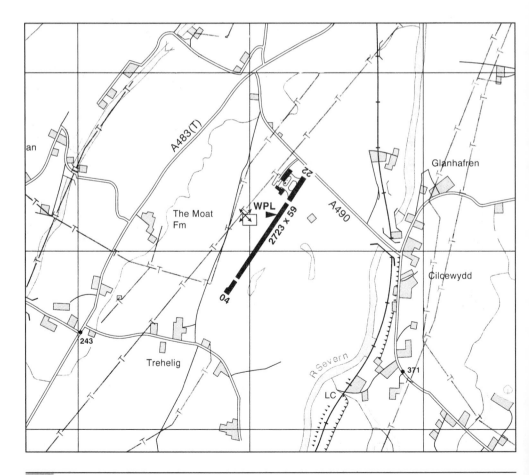

White Waltham

☺☺☺

Location: N51 30.05 W000 46.42 (2nm SW of Maidenhead)
Tel: 01628 823272

Runways:
03/21 3,363ft (grass)
07/25 3,642ft (grass)
11/29 3,051ft (grass)

Radio:
122.6

Notes:
Opened in 1935 as the home of the de Havilland School of Flying, White Waltham is best known for its association with the Duke of Edinburgh, who learned to fly here, on Chipmunks and Harvards. As the wartime headquarters of the Air Transport Auxiliary, a wide variety of aircraft used the site during World War Two. Today the airfield remains very active as a general aviation base, with flying schools and clubs, privately owned aircraft and plenty of visitors.

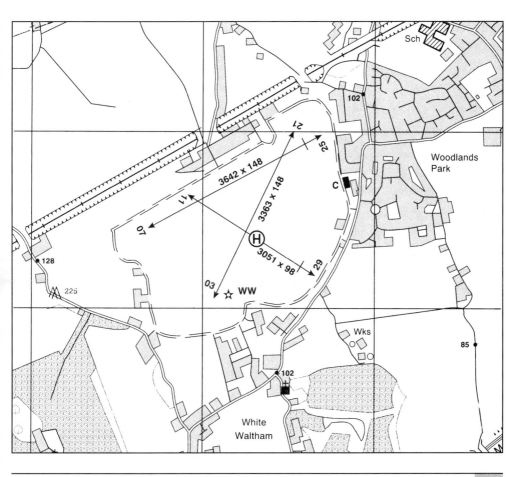

Wickenby
☺

Location: N53 19.00 W000 20.98 (8nm NE of Lincoln)
Tel: 01673 885345

Runways:
03/21 2,133ft
16/34 2,178ft

Radio:
122.45

Notes:
Wickenby is a well-known former RAF bomber base from where countless Lancasters flew during World War Two. Much remains of the old airfield, but a public road now intersects the airfield and only the northern portion beyond the road is used. Housing a flying club and a few residents, Wickenby is fairly quiet, although the airfield does play host to occasional visitors. Close to Waddington and Coningsby, RAF aircraft are still very much in the vicinity, and occasionally the RAF's Lancaster passes overhead, stirring memories of Wickenby's wartime history.

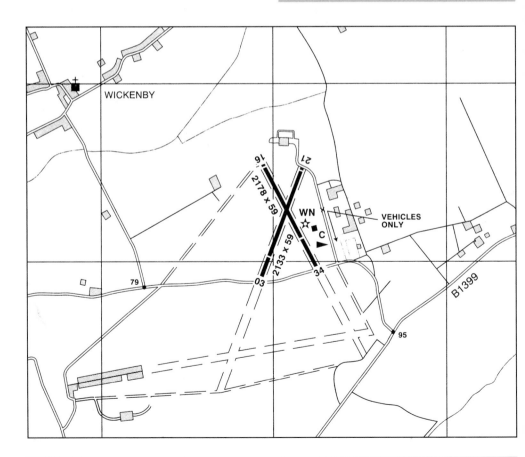

Wycombe Air Park/Booker

☺☺☺

Location: N51 36.72 W000 48.68 (2nm SW of High Wycombe)

Tel: 01494 529261

Runways:

07/25 2,411ft
07/25 2,001ft (grass)
17:/35 2,582ft (grass)

Radio:

126.55

Notes:
Utilised as a training base during World War Two, Booker was also often used for communications flights connected with the nearby headquarters of Bomber Command, at High Wycombe. Today the airfield is one of the busiest general aviation sites in the country, with a variety of flying clubs, resident aircraft and numerous visiting types. Aircraft restoration and maintenance also takes place here and even aerobatic aircraft can be found on the airfield. Spectators are welcome and the airfield is almost always busy.

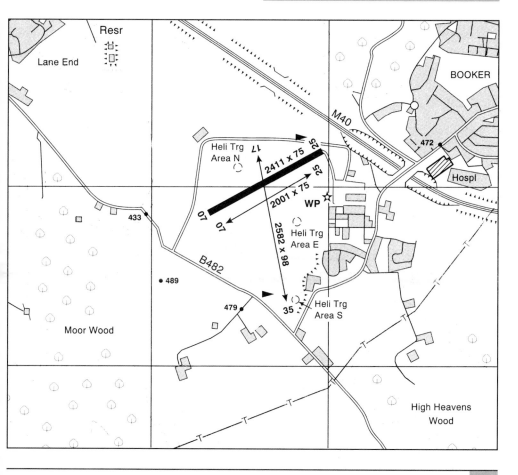

Wyton
☺☺

Location: N52 21.42 W000 06.47 (3nm NE of Huntingdon)
Tel: 01480 52151

Runways:
09/27 5,000ft
16/34 2,500ft

Radio:
134.05

Notes:
A well-known Royal Air Force bomber base dating from World War Two, Wyton is best known for its status as a V-bomber base, with Valiants and Victors based here through the 1960s. More recently, Wyton became the RAF's main Canberra base, but flying has now virtually ceased at the airfield, and all of the operational flying units have been disbanded or relocated. The base is still occasionally used for communications flights connected with nearby RAF Brampton, but most aerial activity is confined to light aircraft, microlights and model aircraft. The huge V-bomber runway can still be used if necessary, so perhaps Wyton may eventually be re-activated as an active flying base.

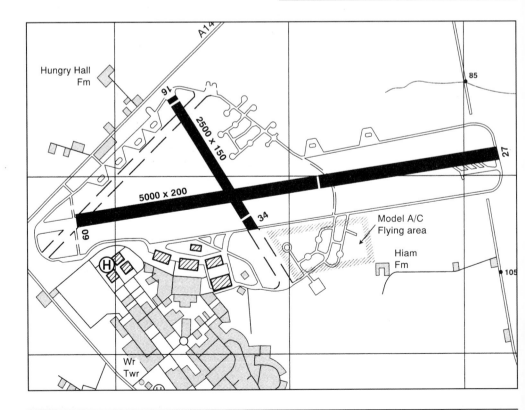

Yeovil

☺☺☺☺

Location: N50 56.40 W002 39.55 (1nm W of Yeovil)

Tel: 01935 475222

Runway:
10/28 4,547ft (grass)

Radio:
130.8 369.975 300.675 125.4 372.425

Notes:
The home of Westland Helicopters, most activity at Yeovil is, not surprisingly, connected with rotary-winged aircraft. Helicopter test flying takes place on most days, sometimes at night, and occasional fixed-wing flights are made, mostly by visiting business aircraft. Surrounding roads offer good views of the airfield, but activity is sporadic.

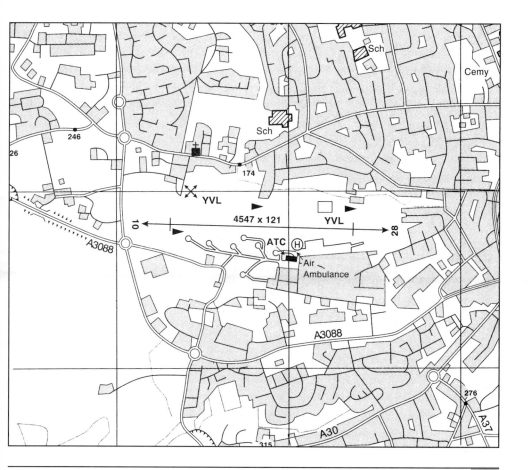

York/Rufforth
☺

Location: N53 56.83 W001 11.24 (3nm W of York)
Tel: 01904 738694

Runways:
18/36 3,937ft
06W/24W 2,073ft (asphalt/grass)
06E/24E 1,969ft

Radio:
129.975

Notes:
A World-War-Two-era Royal Air Force bomber base, Rufforth closed shortly after the end of the war. It remained disused until fairly recently, when a small number of light aircraft began to operate from portions of the former bomber base, alongside gliders and microlights. Flying activity is fairly low, but the airfield may become more popular with the general aviation community as it becomes more familiar.

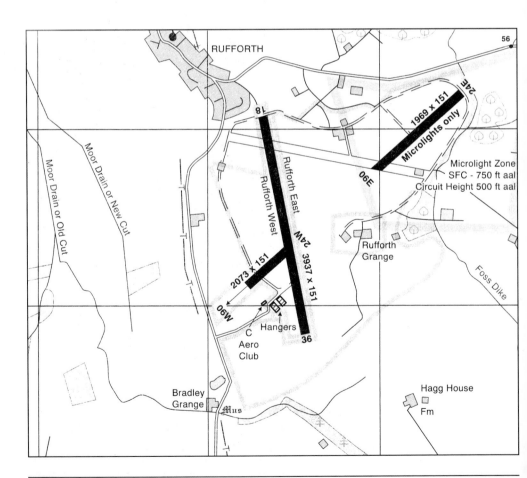

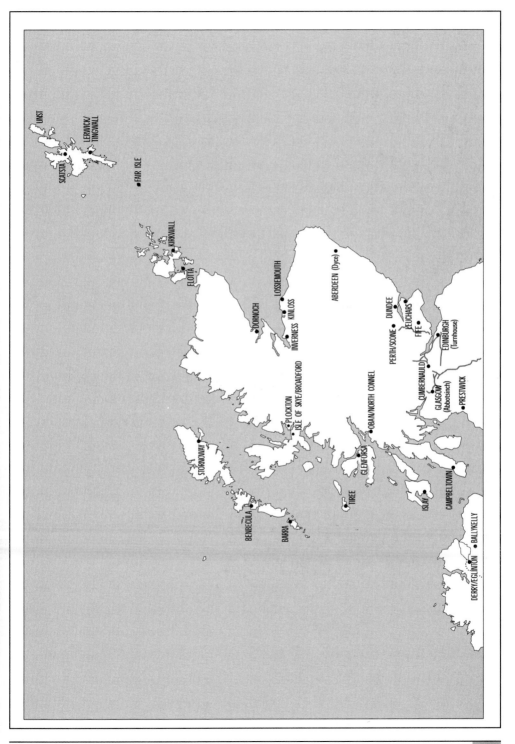

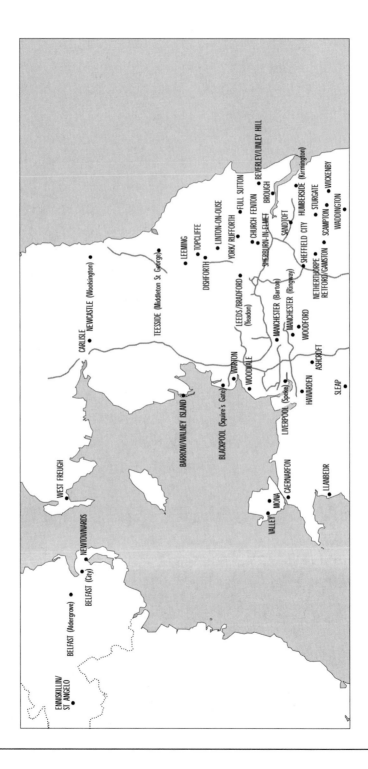

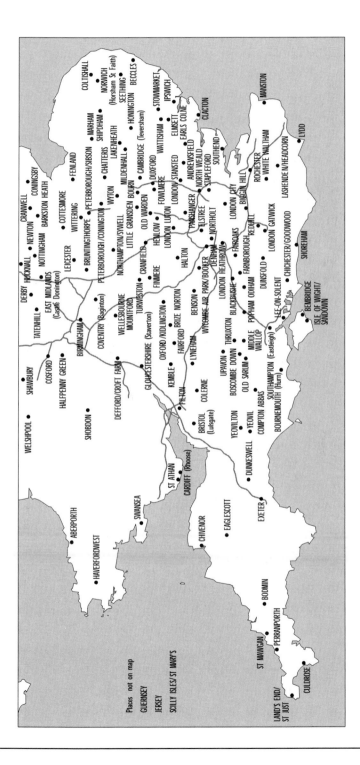